(continued from front flap)

tically about the advantages a liberal education offers to business careers. Sponsored by the Association of American Colleges.

"Now that the technical, economic and political environment of business is changing so fast, executives with broad vision, historical perspective, and the ability to learn—that is humanistically educated executives—will be increasingly needed. This book is particularly valuable because it not only tells us why we need liberally educated managers, but how to develop them"—*Peter F. Drucker.*

"The book musters persuasive evidence that liberal learning is excellent preparation for leadership in the corporate world and the larger society. Descriptions of exemplary programs on campuses across the country will also make this book an important resource for those of us engaged daily in providing liberal education to our students"—*Harriet W. Sheridan, dean of the college, Brown University.*

THE AUTHORS

JOSEPH S. JOHNSTON, JR., director of national affairs of the Association of American Colleges, has designed a range of programs to integrate liberal education and the professions.

The other authors are identified in the front of the book.

Educating Managers

Executive Effectiveness
Through Liberal Learning

Joseph S. Johnston, Jr.
Stanley T. Burns
David W. Butler
Marcie Schorr Hirsch
Thomas B. Jones
Alan M. Kantrow
Kathryn Mohrman
Roger B. Smith
Michael Useem

Foreword by Thomas H. Wyman

Educating Managers

Executive Effectiveness
Through Liberal Learning

Jossey-Bass Publishers

San Francisco • London • 1986

EDUCATING MANAGERS
Executive Effectiveness Through Liberal Learning
by Joseph S. Johnston, Jr., Stanley T. Burns, David W. Butler,
Marcie Schorr Hirsch, Thomas B. Jones, Alan M. Kantrow,
Kathryn Mohrman, Roger B. Smith, Michael Useem

Copyright © 1986 by: Jossey-Bass Inc., Publishers
433 California Street
San Francisco, California 94104
&
Jossey-Bass Limited
28 Banner Street
London EC1Y 8QE

Library of Congress Cataloging-in-Publication Data

Educating managers.

(The Jossey-Bass higher education series) (The
Jossey-Bass management series)
    Bibliography: p. 219
    Includes index.
    1. Management—Study and teaching—United States—
Addresses, essays, lectures. I. Johnston, Joseph
Shackford (date). II. Series. III. Series:
Jossey-Bass management series.
HD30.42.U5E39   1986   658'.007'1173   86-1441
ISBN 0-87589-684-7

Manufactured in the United States of America

The paper in this book meets the guidelines for
permanence and durability of the Committee on
Production Guidelines for Book Longevity of the
Council on Library Resources.

JACKET DESIGN BY WILLI BAUM

FIRST EDITION

Code 8614

A joint publication in
The Jossey-Bass
Higher Education Series
and
The Jossey-Bass
Management Series

Foreword

We live and work in an increasingly complex world character-ized by dramatic change and accelerating rates of change. Busi-ness decisions affect, and are affected by, many parts of society. With such a premium placed on thoughtful, sensitive, creative, and flexible management there is no place for leadership with limited perspective. This book reminds us that corporate Amer-ica needs even its specialists to have a general liberal education. Liberally educated managers—especially managers with excel-lent written and verbal communications skills—are increasingly recognized as critical to the successful corporation.

It is surprising that we in corporate America have not paid more attention to the value of this type of background. Few corporations have given serious attention to this important issue. As Joseph S. Johnston, Jr., points out, one of the reasons for this neglect has been an unhappy preoccupation with short-term profits.

Regrettably few in the business world or in academia see their relationship clearly. There has been too little research on the connection between a liberal education and business leader-ship. We have not satisfactorily addressed the questions that Johnston and his associates ask: Are liberally educated man-agers more effective managers? Should business place priority on their recruitment and development? If there is an unfulfilled need for liberally educated managers, what changes must be made—in business and higher education—before this need can be met?

The failure to answer these and related questions has made it difficult for the business and academic communities to combine resources to put the value of liberal learning on the corporate agenda in a useful way. As a result, young people who are entering college—and their parents—are concerned that a liberal arts education may not provide adequate preparation for the job market. When this happens, we lose the potential of a large personnel resource. The alert sounded in this book makes a compelling case for a change of perspective.

Educating Managers offers provocative arguments, insightful analyses, data, personal accounts, and recommendations. The breadth of experience of the authors is impressive. I have seen no more persuasive case for the liberally educated manager in business.

All companies need more people who know how to read, write, talk, and think clearly. For this reason alone, *Educating Managers* will be read with great interest inside the corporation. It should also find a warm reception in the liberal arts institutions and business schools across the land. This is a book about bridges—important bridges.

New York, New York   Thomas H. Wyman
January 1986   *Chairman and Chief Executive Officer,*
                               CBS, Inc.

Preface

A broad liberal arts program [is] fluff and can't be translated into the marketplace.
—President of a personnel consulting firm

If I could choose one degree for the people I hire it would be English. . . . You can teach a group of Cub Scouts to do portfolio analysis.
—Senior vice-president of a large financial institution

The question of liberal education's importance for business has always inspired both controversy and its share of nonsense. We have, for example, had pronouncements on the universal utility of liberal education from faculty innocent of the world of business; we have had glowing testimonials to liberal education from executives whose firms seem in practice not to value it at all. The two epigraphs above help illustrate the problem. The first dismisses liberal learning with a proudly "real world" scorn. The second offers an emphatic endorsement. Both kinds of statements are familiar, both find appreciative audiences, and neither can be taken seriously.

What can be said responsibly about the relationship between liberal education and business? Are liberally educated

managers more effective managers? Should business place priority on their recruitment and development? If there is an unfilled
need for liberally educated managers, what changes must be
made—in business *and* higher education—before it can be met?
And what are the roles for professionals in both environments
who want to be agents of that change? These are the practical
questions this book addresses.

*Educating Managers: Executive Effectiveness Through
Liberal Learning* makes the case that business has a critical need
for liberally educated managers. It emphasizes the need for reform in three key environments. The first is business itself, in
which recruitment and management development programs
need to be strengthened. The second and third environments
are the business school and the programs of arts and sciences,
where both curricular and extracurricular offerings need to be
improved.

This book is written by a team of business executives,
management scholars, business and liberal arts faculty, and academic administrators. Each author has wide experience in one
or more of these environments and has been directly involved
in efforts to win a central place for liberal learning in the development of business managers. Impressed by the need for a
comprehensive book on the subject, we have tried to provide
one here.

What is that need? George Bernard Shaw once described
the English and the Americans as two peoples separated by a
common language. In much the same way, business and American higher education are sectors of society separated by a common problem—their mutual doubt and confusion regarding the
practical value of a liberal education. This separation harms
both communities and society as a whole.

The separation, however, is not in the least inevitable.
For the evidence is compelling that business will benefit by
seeking educational breadth in its managers. "That's the good
news," as Charles Brown, chairman of the board of American
Telephone and Telegraph, has commented. "The bad news is
that the good news is not better known."

The majority of publications—and other efforts—addressing this failure to disseminate "the good news" have come from those who teach in or administer liberal arts programs. These efforts have sought to convince *students,* and others in academia, of the value of liberal education as career preparation.

The emphasis is understandable. As Chapter One points out, widespread belief that liberal education has little practical value for those seeking careers in business has helped produce protracted enrollment declines in the liberal arts—the fields traditionally associated with liberal education. But the limitations of a response that tries to persuade students directly are now apparent. In the economy of the late 1980s educational choices are market-driven, to an extent unparalleled in recent history. The perceived preference of corporations and other businesses has an enormous influence on what is studied. And at present most of these potential buyers of college-educated labor are clearly and accurately perceived to choose predominantly by major, not overall breadth, and to prefer business, economics, and computer science majors to those trained in other fields. Students, no less than businesspersons, have a keen ear for wishful pieties. They will need to see some adjustment in businesses' hiring priorities before making different educational choices. If that adjustment is to come in response to persuasion, it will be persuasion directed to business, not to students.

Educating Managers is unique—and we hope it will be more effective—in that it deals with the issue by addressing the concerns of business. It urges a central role for liberal learning in the development of current and future managers as a matter of simple good sense and enlightened self-interest on the part of businesses and those who lead them. Corporate decision makers are a primary intended audience. They need, as a part of their jobs, to be aware of the case we make. They are also able to implement changes. This group includes top management and all those on the strategic marketing frontier—those responsible at the highest levels for deciding a firm's goals and thinking through the resources, including the human resources, necessary to achieve them. The book can be of assistance to all managers— whether in human resources, marketing, finance, or operating divisions—who are concerned with entry- and middle-level hiring and internal promotion. Those with direct responsibility for the recruitment, training, and development of managers will, we hope, find it especially useful.

Our analysis poses as many challenges to higher education as to business, and campus decision makers are our other primary audience: presidents, provosts, vice-presidents, and other senior academic officers responsible for institutional planning and other external relations with the corporate community; deans and faculty with responsibility for curriculum, teaching, and advising, both in liberal arts and in business management programs; and, finally, administrators in college relations, admissions, student advising, career planning, and continuing education who need to explain the practical value of liberal education, often to skeptical audiences.

Others we hope to reach include foundation officials, public policy makers, association executives, accrediting agency officials, and college and university trustees. All have roles to play in the development of institutions capable of preparing better managers.

This volume should serve all these professionals—in corporations, on campuses, and elsewhere—as a resource on liberal education's role in the development of managers. Differences in their responsibilities notwithstanding, the senior business executive and the university dean, the corporate recruiting manager and the faculty member have similar needs as they confront this issue. First, they need to know what credible evidence there is that, as Ralph Saul, chairman of CIGNA, once observed, it is no longer enough for managers to be well trained; they also need to be well educated. Second, they need to know the practical steps to take to ensure that more such managers are developed or employed.

Overview of the Contents

The structure of *Educating Managers* reflects an emphasis on these two broad needs. Part One, "The Need for Liberally Educated Managers," begins with a look to the future. Chapter One, by Joseph S. Johnston, Jr., reviews what we know of the likely needs of tomorrow's profit-making organizations. It asks what kinds of skills and abilities—and, by extension, what kind of education—their managers will require. The chapter concludes with a definition of liberal education in relation to the study of both business and the liberal arts that clarifies its potential in helping to meet these business needs.

Chapter Two, by Roger B. Smith, chairman of General Motors Corporation, is the first of three that give what might be termed arguments from experience. Smith's view carries particular weight because of his own rise through the operational world of one of the world's largest manufacturing firms. The question of the usefulness of a liberal education usually turns, of course, on the particular case of the liberal arts, and of the humanities even more than the sciences and social sciences. Smith's essay is of interest in that he not only finds practical value in the knowledge and competencies gained from studying all of these fields but relates this directly to key managerial attributes spelled out in Peters and Waterman's *In Search of Excellence.*

Chapter Three features interviews with five executives in various industries and at different stages in their careers. Collected and edited in large part by Alan M. Kantrow of the *Harvard Business Review* and Stanley T. Burns of Chase Bank of Maryland, and introduced by Joseph S. Johnston, Jr., these accounts move beyond testimony to illustrate, with reference to actual business situations, just how a liberal education is of value in management.

Chapter Four, written by Michael Useem of Boston University, concludes Part One by examining experiences in a more collective form. It is a substantial and up-to-date review of empirical evidence on the actual performance of the liberally educated as a class of corporate manager and of what is known about why they so often excel.

Part Two, "Effecting Change in Business, Business Schools, and Liberal Arts Programs," looks at efforts in business, business schools, and liberal arts programs to integrate liberal learning and professional education. It begins with Michael Useem's report in Chapter Five on the reasons why, and the vehicles through which, more and more corporations are now providing or sponsoring liberal education for their employees.

Chapters Six and Seven turn to the business school, criticized now from all sides for producing graduates who are narrowly trained. In Chapter Six, Thomas B. Jones of Metropolitan State University surveys historic and persistent obstacles to the integration of liberal learning and undergraduate management education and then describes a number of innovative programs that offer models for change. In Chapter Seven, David W. Butler draws on his experience directing the Claremont Graduate School's management programs to reflect on the potential contribution of the humanities to graduate management education.

There are many routes through the university to a business career, and Chapter Eight, by Kathryn Mohrman of Brown University and Marcie Schorr Hirsch of Brandeis University, should help orient recruiters to a rich and as yet largely untapped market. Focusing on the many different kinds of initiatives, curricular and extracurricular, by which programs in the arts and sciences are preparing interested graduates for management careers, it will also alert liberal arts faculty and administrators to some proven strategies for change.

Part Three, "Strategies and Resources for Action," consists of two chapters. Chapter Nine, by Joseph S. Johnston, Jr., sums up the need for reform and spells out those steps that different professionals in business and higher education need to take in order to bring it about. Finally, Thomas B. Jones provides a list of other resources—publications and organizations—that will help equip the reader to meet that challenge.

There are those in the academic world who may object to this volume's emphasis on the utility of a liberal education. Some prefer to define liberal learning exclusively as learning pursued for its own sake and hold that to explain the practical value of liberal learning is to grant validity to an invalid question. Still others may regret our relative inattention to liberal learning's role in personal enrichment and in the production of an educated citizenry. The authors understand these positions and concerns, and they themselves believe both in the intrinsic worth of liberal learning and in its personal and civic value. Our purpose here, however, is to correct a widespread underestimation of its value in professional life.

Even on this narrower topic, some would write a different book. It would emphasize that liberally educated graduates serve the needs of a variety of professions, including law and medicine, and that, insofar as management is concerned, a range of governmental and other nonprofit institutions can benefit from their skills. The authors, again, would be unlikely to disagree. But then who would? The liberal arts already encompass the majors of choice for prelaw and premedical study, and government, the arts, most education, and other sectors of the nonprofit world continue to employ the liberally educated in large numbers. The real area of misunderstanding is business management. Both in business and on campuses, doubt about liberal education's relevance to management is widespread and costly. We have directed our efforts, therefore, to clarifying and strengthening the connections between these two and thereby making the case that most needs to be made.

All of the chapters in *Educating Managers* were commissioned expressly for this publication. Depending on their needs, readers may wish to read the book in sequence or turn instead to individual chapters on particular topics. The book has been prepared under the auspices of the Association of American Colleges as an integrated volume, but the chapters all draw on the personal perspectives of their authors.

Acknowledgments

This book is itself the product of an encouraging collaboration among professionals in business and liberal education. Foremost among them are the authors. As their editor and coauthor, I appreciate immensely their ready agreement to this project, their support in planning it, and the skill and good humor with which they brought it to completion.

For the executive interviews that comprise Chapter Three, we all wish to thank William Hazen, Nancy Zimmerman, John Gidding, Charlotte Kuenan, and Patrick Coady. They have been most generous with their time, and their participation has made this a more useful and interesting book.

Special thanks are due to Michael Useem and Kathryn Mohrman, who took a helpful interest in the book as a whole and gave good advice at many points; to Alan M. Perlman, whose role included securing and coordinating the involvement of General Motors; and to Wayne Broadbent of General Homes Corporation for his generous assistance in the development of material for Chapter Three.

   The book was prepared under the auspices of the Association of American Colleges. Mark H. Curtis, president of the association from 1978 to 1985, generously provided from his discretionary funds the financial support that made the undertaking possible. His own writings on liberal education also helped point us on our way. Other senior staff members who lent their support and encouragement include John Chandler and William O'Connell, the association's current president and former vice-president, respectively. Irving Spitzberg, executive director of the association's Council for Liberal Learning, has given much helpful advice and reaction.

   Daphne Layton was a full and valued partner in the coordination of the project. She was instrumental in developing the material used here, including the interviews in Chapter Three, and repeatedly brought order out of a near chaos of memos and manuscripts. On behalf of all the authors, I thank her.

   The drafts of many chapters profited from close, informed reviews by Donald A. Cress, chairman of the philosophy department at Northern Illinois University. Lauran Nohe's expert copyediting, and William Melvin's and Kimberly Schlenker's generous assistance in preparing the manuscript are also appreciated.   .

   J. Fred Beamer of the National Center for Education Statistics provided up-to-date statistics on enrollment trends. Russell Edgerton of the American Association of Higher Education generously made available the preliminary results of unpublished research, and Milton Blood of the American Assembly of Collegiate Schools of Business kindly provided documentation on the assembly's accreditation standards.

   Finally, I want to acknowledge the importance to this book of two grants from the National Endowment for the Humanities. During 1983 and 1984, the National Endowment for the Humanities supported a series of national and regional meetings on the humanities and careers in business, sponsored by the Association of American Colleges. The contacts, insights, and recommendations provided by these four working conferences have been invaluable to this project. The authors' hope for their work is that it, in turn, has something of the same continuing and multiplying effect.

Washington, D.C.   Joseph S. Johnston, Jr.
January 1986

Contents

The Authors

Joseph S. Johnston, Jr., is director of national affairs of the Association of American Colleges, where he is responsible for a range of programs connecting liberal education and the professions. His degrees include a Ph.D. degree (1978) in English language and literature from the University of Chicago and an M.B.A. degree (1982), with a concentration in finance and planning, from the Wharton School of the University of Pennsylvania. The author of a number of scholarly articles on seventeenth-century literature, Johnston has taught at Temple University, Villanova University, Bryn Mawr College, and the University of Maryland. His principle work has been as an administrator—as assistant to the president at Bryn Mawr, visiting associate examiner at the Educational Testing Service, research associate with the Higher Education Finance Research Institute of the University of Pennsylvania, and, immediately before joining the Association of American Colleges in 1983, director of planning and development at Washington College. Johnston is also cofounder and president of Severn Investments, Inc., a Maryland-based registered investment advisory firm offering investment planning and management services to individuals and institutions.

Stanley T. Burns is president of Chase Bank of Maryland. Prior to assuming that position in 1985, he served for nineteen years in a variety of positions with the Chase Manhattan Bank, N.A., most recently as vice-president and eastern regional executive of the bank's commercial sector. His previous experience involved a variety of commercial banking activities, including corporate banking and real estate finance. He has also been responsible for the training and development of marketing officers and has implemented a coordinated approach to professional education at Chase for entry-level and experienced bankers. Active in a variety of civic and charitable organizations, Burns was educated at Duke University, from which he received a B.A. degree in political science in 1966.

David W. Butler is executive director of the Graduate Management Center and associate professor of business administration at the Claremont Graduate School. He is responsible for the administration of the graduate school's three major graduate management programs. As professor and consultant, Butler focuses on the role of language in managerial problem solving, on executive rhetoric, and on the design of management development programs. Butler was formerly assistant professor of English and director of undergraduate studies in the Department of English at the University of Kentucky, Lexington. He holds a B.A. degree (1965) in English from Stanford University, a Ph.D. degree (1972) in English from the University of Wisconsin, Madison, and an M.B.A. degree (1979) from the Claremont Graduate School.

Marcie Schorr Hirsch is the director of the Hiatt Career Development Center at Brandeis University. Recipient of a B.A. degree (1971) in theater arts from Brandeis and an Ed.M. degree (1974) from Tufts University, she is currently a doctoral candidate at the Harvard Graduate School of Education, where she is conducting research on successful organizational careers. Hirsch has written for numerous magazines and has frequently appeared on national television to speak on human resource management and work issues, topics on which she also lectures and serves as a consultant to industry and higher education.

Thomas B. Jones is professor of humanities at Metropolitan State University. He received his B.A. degree (1964) in his-

tory from the University of Minnesota and his Ph.D. degree
(1968) in American history from Cornell University. At Metropolitan State University, he teaches American history, designs
curricula for nontraditional adult students, and works with the
individualized degree planning program. His published works include writings on American history, nontraditional education,
and liberal education. Recently, he received a Chancellor's Fel-
lowship from the Minnesota State University System for a year
of research and writing on liberal education and business study.

Alan M. Kantrow is associate editor of the *Harvard Business Review* and senior research associate of the Harvard Business School. He holds a B.A. degree (1969) in anthropology and
a Ph.D. degree (1979) in the history of American civilization,
both from Harvard University. He is the author or editor of numerous publications on such topics as corporate research, technology management, and industrial revitalization. A frequent
speaker and consultant to industry groups, he is a principal and
director of The Winthrop Group, Inc., a business history consulting firm.

Kathryn Mohrman is associate dean of the college at
Brown University. Earlier she was director of programs and national affairs at the Association of American Colleges, where she
initiated a number of programs linking higher education and careers. In both research and administrative work, she focuses on
the relationship between colleges and universities and other social structures; she has interests in federal policy and higher education, campus-corporate connections, and adult education and
training. After earning her B.A. degree (1967) in history at
Grinnell College, she continued her work in American history
for an M.A. degree (1969) at the University of Wisconsin at
Madison. She received her Ph.D. degree (1982) in public policy
at George Washington University.

Roger B. Smith became chairman and chief executive officer of General Motors in 1981. Born in Columbus, Ohio, he
received his B.A. degree (1947) and M.A. degree (1949) in busi-

ness administration from the University of Michigan. Smith began his career with General Motors in 1949 as a general accounting clerk in the Detroit central office. After a series of promotions, he became treasurer of the financial staff and a member of the administrative committee in 1971. Prior to being elected chairman, Smith had served as an executive vice-president and a member of the board of directors since 1974. He is credited with foreseeing the critical role that computers and electronics would play in the automotive industry—in the manufacturing processes and in the products themselves—and he has engineered several high-technology acquisitions and other strategic moves that have helped to transform General Motors into a broader, more effective organization.

Michael Useem is associate dean of the College of Liberal Arts at Boston University and director of the university's Center for Applied Social Science. He holds a B.S. degree (1964) in physics from the University of Michigan and an M.A. degree (1966) in physics from Harvard University. He received his Ph.D. degree in sociology from Harvard University in 1970. Useem's research has been supported by grants from the National Endowment for the Arts, the United Nations, and the National Science Foundation, among other agencies. He is the author of numerous articles on the social and political activities of corporations and managers that have appeared in the *Administrative Science Quarterly, Sloan Management Review, California Management Review,* the *New York Times,* and elsewhere. His recent book on the subject, *The Inner Circle: Large Corporations and the Rise of Business Political Activity in the U.S. and U.K.,* was published in 1984.

Educating Managers

Executive Effectiveness
Through Liberal Learning

To Mark H. Curtis,
president of the Association of American Colleges
from 1978 to 1985 and
lifelong advocate of liberal education

Joseph S. Johnston, Jr.

Educating
Managers for Change

Why should anyone—business executive, faculty member, or administrator—be concerned with the connections between liberal education and business management? This book is an attempt to answer the question fully. But a briefer explanation can begin, even for business readers, with the sharp and continuing enrollment declines in the liberal arts.

The liberal arts include the sciences, the social sciences, and the humanities. These are not the only fields that lend themselves to liberal education; the breadth and open-ended style of inquiry that characterize liberal education can and should be central to professional education as well. Nor do the liberal arts (or arts and sciences) disciplines always fulfill their promise as vehicles for liberal learning; they can be taught and approached quite narrowly. Nonetheless, far more than other fields, they have traditionally been expected and assumed to prepare liberally educated graduates, and their recent experience is telling.

The National Center for Education Statistics (1985, p. 84) neatly sums up the changing patterns in undergraduate majors: "During the 15-year period ending in 1981–82, the undergraduate majors of college students shifted significantly. There was a clearly discernible movement away from a number of the traditional arts and sciences, while the number and percent of students who majored in business and management and some other occupationally oriented fields increased substantially." At the beginning of that period, in 1966–67, degrees in a representative sample of liberal arts disciplines—mathematics, biological and physical sciences, history, English, and foreign languages—constituted 28 percent of all bachelor's degrees conferred. By 1981–82 they accounted for only 14 percent (National Center for Education Statistics, 1985, p. 85). Certain disciplines have been severely hit. Between 1970 and 1983, while the number of bachelor's degrees awarded annually increased by 22 percent, the numbers of graduates in some areas plummeted—in philosophy by 39 percent, in modern languages by 52 percent, in mathematics by 55 percent, in English by 57 percent, and in history by 63 percent (personal communication from staff statistician, National Center for Education Statistics [NCES], July 1985). But the decline, again, is general. Even the once-popular natural sciences have fallen behind in percentage of degrees awarded (National Center for Education Statistics, 1985, p. 132).

The flight has been into business and management and, to a lesser extent, other occupationally oriented fields, such as engineering and the health professions. Between 1966 and 1983, the number of business degrees conferred each year increased enormously—from 64,000 to 227,000. This 257 percent increase is outstripped only by the rate of growth in computer science degrees, up ninefold to 24,000 since 1971, the first year figures on that field were collected (personal communication from staff statistician, NCES, July 1985). Each year now, virtually one in every four of the nation's nearly one million new graduates takes a degree in business. Business enrollments dwarf those of all other fields of study.

Before returning to our opening question and suggesting why these trends matter, especially to business and business schools, we need to note one other fact: Not only is the movement toward preprofessional study a major one; it shows no sign of abating. Research by Alexander Astin and associates (Astin, Green, Williams, and Maier, 1984, p. 5) disabuses us of any notion that a change in these trends is imminent. The latest of their annual surveys of college freshmen indicates that the percentage of students aspiring to careers in business continues to rise. It reached an all-time high of 22.2 percent in 1984, up from 10 percent in 1966. The percentage of women aspiring to business has increased fivefold (Astin, 1984, p. 12). Indications from the high schools foretell still more of the same. The College Entrance Examination Board's annual survey of high school students collects information on the academic aspirations of about two-thirds of all college-bound seniors. In 1985, for the seventh consecutive year, business and commerce was the most popular area of intended college study (College Entrance Examination Board, 1985, p. 10).

Some observers assume that demographic changes over the next ten years or so will bring students back to the liberal arts. There being fewer 18- to 22-year-olds, this line of thought goes, they will face less competition for jobs and will thus be in a position to major in whatever they wish and still be assured of good employment. The facts, however, provide little support for this hope. It is true that over the period 1982–1995, an average of 36,000 fewer new graduates will enter the job market each year than in 1982. This drop, however, will be more than offset by growth in the number of other entrants. Indeed, the Bureau of Labor Statistics (BLS) tells us that, thanks to a tremendous hidden supply of graduates entering or returning to the labor market after delays caused by family responsibilities, graduate education, or military service, the availability of educated workers will exceed demand by an average of about 300,000 annually (Sargent, 1985, pp. 5, 7). Peter Drucker even predicts that, because of shortages of work in the knowledge industry suitable to their education, finding jobs for college graduates will be "the central employment problem in the United States in the next 20 years" (Career Placement Council, 1985, p. 1). No one knows what the dimensions of the problem will be. But it does seem clear that, as the BLS predicts, the entry-level job market will be more competitive. And in the absence of a change in corporate hiring policies, students will be under more, not less, pressure to specialize as a way of gaining a competitive edge.

Why, then, should these trends or the connections between liberal education and business practice concern business? Like it or not, it is toward business that more and more of the products of today's education are bound. They will, with all the strengths and defects of their preparation, soon have large roles in determining corporate performance. And the managers who have such roles now are drawing on education in which liberal learning could, today, be made a larger part. *The Cox Report on the American Corporation* (Cox, 1982, pp. 251-252) has already found that the trend among corporations to hire on the basis of particular and specialized areas of study "results in executives who are not properly developed to assume general management responsibilities later on." What, then, will it mean for a corporation when even larger numbers of its managers know more and more about less and less? Obviously, business needs specialists. (Even its generalists need applied skills.) But firms need to consider whether the soundest policy may be to hire specialists only when their particular expertise is essential—or, better, see that the specialists that they do hire are themselves liberally educated. Companies need to know what liberally educated managers offer. How have they actually performed? How can business do a better job of recruiting and developing them?

The figures on enrollment declines and the future of the job market go far, of course, toward explaining the relevance of this book to faculty in the liberal arts, who need to do more than they have been doing to clarify and enforce the importance of a liberal education in preparing managers. They need to know how work in their disciplines can develop skills and abilities used in business and how, through curricular and other initiatives, they can improve their offerings, better assist their students in considering and preparing for careers, and reach more of those whom they are prepared to serve.

Thoughtful business educators will see in these figures a vastly increased—and not entirely comfortable—responsibility for the education of tomorrow's leaders. Fifteen years of growth have brought their programs pre-eminence on their campuses but increased scrutiny and criticisms from both the academy and the business world also. They need to know what they should be paying attention to now. Is liberal learning really important to managerial success? What steps can faculty and administrators take to ensure that their graduates are liberally educated?

Top administrators of colleges and universities need to think through the implications of enrollment trends and job-market prosperity for entire institutions. Some schools are experiencing shifts in their intellectual centers of gravity and others outright dislocation. Their leaders are recognizing a need to reassert control. Through what comprehensive integration of liberal and professional education can they meet the growing demand for career preparation without risking the centrality of liberal learning?

There are compelling reasons for business executives, faculty, and administrators to attend to the issues dealt with in this book. It offers arguments, analyses, data, personal accounts, models, and recommendations that can help them deal with an important problem. All its parts, however, are grounded in some common ideas, to which we now turn, about the future confronting business and the skills and the capacities that a strong liberal education fosters.

"Sustained excellence in management will require, above all, adaptability to change." Thus concludes a 1985 report by the Business-Higher Education Forum (1985, p. 2), an organization for leading corporate and academic chief executives. In emphasizing this point, the forum echoes virtually every study of the future of American business. It is generally agreed that nothing is more important to the nation's ability to meet the competitive challenge of the future than what Samuel Ehrenhalt (1983, p. 43) of the Department of Labor has termed a "flexible, adaptable, labor force."

It is when we ask what that truism means for the education of future managers that consensus breaks down. Clearly, many people in our society would take observations such as the forum's as a mandate for more and more specifically preprofessional and technical training. Indeed, many subscribe to the view of high-tech training advocate Lewis J. Perelman (1984, p. xvii) that the "irrelevancy" of formal education today "has led to a growing mass of overeducated and underemployed adults" and that America's growing crisis of obsolescent human capital will leave traditional education "almost as little place in the twenty-first century's learning enterprise as the blacksmith shop has in today's transportation industry."

The authors of this book take a different view. Briefly, we, too, are struck by the pervasiveness and increasing rapidity of change and the need for adaptability. But we see in all this a strong case not so much for job-specific skills training as for educational breadth. We recognize most future managers' need for directly job-related and, in some cases, technical skills. We recognize the practicing manager's need for frequent retraining. But, largely because it fosters adaptability, we regard a broad— or liberal—education as the best possible foundation for sustained managerial productivity. For that reason, in turn, we think businesses have few more compelling needs, as they prepare themselves for the future, than their need to recruit and develop liberally educated managers.

The association of liberally educated managers with adaptability is one that has been made before. Charles Brown (1983) of AT&T, for example, recently gave this explanation for the superior performance over time of liberal arts graduates in that company's management: they "were most suitable to change, the leading feature of this kind of high-speed, high pressure, high tech world we occupy." But, however familiar and whatever its source, this kind of statement strikes many people as counterintuitive. What better way for a manager to stay atop the changes occurring in business, they reason, than to concentrate on mastering the technology that seems to drive it, as well as on acquiring specific business skills? And, they wonder, what could be less useful to a manager than studying languages, philosophy, sociology—the kinds of subjects they associate with a liberal education? The questions are good ones. They also have good answers. This introductory chapter sets out some of the principal ones. In the process, it looks closely at a number of things—the nature of the changes facing business and the nature of liberal education among them.

Directions of Change in the Business Environment

"Never make predictions," Sam Goldwyn once said, "especially about the future." Yet, as business has discovered, projections are more essential than ever in a world where change is so rapid that it is not enough merely to react to it—it must be anticipated. They are essential, too, to our explanation of why a liberal education equips managers for tomorrow's world—and why a company with liberally educated managers will probably be a more competitive company over time. Fortunately, economic analysis, management scholarship, "futures" research, and observation of the evolving world around us support some generalizations. This section briefly reviews seven broad directions of change in the business environment in which managers will function for the rest of this century.

An Information Economy of Accelerating Change. We have all heard the figures. The amount of human knowledge is doubling every seven years. Scientific information alone is increasing at a rate of 65,000 words a minute (Stine, 1984, p. 45); now doubling every five and a half years, it will soon be doubling, it is said, every twenty months (Naisbett, 1984, p. 16). Only slightly less familiar by now is the fact that the exponential increase of information that these figures reflect is both symptom and cause of a fundamental restructuring of our economy. Once "Smokestack America," the United States is now, in Daniel Bell's (1967) phrase, a "post-industrial society." Overall, only two in eight American workers are now employed in the goods-producing sector, and only one of these is in manufacturing (Naisbett, 1984, pp. 4-5). The drop in employment in the iron and steel industries is indicative of the trend; employers of nearly a million workers in 1957, they will claim by 1995 a work force of about 570,000 (Interindustry Forecasting Project of the University of Maryland, 1983). Of the nineteen million new jobs created in the 1970s, only 5 percent were in manufacturing and only 11 percent in the goods sector as a whole (Birch, 1981, p. 9).

The services sector, however, has experienced more than commensurate growth. That growth has come, moreover, from one source: that burgeoning part of the economy that deals in the creation, processing, and distribution of information. Since 1950, noninformation services have accounted for a constant 11 to 12 percent of employment; the information sector's share of the work force has grown from 17 to 65 percent (Naisbett, 1984, p. 4). Information-sector workers include accountants, librarians, brokers, and journalists. They include teachers and lawyers, secretaries and clerks, computer programmers and researchers. They are, in disproportionate numbers, professionals and manager/administrators—groups whose numbers have seen unusually rapid growth in the last twenty years (Naisbett, 1984, pp. 5-6).

Not only will still more of us devote our energies to information in the future, but the technologies with which it is conveyed will continue to speed its transfer dramatically. Already, global telecommunications instantaneously alert the Hong Kong financial community to the London gold fix and United Nations representatives in New York to election results in New Delhi. And, already, computerized management information systems put unprecedented amounts of up-to-date information at the disposal of corporate managers—data, for instance, about purchasing, inventory, production, shipping, sales, personnel, and finance. Corporate managers of the future will thus be awash in information—from both within the business and without. This, typically, they will use and pass quickly on in new forms—magnifying the information explosion and hastening the pace of change still more.

A Rapidly Growing but Limited Role for High Technology. Laser technology, supercomputers, computer assisted design–computer assisted manufacturing (CAD-CAM), telecommunications, robotics, biogenetics—high technology in its many forms is revolutionizing our world. It is transforming both the goods and services sectors of the economy—transforming, in many instances, both the work we do and the way we do it.

High technology is being introduced into old industrial tasks. Design, manufacturing, and control are increasingly computerized. "Flexible"—that is, computer-controlled and reprogrammable—manufacturing systems in particular confer a prized competitive advantage in a dynamic marketplace. And the robot is a fact of industrial life. Some experts predict that there will be 160,000 robots in the workplace by 1990 (Shaiken, 1981, p. 10). In a matter of decades, computerization will displace millions of workers, creating fully automated factories and a new "steel-collar" class (Sheils and others, 1980, p. 51). The office, obviously, will become more automated. By some estimates, 75 percent of jobs already involve computers in some way (Naisbett, 1984, p. 27). The introduction of still more technology will, according to James O'Toole (1984, p. 43), actually begin blurring distinctions between the secretary and the boss (and present new opportunities to those prepared by experience and education to accept increased responsibility).

We need to distinguish, of course, between industries that are themselves high-tech and those that are, more properly, affected by the new technology. In 1980, fewer than 2 percent of the businesses in the United States were in high-technology industries. Between 1976 and 1980, employment in this sector grew by 19.4 percent, compared with only 11.7 percent in other manufacturing and business services. But, at the end of that period, the sector still employed less than 10 percent of the work force, and a few companies with more than ten thousand employees accounted for more than 60 percent of that employment (American Society for Training and Development, 1984a, p. 3). Between 1982 and 1995, it is estimated, high-technology industries will account for only 1 to 4.6 million of the 23.4 to 28.6 million new jobs in the economy (Riche, Hecker, and Burgan, 1983, pp. 54–55).

A related, critically important point is that demand for college-educated high-technology workers overall in the economy will be far less than is often assumed. Here, too, the growth will be exceptional—double the average for all jobs—but on a small base. In the period 1982 to 1995, new positions requiring an in-depth knowledge of the principles of science, engineering, and mathematics underlying technology (as opposed to relatively lower-level skills in the technology's operation and repair) will total only 1.5 to 1.6 million, or no more than 6 percent of all new jobs (Riche, Hecker, and Burgan, 1983, p. 55).

Changing Markets and Industry Boundaries. In recent decades, as competition for their customers has intensified, American companies have abandoned their orientations to products and sales for a new orientation to their markets. Demand considerations have assumed a new prominence; they shape long-range corporate planning and new product development no less than they do sales-force deployment and the choice of media for advertising.

The markets themselves have meanwhile grown increasingly elusive, as consumers have come to expect and depend on products responsive to their changing needs and desires. There seems no reason to expect a change in this trend in the future, and its implications for business are clear. Product lines will be more and more diversified, needing to provide choice to a marketplace that demands it, whether in heavy equipment or ice cream, investment vehicles or mortgages. And the life cycles of products will continue to grow shorter as they fall victim to the same general kind of change that creates them in the first place. As whole markets change—appearing and disappearing—and as aggressive firms move to exploit perceived opportunities, industry boundaries will blur. Ours is already a world where consumers can get discount brokerage services from their banks and withdraw cash from automated tellers in their grocery stores. A premium will be placed on a firm's ability continuously to define the business it is really in and the business it should be in and to see that the two are constantly made one. Had slide-rule manufacturers realized that their real business was the production and sale of calculation devices—manual or electronic—they would perhaps have thrived to our own day. As it is, they did not, and for all practical purposes, they now occupy a place in what Walter Wriston (1981) of Citicorp has called the "corporate graveyard." It is the resting place of companies that, believing in some "divine right of inherited markets . . . failed to change with a changing world."

Global Competition and Cooperation. We can expect to see in the years ahead a continuation of the trend toward a more internationalized economy. Broadly, other countries will figure more and more in the future of American business in three ways: as competitors, as markets, and as partners. Built largely on the ideal domestic market once afforded by this country's homogenous, growing, and prosperous population, America's post-World War II dominance of the world economy has ended. Japan now enjoys industrial pre-eminence. It has surpassed the United States in such key industries as automobiles and steel and enjoys a more rapidly growing gross national product (GNP). But other nations, from established powers such as Germany to emergent ones such as South Korea, offer both powers keen and growing competition. Foreign manufacturers of products ranging from railroad equipment to textiles and from appliances to steel will, we are told, continue to make inroads into traditionally U.S.-dominated markets both here and abroad (Naisbett, 1984). Minimizing or reversing that trend will require understanding of and attention to the needs of international markets too often in the past regarded as convenient dumping sites for goods with no domestic market.

The new global character of business activity will have a cooperative as well as a competitive dimension. Peter Drucker has termed production sharing the prevailing form of worldwide economic integration. It is commonplace now to discover that a product bought in the United States was made with raw materials from, say, two other countries, partly assembled in a third, and finished in a fourth. Even the U.S. auto industry is increasingly entering into cooperative ventures with foreign manufacturers (Naisbett, 1984). Some of these are in the Third World, which, by some estimates, will so benefit from the global redistribution of production that by the year 2000 it will manufacture some 30 percent of the world's goods (Naisbett, 1984, p. 60).

Entrepreneurism, Intrapreneurism, and the Small Company. The economy's need for managers will be centered, it is clear, in business units dependent on entrepreneurism. This trend will result from two phenomena: growth among small companies and the decentralization of large ones.

Small businesses are the true growth sector of the American economy. They currently account for 10.8 million of the 11 million U.S. businesses and employ 60 percent of the labor force (Naisbett, 1984, p. 161). Moreover, despite great attrition, their ranks are growing at an increasing rate: 630,000 of these businesses were created in 1984, according to Dun and Bradstreet, up from 520,000 just five years before (Dobrzynski, Tarpey, and Aikmann, 1985, p. 89). In one recent seven-year period, the *Fortune* 1,000 companies produced only 3 percent of the new jobs in the economy (Whitelaw, 1982–83, p. 7); small companies of less than a thousand employees, by contrast, are currently generating almost 82 percent (Dobrzynski, Tarpey, and Aikmann, 1985, p. 90). Women, interestingly, get much of the credit for this growth. Many have started their own firms in preference to climbing the corporate ladder. Between 1974 and 1984, women set up enterprises at a rate six times faster than men (Ansberry, 1985, p. 19).

As the trend toward small business continues, so should the intensification of demand for entrepreneurial management capable of leading these enterprises. But small business will have to compete for such management. More and more large businesses, impressed with the merits of decentralization, are creating competing profit centers or "intrapreneurial" groups within the corporation. Here, too, in large corporations restructured into smaller and smaller units to encourage mobility and risk taking, the enterprising, opportunity-minded motivator will be in great demand.

New Styles of Management for a New Work Force. No trend in American business is more important than that toward participative, "people-oriented" management. It is a trend born of several other trends—including several already mentioned. An information economy, for example, requires more, and more varied, interaction among workers. And competitive viability in such an economy requires, in particular, a speed and flexibility of communication difficult to achieve in a rigidly structured, hierarchical organization. Other things being equal, the more successful firms will, without abandoning formal controls, foster constant, informal lateral and diagonal communication across

functions (Naisbett, 1984). The trend toward smaller companies
and smaller, relatively autonomous units within larger companies works to the same end. So do the increasing fluidity of
markets and the increasing encroachment of technology into
the workers' world. All these developments will in the years
ahead conspire to put a premium on humane modes of management that encourage workers' personal commitment to collective enterprise, draw creatively on their ideas, and build a foundation for cooperation and flexibility in the face of necessary
change.

Yet perhaps the most compelling reason for more collaborative management will be the labor force itself. It has been
said of the post–World War II "baby boomers" that they have
transformed every institution through which they have passed
(Jones, 1980); if so, it should be a fact of considerable interest
to American business that one-half of all its work force is now
from this age cohort. They are better educated workers than
those they replace, 40 percent of them having attended college.
They are also bringing new values with them into the workplace. As a group, they are relatively more conscious of "worker rights"—for example, privacy, due process, free speech—and
less responsive to authoritarian directives (Naisbett, 1984). Today's workers are also more likely to be females and members
of minority groups. The number of women entering the work
force is growing rapidly, and by 1989 they will outnumber the
men there. One out of every six workers is a member of a minority group (Wolfbein, 1985). Whatever their gender or race,
today's workers are more inclined to protest perceived inequi-
ties. It is probably no coincidence that a number of recent surveys have begun to show sharp drops in the percentage of
workers who think they are treated fairly and who have confidence in management (Morgan and Schiemann, 1984).

Confronting all these trends—and, some would admit,
following the example of the Japanese—American companies
are dramatically changing their management of work and
workers. A recent Conference Board report (Gorlin and Shein,
1984) indicates that virtually all of fifty-two "pace-setting"
companies studied try to increase productivity and product

quality by involving workers in the management of their work and the overall goals of the company. Techniques include the redesign of jobs, the granting of increased autonomy to work teams, a commitment to retraining, and the establishment of various kinds of cooperative problem-solving groups, including quality circles and so-called quality-of-work-life (QWL) groups. Companies cited as having impressive records in this area include such large and mainstream enterprises as TRW, Hewlett-Packard, Dana, General Foods, and IBM.

More Sophisticated Decision Making. Under this last rubric we can group several important developments, all of which pertain to the sophistication with which business makes decisions. One is a growing recognition of the limitations of current, largely quantitative decision-making models. This dissatisfaction takes many forms. As Ian Mitroff and Ralph H. Kilmann (1984, p. 52) have written, today the bulk of business practitioners have been trained to "solve exercises predicated on a simple, stable view of the world"—exercises "designed to have a single correct answer" in light of "a single criterion, the 'bottom line.' " As a result, managers today are unprepared "to face the . . . intellectual and emotional challenges" that actual business situations present. Others, such as Alan Kantrow of the *Harvard Business Review,* are calling attention to our need to know more about "how implicit values and assumptions structure not only judgments and decisions, but also the common understanding of what constitutes evidence and what serves as a source of authority in a debate" (personal communication, January 1985). Calls are heard for more attention to the development of institutional memories to "bring the lessons of the past to bear on specific business problems" (Committee on Public History, 1983, p. 3).

Closely related and more widely reported is a growing conviction (expressed by 76 percent of one thousand top executives in one recent survey) that U.S. business is ill served by the short-term bias of its decisions (Heidrick and Struggles, Inc., 1981, p. 3). The dynamics of the nation's capital market continue to give managers strong reason for that bias, but one sees in a growing number of areas evidence of longer-term perspective. Experts report "more concern, particularly at the board level, for structuring compensation packages to motivate executives to think long term" (Naisbett, 1984, p. 87). Long-term plans—albeit honored as much in the breach as in the observance—are now a fixture of corporate life. Finally, increasing numbers of firms are regarding employment decisions as long-term commitments to repeated retraining. IBM now spends approximately $500 million a year on employee training and education (Naisbett, 1984, p. 32). One management organization specialist has recently estimated that training costs in the services sector may, by 1990 to 1995, approach 10 percent of a company's gross revenues (American Society for Training and Development, 1984b, p. 1).

Finally, and still more pervasive and well known, is business's resolve to avoid decisions that fail to take sufficient account of its political environment. Sometimes victimized in the past by their own insensitivity or naivete, businesses have made great efforts to anticipate and meet appropriately the concerns of a range of external agents, from legislators, government agencies, and the courts to shareholders, suppliers, and consumers. Few things being less welcome to business than surprise and disruption, the priority placed on environmentally sensitive, proactive decision making is only likely to increase in the future.

To this point, we have surveyed a number of developments in the corporate world with an eye to identifying the ways in which the environment confronting tomorrow's manager will differ from our own. We have skimmed the front pages, as it were, of tomorrow's *Journal.* Now we can look at the want ads. What has our survey told us about the capacities that companies will increasingly need in their managers? What skills and abilities will spell managerial adaptability in the future? Some of the key ones are briefly enumerated here.

- The growing role of high technology will increase the importance of a basic understanding of mathematics, science, and technology; it will not, however, require most managers to become high-technology workers themselves.
- The emergence of an information economy marked by accelerating change will place a premium on the abilities to synthesize, organize, and analyze masses of information, to

communicate accurately and compellingly, and constantly to
learn anew.

- Shifting markets and industry boundaries will call for creativity, an ability to see things whole and to reconceptualize
  a firm's role in the context of a vision for the future. They
  will test the manager's understanding of the firm's social
  milieu, especially of people and their needs and desires.
- The internationalization of the economy will place new priority on a grasp of world affairs and an understanding of the
  mores and needs of other cultures.
- The growth of small companies and entre- and intrapreneurism will require managers who are independent-minded problem solvers, motivated to lead.
- The evolution of the work force will increase the need for
  managers sensitive to the central importance of people in the
  enterprise and adept at collaborative and empathic supervision.
- Finally, the commitment to more sophisticated decision
  making will require managers with an ability to ask questions
  and think critically and to recognize and deal with the un-
  quantifiable; it will put new importance on a sense of history
  and an awareness of ethical as well as political implications—
  in general, maturity of judgment.

A tall order: companies might sooner expect the manager who
qualifies to spring full grown from the brow of Zeus than to
stroll off a college campus. Nonetheless, environmental change
is a certainty, and firms need to find or develop managers who
come as close as possible to the mark. The central premise of
this book, of course, is that they can maximize their chances of
doing so if they are alert to the potential of liberal education.
Let us turn now to a definition of that kind of learning and
trace its connections to the capacities we have identified.

Liberal Education

Liberal education is best defined by the spirit and style
of its enquiry and by the results that it seeks—not by any association with a particular subject matter. Although definitions

differ, most agree that its hallmark is a kind of learning that can take place in schools of business—and in a wide variety of other curricular settings—as well as in programs in the traditional liberal arts.

Liberal education emphasizes a rigorous but broad and open-minded approach to subject matter; it encourages an active and questioning role for the learner, the exercise of individual judgment, and the development of broadly applicable skills. The antithesis of narrow—or illiberal—education, it ranges across many disciplines, grounding poets in science and technology, programmers in political philosophy, and economists in the history of art. It exploits each subject's potential for posing value questions and for displaying problems, facts, ideas, events, and situations in their full contexts—cultural, scientific, esthetic, political, historical, technological, and so on.

Some believe that the liberal arts—the disciplines within the humanities, fine arts, social sciences, and sciences—are especially conducive to liberal learning. Certainly, as Thomas Jones (1982, p. 6) has elsewhere pointed out, few courses in the liberal arts can be taught (or their subject matter researched) without attention to liberal learning's objectives. "While a course in modern art might try to teach only names and dates, it is unlikely that students will go far without asking: 'What is good art? Who is an artist as opposed to a technician? Why do we need art?' " By contrast, as Jones writes, there may be an equally natural tendency in business courses to "concentrate on how to do something—better, quicker, more cheaply." Too seldom do they "raise questions of 'Should we? Might it not be better to . . . ? What are the human implications of . . . ?' "

It is a fallacy, however, to think that the liberal arts have a patent on liberal learning's distinctive spirit and approach. First, the liberal arts can be taught and studied as illiberally as any other subject matter. There are too many boorishly narrow liberal arts professors and graduates for us to pretend otherwise. Secondly, as Chapters Six and Seven suggest, preprofessional programs can be powerful vehicles for liberal learning. Although study for a real estate license is unlikely to further liberal learning, many business school courses can. Marketing courses can move easily beyond technique, forcing students to grapple with the ethical implications of advertising or the sensitivity of a marketing strategy to different cultural contexts. Management courses lend themselves especially well to searching enquiry into the social sciences that provide this more applied discipline its intellectual underpinnings. And, to cite a final example, the entire business curriculum can enforce attention to oral and written communication. The best business and other preprofessional programs will, in the words of Cornell University president Frank H. T. Rhodes, "embrace . . . liberal education, not as an 'add-on', but as a vital component of professional study" (Rhodes, 1985, p. 80).

I have been more explicit to this point about the "spirit and style of enquiry" that defines liberal learning than about the distinctive results it seeks. But it will be apparent by now that the capacities we have identified as requisites for future managerial success are all among the objectives for liberal learning. Uniquely ambitious, liberal education aspires to foster other outcomes, too: civic responsibility, for example, and personal enrichment. But the list of commercially applicable traits that emerges from our survey of change very closely approximates even the most detailed enumerations of liberal learning's aims. (That the stated aims of most vocationally oriented courses of study look quite different is also noteworthy. For achieving liberal learning objectives is difficult enough for programs that seek them above all else; the likelihood of their being realized as by-products is slim.)

The Yale report of 1828 spoke of educational outcomes as "the furniture and disciplines of the mind" (Edgerton, 1984, p. 18). Both outcomes are essential. A liberal education, like our managerial profile, certainly includes the acquisition of specific knowledge—"furniture of the mind." But business faces a future in which what is known will change more and more rapidly. Even now, half of the engineer's knowledge is said to grow obsolete every five years (Alfred and Hilpert, 1985, p. 30), and a focus on content "threatens to equip us with solutions to yesterday's problems" (Mandt, 1982, p. 49). Thus, liberal learning is especially timely in that broad generic competencies—the "disciplines of the mind"—are its primary aims. There is much appeal in the waggish definition of liberal education as "what the student has left after he has forgotten what he has learned."

Finally, the question arises of what success liberal education has had in actually achieving—as opposed to seeking—its objectives. Chapter Four covers this issue at length. As we shall see, however, the available evidence is encouraging. The research of Winter, McClelland, and Stewart (1981), longitudinal studies of AT&T managers (Beck, 1981), the Chase Bank's studies of management trainees (Burns, 1983)—this work and more provide impressive empirical proof that liberal education is for the most part doing the job it sets out to do.

Conclusion

Business executives are trained, quite properly, to make decisions "at the margin." They concentrate on the relationship of costs to benefits from a current time—or current level of production—forward. It is only at the margin, typically, that they have their opportunities for effective intervention—and even there, the levers they control are few. Viewing their options from this perspective, business decision makers may wish to give the arguments reviewed here special weight. First, the selection and development of managers can clearly have great influence on a firm's future, and they are within business's control. Second, we have identified as potential criteria for selection management competencies that seem likely to take on increasing importance over time.

John Kemeny (1980), eminent mathematician, computer scientist, and former president of Dartmouth College, spoke as an educator when he said that "neither you nor I knows what the big issues will be when today's students are at the height of their careers. . . . We have to give them a breadth of education that will prepare them, not for the problems we know today, but for the problems that we *don't* know today." Alert to opportunities for effective intervention at the margin, businesses may, for entirely self-interested, competitive reasons, reach the same conclusion. Those that do give liberal education a more

central place in the preparation and development of their management should be well served. For, in the words again of the
forum report (Business–Higher Education Forum, 1985), they
will have moved to secure that first requirement of "sustained
excellence" in the future: adaptability to change.

The Liberal Arts
and the Art of Management

There are many paths to educational breadth, but none, I think, better than the liberal arts. A strong grounding in these fields can greatly enhance a manager's effectiveness. The reasons for this are probably as old as the liberal arts themselves, but my own explanation begins with an observation about a current best seller.

In Search of Excellence (Peters and Waterman, 1982) was, and continues to be, a phenomenal success. But in the four years since the book appeared, business realities have changed. Some of the companies cited for their excellence are, for various reasons, excellent no longer. Part of the problem may have been a tendency to take the text too literally. As *Business Week* recently noted ("Who's Excellent Now?," 1984, p. 78), a company does itself little good if it adheres strictly to the book's eight commandments but fails to react to broad economic trends. Furthermore, *In Search of Excellence* was essentially "a response to an era when management put too much emphasis on number-crunching," whereas good management in fact "requires much more than following any one set of rules."

Does all this mean that the book was worthwhile only be-

21

cause it gave the pendulum a much-needed shove in the "people/simplicity/values" direction? I think not, and my reasons begin with a statement by one of the authors, Robert Waterman ("Who's Excellent Now?," 1984, p. 78): "The book has been so popular that people have taken it as a formula for success rather than what it was intended to be. We were writing about the art, not the science, of management."

I believe that Waterman's statement is valid—and not as an apology, either. Management *is* an art, very much like the creation of a painting, a sculpture, or a work of literature. Whether you are carving a statue or reorganizing a corporation, you have a vision of what you want to create, as well as a sense of how to make that vision real by bringing different elements together according to an overall pattern. There are, in fact, specific parallels between management and the fine arts, as Henry Boettinger (1975, p. 57) has noted in an article in the *Harvard Business Review.*

Both the artist and the manager, Boettinger says, must have technical mastery of their materials and their crafts. Managers' materials are human talent, including their own, plus "the drives, anxieties, and reactions of those beyond the perimeter of [their] control—stockholders, customers, competitors, and government officials." Managers' craft is their ability to organize that talent to fulfill their vision. And just as artists communicate their intent through their works, managers must be able to convey their vision in an inspiring and forceful way—in other words, to lead—or else that vision will never be fully realized. Seen in this light, Waterman's (and coauthor Thomas Peters's) attributes of excellence are nothing more than specific expressions of management art. Some of them involve a vision of what the organization should be. The management of an excellent company:

- fosters autonomy and entrepreneurship (it breaks the corporation into small companies and encourages them to think independently and creatively);
- achieves simultaneous loose-tight properties (it encourages dedication to the central values of the company, with tolerance for all employees who accept those values);

- sticks to the knitting (it remains with the business that the company knows best);
- is "hands-on" (it insists that executives keep in touch with the firm's essential business).

Other attributes rely on the manager's craft—on his or her ability to motivate people and orchestrate their talents. Thus, the excellently managed company:

- stays close to the customer (it learns his or her preferences and caters to them);
- achieves productivity through people (it creates in all employees the awareness that their best efforts are essential and that they will share in the rewards of the company's success); and
- is value driven (it promotes a strong corporate culture).

Furthermore, if you accept, as I do, the parallels between fine art and management art, then it quickly becomes clear that the study of the liberal arts—of nature and of human beings and their works—can lead to an understanding of what the successful manager does so well. Contrary to what is widely believed, liberal arts students are far from ignorant of the art of management. They know quite a bit about it.

Even more important, we in business can benefit from having such people within our ranks. Granted, most business activities must be performed by individuals trained in finance, engineering, accounting, and so on. But those people do not perform in a vacuum. It is up to their managers to motivate them and coordinate their efforts in ways that maximize personal satisfaction and achieve the organization's goals. And they, as managers, must do the same for the people who work for and with them. Thus, the practice of management art and the pursuit of business excellence call for an entirely different, but parallel, set of nontechnical skills—skills that we urgently need today.

These abilities can readily be acquired through liberal arts training. To support this idea, I will explore the connections between management art and the liberal arts disciplines that underlie it. As I do that, I will offer examples of the ways in which these skills are helping GM to achieve some of its key objectives. Then I will discuss some other business goals to which a liberal arts education seems relevant.

The art of management begins with vision, a quality that has never been so critical as it is today. In the auto industry, for example, new foreign competition, government regulation, and wide swings in economic conditions and consumer preference have created an environment of rapid and constant change. In this context, competitiveness—and, for some companies, survival itself—depends on the manager's ability to envision new things (as well as new ways of doing old things), to extrapolate on the basis of what worked in the past, to organize and reorganize operations so that economy is achieved and redundancy eliminated, and to imagine how the course of events might be changed, and by what kind of interventions.

Early in 1984, General Motors undertook a massive reorganization of its North American passenger-car operations. The basic thrust has been to reduce five car divisions to two "supergroups," each with a different market orientation, and each responsible for the design, manufacturing, and profitability of its products. The reorganization was carried out over a period of many months by a team that at times numbered as many as 1,400 people. Over and over, we asked ourselves how the same functions could be performed more effectively with less overlap and more accountability. Dozens of manufacturing and staff operations had to be reassigned to one or the other of the new car groups or to one of our component operations. And from preliminary research to final implementation, the reorganization has called upon the creativity of our people, in the senses in which I just defined it.

The same kinds of mental processes can be acquired and sharpened in the study of the liberal arts. When students are trained to recognize recurring elements and common themes in art, literature, physics, and history, they are becoming familiar with what the author William Plomer defined as the ability to "perceive the relations between thoughts, or things, or forms of expression that may seem utterly different, and to be able to combine them into some new forms—the power to connect the seemingly unconnected" (Peter, 1977, p. 123). They are, in other words, learning about the kind of creativity that leads to visionary solutions to business problems.

Now let me focus on some of the ways in which managerial vision creates an excellent company, as Waterman and Peters ("Who's Excellent Now?," 1984, p. 77) define it. Autonomy and entrepreneurship, as well as the "looseness" of a "simultaneous loose-tight organization," have something important in common: both place a high premium on independent thought and action. Some organizations emphasize these strongly, and some ignore them, but most fall in between the two extremes. And I see a clear connection between an organization's competitiveness and its avoidance of bureaucracies in which methods, rules, and procedures multiply and become more important than individual people, organizational productivity, and the attainment of actual business goals. For this reason, we at General Motors are cultivating entrepreneurism and loose-tight organization throughout the length and breadth of our company. One of the main purposes of the reorganization I mentioned earlier is to move products from design to production as quickly as possible, by moving the decision-making factors as far down in the organization as possible and by allowing people more freedom of operation. This decentralized control will go even further in our new Saturn Corporation, where workers will actively participate in many decision areas that used to be the exclusive territory of management.

"Loose-tight" also applies to our pursuit of product quality: we have a corporatewide "quality ethic," but we have allowed each division to decide what quality system it will use to achieve the objectives we have set. It applies to our labor relations: where possible, we are working with the United Auto Workers to reduce the number of job classifications, so that our employees can more freely call upon the full range of their abilities. And we are becoming more and more open to our employees' suggestions, since we regard everyone as a potential expert on how to do his or her job. Finally, the "loose-tight" description applies to our newly acquired high-tech subsidiaries—to Electronic Data Systems, to Hughes Aircraft, and to the machine-vision and artificial-intelligence firms in which we have invested: while we expect that each of them will benefit General Motors in its own way, we will do nothing to interfere with the highly entrepreneurial and performance-oriented cultures that have been responsible for the outstanding success of these companies.

People trained in the liberal arts would be able to understand, function in, and contribute to the loose-tight, entrepreneurial organization that General Motors and so many other businesses are striving to become. They would feel little tension between outward nonconformity and inner commitment to common goals. That is partly because their studies have exposed them to a diversity of human experience and, perhaps even more important, to a research and discovery process that, as I understand it, is relatively unstructured and unsupervised. During this process, students acquaint themselves with scholarly methods and findings; then they often work alone, reading documents, evaluating and comparing ideas, observing behavior, recording data, and formulating hypotheses. They learn to tolerate ambiguity and to bring order out of apparent confusion. Intellectual integrity is paramount, and reasoning processes are just as important as the conclusions to which they lead. Accordingly, the liberal arts can prepare the student for a work environment of clear, strong values that are interpreted and implemented in an individual, personal way.

The liberal arts can also prepare the student to contribute to another attribute of excellence that expresses a managerial vision—"sticking to the knitting" and "keeping in touch with the firm's essential business" (the "hands on" aspect of "hands on, value driven"). To achieve and practice these, you need the kind of "sideways" thinking and cross-classifying habit of mind that comes from learning, among other things, the many different ways of looking at literary works, social systems, chemical processes, or languages. I make this point because "sticking to the knitting" is not always as simple as it seems. The answer to the question of what business a company is "really" in depends, to a great extent, on when and in what context the question is asked. If the early-twentieth-century railroad magnates had understood that they were in the transportation business and had invested in the fledgling aviation industry, the entire face of corporate America would be radically different from what it is today. On the other hand, the makers of cash registers and adding machines did see that their real business was information; consequently, they leaped upon the surging wave of the computer industry and were able to ride it to its crest.

In these times of rapid and complex change, it is getting harder and harder to stick to the knitting. Home computers may seem to resemble toys, but the gap between the two products, as Coleco recently found out, turned out to be a lot wider than it looked. At General Motors, we are determined to keep on doing what we do best—but we are always looking for ways to do it better. This strategy may require indirect approaches to more effective knitting. We do not consider ourselves to be a software writing and marketing firm, but we saw that our manufacturing automation systems were so diverse that it would simply have been wrongheaded *not* to pursue an overall compatibility. That is why we developed Manufacturing Automation Protocol (MAP), a computer program that allows different manufacturers' systems to communicate with each other. It is only tangentially related to our core business—but it responds, in important ways, to our unique needs.

Let me turn now from the manager's vision to his or her craft—to the way in which he or she makes the vision a reality. Here, the attributes of excellence—staying close to the customer, achieving productivity through people, and being value driven—all depend on communication skills and sensitivity to people. Without the ability to communicate in a clear, concise, and humane way, managers will have a hard time staying in touch with customers, conveying the organization's values to employees, and establishing the connection between individual and corporate success. And without a sensitivity to people, they will find it difficult to harmonize individual differences, needs, and work styles with the common goals and values.

Effective communication is the vehicle for all other forms of business competence. Everything we do depends on the successful transfer of meaning from one person or group to another. In fact, it is not much of an exaggeration to say that communication is really what business is all about! All too few businesspeople understand this principle; all too few practice it in the daily performance of their jobs. But successful students of drama, language, literature, speech, and rhetoric have learned to arrange their thoughts in logical order and to write and speak clearly and economically. The best of them can communicate with a real feeling for the flexibility and power of language and with a sensitivity to their own purposes and to the needs of their audience.

The connection between highly developed verbal skills and effective management is not only desirable—it is real. I recently read that, in 1983, only 20.6 percent of the *Forbes* 500 chief executive officers (CEOs) had a technical background ("Harper's Index," 1984). And the connection between literacy and leadership goes back many centuries, according to an article entitled "The Literacy of Power" (Pattison, 1983). The author, Robert Pattison, notes the connection between verbal fluency and high office in ancient Rome, medieval China, and nineteenth-century Britain. America, he says, "has two literacies. One, the literacy of the great majority, is defined by the ability to read and write. The other, the literacy of power, demands the capacity to manipulate language in profitable and intelligent ways" (p. 48). Pattison consulted *The Reference Book of Corporate Managements* (Dun and Bradstreet, 1982) and found that "the institutions that provide the manpower for American [business] leadership are marked by a commitment to programs in languages and literature." And he observes that "the hegemony of these literates continues, even in the age of software. Executives in industries that rely on new computer technologies tell me that when they want someone to run a computer center or oversee a program design, they look for humanities majors, because [it is] they [who] are adept at manipulating systems of thought and verbal patterns" (Pattison, 1983, p. 49).

A sensitivity to people is also basic to the manager's craft. Here, too, liberal arts skills can help managers achieve their organizations' goals. The liberally educated manager has been exposed to a wide variety of peoples, places, and historical periods. He or she has become acquainted with the achievements—the tales of epic courage, the magnificent cathedrals, the groundbreaking scientific discoveries—that transcend their eras and reverberate down through the ages with their message that the worth and dignity of men and women can be found in any time or place. And the social sciences in particular confront the student with the astonishing diversity of human societies and cultures—and with the similarities between them, as they search for answers to the same eternal questions. This kind of exposure helps develop the interpersonal skills that, for the effective manager, are nothing less than business fundamentals. Geniuses in finance or production processes are not much good to us unless they can also understand people, treat them with dignity and courtesy, respect their opinions about the work they do, and appreciate their differences in age, gender, and culture. And it almost goes without saying that employees are happiest and most productive when they are treated with these kinds of considerations.

At General Motors, through our quality-of-work-life programs and our massive new emphasis on training, we are moving to become an organization that is committed to a set of shared values. In our manufacturing facilities, we are replacing confrontation with cooperation, and we are instructing people at all levels in the principles of conflict resolution. In this context, skill in communication and interpersonal relations is not merely a "nice to have" managerial talent. It is the vehicle by which the organization's goals are conveyed to each employee, and by which each employee's support and commitment are secured. And gaining that support and commitment is nothing less than a pivotal competitive issue, essential to our attainment of higher quality and productivity at lower cost.

Let me turn now to three other management ideals that I think are critically important, as well as closely related to elements of liberal arts education.

The first is corporate social responsibility. In discussions of corporate policy making nowadays, we often find the word *stewardship*. And with good reason. Certainly, a corporation must serve the interests of its customers, employees, and shareholders. But that alone is not enough. In the cities and towns where its facilities are located, it must also act with a sense of responsibility for the natural environment and for the economic health of the community. In all of its personnel policies, it must practice a concern for the rights and opportunities of minority groups. In proportion to its size and influence, it must promote the economic vitality of the nation and, ultimately, the welfare of future generations. Scholarships and other forms of aid to education, driver-training programs, contributions to hospitals, support of cancer research, contributions to the arts, funding of educational and public-interest television programs, sponsorship of intercollegiate competition in marketing, special programs for the education and training of minorities and for the development of minority dealers and suppliers—these are but a sampling of the ways in which General Motors seeks to enrich the life of the society in which it operates.

The higher one rises in the managerial/executive ranks, the more far-reaching his or her decisions are likely to be, and the more critical it becomes that these decisions be colored by a strong sense of stewardship. And this is another area in which liberally educated people come to us already prepared, at least conceptually. People who have studied history and philosophy find it easy to maintain a broad perspective. They know that what a corporation does can have moral implications that may reach far beyond the making of goods and the earning of profits. They understand the inherent worth of our philanthropic activities, and they can be counted on to carry these projects forward and to devise new ones as well.

The second management ideal is product quality. There are three dimensions here, all of them essential, all of them the focus of considerable attention and investments at General Motors and, of course, at many other companies as well. Fundamentally, quality is the result of specific tools and techniques, such as statistical process control. But it also requires management systems that encourage input from line workers and reward quality in tangible ways. And its third dimension is an individual and ethical commitment: a universal, sincere belief that a quality product—and this notion includes whatever moves from one person or group to another within the organization—is the only product worth striving for. Thus, it is not enough to teach techniques for building to specifications. The people who apply these techniques must do so in the context of an organization that demonstrates, by management systems and management example, that it supports the goal. And these two factors, operating together, kindle the individual commitment that perpetuates itself and becomes entrenched as a "quality culture." This is another area in which liberal arts graduates already have a grasp of the basic issues. The study of literature, arts, esthetics, or music has almost certainly offered insight into the fit of form with function. No doubt it has also nurtured a respect for attention to detail and for doing things with perfection as the goal. Thus, the liberally educated manager understands the nature of quality in its broadest sense: the result of an attitude—a pride of workmanship—that permeates the entire organization and touches every task.

The third ideal is the effective management of change. Charles F. "Boss" Kettering, a prominent GM scientist and executive of the 1920s and 1930s, maintained that "change is the only thing that has ever brought progress." True, but change is getting harder and harder to keep up with. An engineer who graduates today and makes no effort to stay current will find his or her skills obsolete in only five to ten years. We need people who are receptive to new information, to new paths to the traditional goals, even to new goals. And I believe that liberal arts graduates are indeed such people. They have learned to uncover truth in many forms. They know that although some principles endure from one time and place to another, no answer need be final.

All throughout this chapter, I have spoken of a need for skills, not for a particular head count. My argument is not a recruiting plea, and it should not be construed as such. But make no mistake about it: we do need the skills that a liberal education confers. We must import them by hiring liberal arts graduates. And we must impart them to the technical people we already have. Neither process is simple. Certainly, we can recruit liberal arts graduates. Still, the candidates themselves must be resourceful, ambitious, and energetic. These are personal characteristics, unrelated (as far as I know) to liberal education. And the college placement counselors must meet us halfway, by identifying those students who are interested in business careers and by preparing them—in ways their liberal arts training alone typically does not—for the transition to corporate life.

Making changes among our own people is not easy, either. In some cases, the habits of mind developed by the liberal arts directly oppose some strongly established ways of doing things; that is a situation that we are trying hard to change. And, in any case, the technical people cannot stop their work for six months while they learn new ways of doing it. We must help them cultivate these new skills day by day, as they do the jobs for which they were hired. We are, in fact, doing just that: our Education Training Department carries on a wide variety of programs in communication skills, interpersonal skills, quality, creativity/ innovation, and (for plant managers and others directly concerned) community impact and corporate social responsibility. And, despite all the difficulties and obstacles, we have to go forward—because of what I see as the ultimate impact of liberal arts on the art of management.

Capitalism seems to me a demonstrably superior system for the creation of wealth, and it has certainly come a long way since the excesses of years past. Still, it can be fine tuned and improved, so that it works even more effectively, through constructive attention to the human element. That attention will lead the organization to more effective problem solving, a more acute awareness of its surroundings, and a rededication to product quality and value. And it can lead to something else: corporations can clarify, for themselves and their people, the nature and value of work. This process is at least as important as the others, but it has received comparatively little recognition among business leaders. My point is that we do not get the levels of loyalty and performance that we need by asking people to work for a paycheck and benefits alone. Rather, employees need to see the value and impact of what they do. They need to understand its place in the larger scheme of things. They need to be recognized for doing it well. And they need to be encouraged to be creative about doing it even better. Furthermore, by pursuing these goals through people-oriented systems, we managers can oppose the depersonalization of work, and even reverse it, so that people can identify with what they do, and—even as our computers and robots deliver greater and greater efficiency, precision, and productivity—our employees can aspire to the individual, craftsmanly excellence and satisfaction of the silversmith or the potter.

The ultimate impact of the liberal arts on the art of management, then, is a major contribution to the evolution of an ethical and humanistic capitalism—a system that stimulates innovation, fosters excellence, enriches society, and dignifies work. Pressed as we managers may be by our day-to-day concerns, we must nevertheless serve this higher obligation as well —and we must find and develop the people who can help us to fulfill it.

3

Alan M. Kantrow
Stanley T. Burns

Conversations
with Five Managers

Chapters One and Two have stated in general terms the case
that liberal education has value in management. For a more detailed and vivid sense of just how it does so, we turn now to
some individual histories. The five executives interviewed on the
following pages are a diverse group. Three are men, two women.
They range in age from the late thirties to mid fifties and in
level of responsibility from middle to top management. Their
undergraduate institutions range in type from small liberal arts
colleges to large research universities, and most have taken at
least some courses at the graduate level. They work now in
small to midsized companies in a variety of (mostly service-
sector) industries—life insurance, investments, information systems consulting, electronic publishing, and wine importing.
Most have come to their present positions through a variety of
work experiences and by paths they could not have foreseen as
undergraduates. In all these respects, they are not unrepresenta-
tive of liberally educated managers generally, especially those
with backgrounds in the liberal arts.

  Like the rest of this volume, these interviews pose challenges to those responsible for the provision of higher educa-

tion. We hear in one interview dissatisfaction with institutional neglect of liberal education and in another concern over a lack of curricular coherence. Several of the five deplore the frequent elevation of research over teaching as a faculty priority, and one criticizes a rigidity in our entire educational system that forces students to concern themselves far more with accumulating credentials than with self-discovery.

On balance, however, the interviews are very positive. What may strike one most is their subjects' enthusiasm for liberal learning as a form of personal enrichment. Several convey a sense of the intrinsic interest of favorite courses and fields of study and the curiosity and excitement with which they approached them. One speaks of a liberal education as "a development process, a growth process," and relates it to the development of the personal goals and values of the whole human being. The suggestion is clear, however, that even here, where the value of liberal learning is most personal, it is not only that. Managers are people; they manage with and through the strengths and weaknesses of their humanity and individuality, and to the extent that liberal learning affects these last—and it clearly does—we can draw no easy distinction between the personal and practical values of this kind of education.

The executives speak with one voice about the directly practical benefits of their education. They affirm the value of content knowledge—a grasp of history, language, mathematics. But, to paraphrase one of the five, their emphasis is on what one can learn from such subjects besides the subjects themselves. That, they contend, includes the abilities to analyze situations, to understand people and orchestrate their efforts productively, to communicate compellingly in writing and speech, to adapt creatively to changing and ambiguous conditions. Perhaps more than any other practical outcome—and they cite many—they emphasize liberal learning's value as a preparation for further learning, whether in the classroom or on the job.

A thing, said Einstein, should be made as simple as possible, but not simpler. The five managers interviewed cannot, of course, neatly separate the effects of their liberal educations from those of their other academic and work experiences. And who is to say that their career successes and their value to their companies would have been any less had they not had as broad a preparation? These hard questions notwithstanding, the interviews that follow leave little doubt that these five executives see their own liberal learning as a special, and especially valuable, part of their preparations. Its dimensions and precise outcomes may be elusive; but even in a world of commerce, it is not something they would trade.

William H. Hazen
Chief Executive Officer
J. & W. Seligman Trust Company

Q: Why don't you start by talking about where you went to school? How did you choose? What was on your mind?

W. H.:   Well, I'm a good example for you of a liberal arts education, because I came from a family that really had no education at all. I grew up in Danvers, Massachusetts, a little town about twenty miles north of Boston, in the days before it became a suburb of Boston—when it was still a separate community. It had two industries: the Ideal Baby Shoe Company employed a lot of people, and the rest of the folks raised onions or carrots or parsnips or whatever.

I went to Bowdoin College by luck. I was an outstanding hockey player and hadn't even been thinking about college until my junior year in high school, when the hockey coach said I was a good enough student and had this extra skill where I could probably get a scholarship to college. The reason that I went to Bowdoin was simply that it gave me the largest scholarship of the colleges that I applied to. I had never seen the campus. When I applied, everything was done by mail, and I went to Bowdoin as a real hick. I can truthfully say that Bowdoin College educated me, and if it weren't for Bowdoin College I wouldn't be here today. And it was my good luck that Bowdoin is a fine liberal arts college. The long and short of it was that I had four great years at Bowdoin, and my eyes were opened to the world.

Q: How did you decide what you were going to do?

W. H.:   Well, in 1948, when I went, Bowdoin had a much more defined curriculum. Everybody had to take freshman English, either mathematics or Greek or Latin—and I chose mathematics over Greek or Latin. You had to have a foreign language other than Greek or Latin: in other words, French or Spanish. And you had to have a history course. So I didn't have to worry too much about which courses to pick, because my courses were pretty much laid out for me.

Q: You had options, but the framework was pretty clear?

W. H.:   Yes. I might say that Bowdoin went off that standard a number of years ago, and only recently has it come back to distribution requirements. What they found when they let people be completely free in their choice of academic subjects was that they were graduating people who did not have the liberal arts training that they really felt was necessary. Today, there are more core requirements; in my day, until you got to your junior year, you didn't have a hell of a lot of electives available to you. Public speaking was a required course. You had to go to chapel. There were six chapels a week between 10:00 and 10:30, and you had to go to at least three. This was a nondenominational, nonsectarian chapel, which covered subjects all over the field of education. These sessions were not necessarily religious, although they started with a prayer and ended with a prayer. So this educational experience was truly in the fine liberal arts tradition that causes one to think, causes one to question, causes one to read, causes one to speak, causes one to analyze. It does not concentrate on a particular technical field, although in order to be graduated from Bowdoin, then or now, you must master some field, must have a major field and a minor field. I had a double major, government and economics, and a minor in English.

Q: It sounds like you were acquiring these intellectual processes and skills within a certain specialty. You weren't just roaming around and getting a totally random experience.

W. H.:   These are things that I know *now* were happening to me *then,* but I didn't know it then. What I knew then was that I was trying to get through a calculus course or ancient history class, that I was enjoying a constitutional law class, that I was enjoying my English classes, that I enjoyed my biology class, that I loved Casey's lit course (which was a comparative literature course given by the president, Kenneth Charles Morton Sills; everybody called him Casey). It was a fantastic course.

Q: What was it about?

W. H.:   It was comparative literature and ranged all the way from the Bible to Hawthorne. It covered the classics as well as the contemporaries, although it didn't cover people like O'Neill, the more recent contemporaries. And at the same time, in a small college, a lot of other things rub off on you. I was a member of the glee club, and that was an introduction to music that I never had before. Bowdoin has a fantastic art museum. I'd never been in an art museum in my life before I went into Bowdoin's, where there are Sargents and Renoirs.

Q: So now you can see what was happening to you.

W. H.:   I can see that now, but then I wasn't able to capsule what was happening to me. It was a very enjoyable experience, one which offered me a close relationship with the professors. One of the great things about Bowdoin was that professors used to have us over for dinner once a week. We would go to their homes for seminars followed by coffee if it was evening or things of that sort, so you really got to know the professors and they got to know you. But you had to be in class. I later went to Harvard Law School, and whether I was in class or not didn't make any difference. At Bowdoin, if you didn't show up in class for a couple of days, someone went around to the dormitory to find out what the hell was the matter.

Q: It sounds like both discipline and concern.

W. H.:   Right. Discipline and concern.

Q: So you had fun. You liked what you did there.

W. H.:   I liked it a lot there. Then came time for graduation in 1952; and if you recall, the Korean War was on, and everybody who graduated went to war. You went into the army if you didn't choose another course, but I decided that the army was not for me, even though I didn't have any money to go on to school. I figured, what the hell, I might as well go into the navy, which I preferred over all the other services. So I went down to Boston and signed up and got accepted at Officer Candidate School at Newport. There was no single subject at Officer Candidate School that had anything to do with what I had studied at Bowdoin, with the exception of understanding the uniform military code, the justice code, whatever it is. Then I realized for the first time, I think, that the education that I had had at Bowdoin, which really had nothing to do with what I had to learn at Officer Candidate School, gave me the ability to learn the stuff that I now had to learn—things like navigation and gunnery.

I was stuck there for four months until I graduated as an ensign in October of '52 and got immediately assigned to the fleet. When I got to the Pacific and met up with the battleship *Missouri* in Sasabo, Japan, the next thing I knew was that I woke up one morning with our nine sixteen-inch guns going off simultaneously and pushing the battleship sideways in the water. Fortunately, I was assigned to an admiral's staff, the commander of the Seventh Fleet; so, although I was present, I was not behind a gun. I was his communications watch officer, initially, in the radio section of the admiral's staff, translating, encoding, and decoding top-secret messages. Then I graduated from that job and moved into the assistant flag secretary's job (the flag secretary and the flag lieutenant were the aides-de-camp for the admiral), which meant that I had responsibility for all of the enlisted men and, in the absence of the flag secretary, would accompany the admiral to whatever function he had on. After the war was over, it became a much more social position.

That was a fine experience for me. I saw a lot of the Far East; I was out there for two years. After the war was over, we took the battleship and then the cruisers and went into all the warmwater ports in Japan. We went to Hong Kong, Formosa, so on and so forth. I ended up on five different ships and served under two admirals. When I came back, they put me into San Francisco for my last year. And that was another great duty.

I was again assigned to an admiral's staff, but the admiral was in San Diego, and I was on detached duty in San Francisco.

My job was to go aboard the various ships that came into San Francisco for overhaul and repair just before they would go back out to the fleet to make sure that their readiness was established. I was about as popular as a skunk at a lawn party. I'd go aboard a ship to find out what readiness was all about, but the captain and the executive officer were not interested in readiness—they were interested in giving their men their last liberty.

Q: That's not the most popular thing to do. You were talking earlier about being able to analyze a situation and, at the same time, being able to communicate with other people.

W. H.: That's right. I knew that the captain and the executive officer were going to be on board ship at least during the lunch hour. So I arranged to come on board and have lunch with them, because they were there and had to have lunch. It didn't interfere with their day. I could spend an hour with them, and we could fill out the forms together—and I also got a free lunch. After we finished lunch, if we still had a couple of pages left on the form or found some problems that were not quite resolved, I could usually get them to spend another hour. Now, I don't know where that ability came from, but I think it has to do with a competence in analysis. There was a problem— how do you get the captain to talk to you?—and I analyzed it. That was the way to do it. I had to get the captain to sign off. Remember, I was only a lieutenant junior grade at this point and was dealing with commanders and four-stripers. I couldn't say, "Listen, my admiral down in San Diego is going to get mad at you." He'd say, "Horse ——. I'm sailing tomorrow."

Q: What really helped you out here was being able to figure out what's in it for the other guy, how to deal with him on his own terms.

W. H.: Exactly. I learned that well. Later on, I filled out my application for Harvard Law School, took my aptitude test, and got admitted. I got dismissed from active duty in time to enroll in Harvard in September '55. I graduated in '58. Looking back, I can't think of a better training for law school than the liberal arts, because law school is really reading and analyzing and then expounding in class on the different theories that you have picked up from the reading. If you can't read, you can't survive in law school. If you can't analyze, you can't survive in law school. And if you can't see the other side of the picture, you can't survive in law school. That's why I think that liberal arts training is so very important. Even then I realized— maybe not as much as I do today—I was a hell of a lot better prepared for Harvard Law School by having gone to Bowdoin and taking a liberal arts education than if I'd gone to a technical school. Harvard Law School, of course, is different from a regional law school. At a regional law school, one really studies law just for the purpose of passing the bar exam in that state. But in the national law schools like Harvard, Columbia, Duke, and Stanford, there is no training to pass the bar. Again, it's almost like a liberal arts training, but it's more confined and more particular in that it's related to the law. I took courses in accounting, ethics, comparative law. . . .

Q: You took ethics at that time?

W. H.:   Yes. I didn't know it by that name then. It wasn't called ethics; it was called something else—I forget precisely what. The only practical experience that Harvard offered in those days was the court competition. Now that's changed. Now there are writing courses and lots of opportunity for volunteer work. You go out and work with the district attorneys.

Q: It sounds, again, like what you were getting at the time was a lot of breadth, of intellectual stretching, within the framework of one discipline.

W. H.:   Right. Ultimately, though, the question I faced was what do I want to do, where do I want to go? I went to my adviser, and he asked me if I felt I wanted to be a lawyer forever. I said I didn't know, wasn't sure. He said, well, if you do want to be a lawyer forever, pick out the town you want to live in, go to that town, and set up a practice. If you don't and if you're not sure exactly what you want to do, get a job in New York. So I came to New York, got a job with a law firm called Pell, Butler, Hatch, Curtis, and LeViness, which was basically an estate and trust firm but with a little court practice. I took a cram course and passed the New York bar. Here, again, I come back to the discussion of what liberal arts training can do for you. For one thing, it enabled me to sit down and study the New York law in two months of cramming and then to pass the New York State bar exam. I'm not saying that the Harvard Law School education wasn't very helpful; it was, obviously. But it did not cause me to pass the New York State bar exam. What caused me to pass that exam was the application of the ability to think, read, digest, analyze.

After practicing law for three years, I went to the New York State Banking Department, where I was appointed in 1962 by Rockefeller as assistant counsel to the superintendent of banks and, later, his executive assistant. As executive assistant, I did a lot of things; I was sort of the troubleshooter. I was the proponent of legislation that the banking department wanted passed in Albany. I went out on particular cases where someone had to represent the superintendent. A year or two later, my Harvard Law School roommate, who was then at Sullivan and Cromwell, said that Seligman was looking for someone like me to be sort of an in-house counsel on mutual funds. I quickly found out who they were, came down and interviewed, and on May 1, 1964, started at Seligman and have been there ever since. At the time, they relied upon outside counsel for legal advice, Sullivan and Cromwell for mutual funds and Cravath, Swaine and Moore for general legal questions. I really wasn't counsel as such. My job was to distinguish between a business question and a legal question and to send the legal question out to the proper law firm and to handle the business question myself.

Q: That brought you back to the kind of analysis you were talking about before.

W. H.:   That's right. Seligman was a partnership, and the mutual funds that we managed were corporations in their own right with Seligman partners as their executive officers. Within a few years, I became the corporate secretary for all of these corporations, and then I moved out of that into operations and administration. In those days, there were six partners, and the rest of us were employees. I became a partner in 1969, with direct responsibility for the brokerage part of the business. So I had to take another examination, because I had to be qualified as a principal of the New York Stock Exchange. They don't teach you anything about the net capital rule at the Harvard Law School or Bowdoin College or in the navy. In effect, I did another cram course. What the hell *was* the net capital rule? As with the New York bar exam, but on a much more confined basis and in a much shorter time frame, I passed the examination in order to become registered with the New York Stock Exchange.

In 1973 or so, we were located at 65 Broadway. Our lease was up, and we had to find new space or renegotiate with the landlord, the American Express Company. We were perfectly happy to stay at 65 Broadway, but the American Express Company had decided not to renew our lease. So we had to go out and find new quarters. The move was my responsibility. I had to analyze the space available in lower Manhattan. I had to negotiate the lease. I had to be in charge of the entire move. Now, I was smart enough—or the firm was smart enough—to know that I couldn't do all that independently. They hired a firm to assist us, show us what properties were available, and explain the differences among the leases we could get at various properties. I was the person who had to analyze those pros and cons and to make recommendations to the firm as to what we would finally do.

Q: And, again, you had not had a course in real estate.

W. H.:   No courses in real estate, no courses in lease negotiation, no courses in landlords' work letters, no courses in labor negotiations, no courses in interior design. All I knew was that we wanted to keep our image as an old-line New York firm. If we had to move into a new building, which we pretty much had decided to do, even though it was glass, we wanted it to continue to look like what we were. I had the complete responsibility for the move, and it was something I'd never done before, a very enlightening experience. If we move again, I'm going to assign that job to someone else.

The next major change occurred in 1981, when we converted from a partnership to a corporation. We put the brokerage company into a subsidiary called Seligman Securities; we put the mutual fund business, the marketing aspect of it, into another subsidiary, called Seligman Marketing; and the parent, J. & W. Seligman, became the holding company but also the investment adviser and manager. It was a working parent. All of that took a considerable amount of reorganization. We also created a trust company from scratch. We felt it was legal to do it under Glass-Steagall. Further, we had served in our individual capacities as personal trustees and as executors of the estates of families whose money we managed. I was the chief explorer into all of this, and finally in December '82 we filed papers with the controller of the currency to get a national trust charter. I wrote that application. I had some background from the New York State Banking Department days, but a lot of it required doing stuff for the first time. We were the first securities firm to make an application as a nonbank trust company.

Q: You couldn't look at what several others had done and model yours on that?

W. H.: That's exactly right. Although the controller of the currency granted us a federal charter in April of 1983, another federal agency with jurisdiction disagreed with that decision. Rather than get involved with that fight, we went over to see if the New York State banking superintendent would entertain an application from us to convert from a national bank to a state charter. He said yes after he had his counsel look at it. New York law and Glass-Steagall are similar, and we had convinced the state there was no violation of Glass-Steagall. On May 20, we filed our application with the New York State Banking Department to convert from a national trust company to a state charter trust company.

On June 8, we opened for business as a state chartered trust company, and that's what we're doing now. I'm in charge of that. I'm no longer the chief executive officer of Seligman Securities; I'm chief executive officer of the trust company. I've got to learn a whole new set of rules again, a whole new marketing effort. I have the responsibility for seeing to it that the trust company becomes a viable business—in part by going around talking to various people about how they can use trusts in their financial planning. I didn't learn any of that at school, but I did learn to shift gears, to understand the way things are moving, to analyze and think, to write, to speak. One of my functions today is to describe what the Seligman Trust Company is and what it does, and I have to be able to describe that to people whose understanding may be very limited—to someone like a broker-dealer who has never really dealt with a trust company before. The other day, I spoke to a group in Texas, 104 broker-dealers, and I don't think too many of them knew what a corporate trust was.

Q: That reminds me of your comment about dealing with code in the navy: being able to communicate and get messages across to people in different kinds of situations. There is also a lot of curiosity in the way you think that keeps pushing you in different directions. You keep on trying to figure out how to communicate with people who don't understand what you need to tell them. Woven in with that is an analytical thought process, an ability to figure out situations, think them through.

W. H.: I don't know where the curiosity came from, although I'd guess that a great deal of it was generated by my formal education, that the initial liberal arts training provoked it. No question about that. Of course, I am very much in love with Bowdoin and have been a very active alumnus. If I'm prejudiced toward Bowdoin, it's because that prejudice developed out of the background and the strength that it gave me.

Nancy Zimmerman
President and Chief Executive Officer
Zimmerman Associates, Inc.

Q: Why did you choose to go to George Mason University?

N. Z.: I was working part time, and it was convenient, because it was a commuter college and you could live at home, work different jobs.

Q: Did you have an idea when you were going in of a particular kind of education that you wanted to pursue?

N. Z.: At the time, it was definitely liberal arts. When I went through George Mason, the advanced courses in the sciences and engineering were still within the state system, at the University of Virginia.

Q: What kinds of courses did you take at GMU?

N. Z.: I was interested in the political science courses. I regret I waited until my last year to take biology, because I enjoyed it so much. It was a natural for me. After graduation, I pursued research work in some areas of marine biology.

Q: What is it about biology that you liked so much?

N. Z.: I'm fascinated with life—the total picture of systems—and not just human mind and body, but all the animals and plants and their interrelationships. It would have been great to have pursued a medical career. I have always had an interest in reading medical journals about diseases and causes, cures, breakthroughs—the thrill of medical discovery. So biology was probably my favorite course. Shakespeare was second.

Q: You mentioned you enjoyed political science also. Why was that?

N. Z.: Well, for international reasons, like the relationships, or lack of relationships, and structures and policies that existed between countries. I thought it was more structured. It was really enlightening to see how countries either worked with each other or didn't—quid pro quo. International law showed me that countries got away with whatever they wanted —very little peaceful control beyond economic measures. Now I have environmental interests, and I recognize why specific worldwide issues are very difficult to manage, such as endangered species, whale and seal hunts, and the protection of natural wilderness.

Q: And in the middle of all this, you majored in English. Why did you choose that?

N. Z.: Well, I've always been a reader. Literature was something that I naturally would have an interest in. I was interested in novels and plays written by authors from many different backgrounds and countries.

Q: Had you read a lot as a child?

N. Z.: Always.

Q: What was the curriculum structure like at GMU when you were there? Were there a lot of requirements?

N. Z.: The thing that we all joke about now, that we didn't think was so great then, is George Mason was breaking away from UVA and driving toward its own accreditation. The students quickly figured out that we were the only ones that had to take three years of a foreign language in the Washington area. We compared ourselves with George Washington and American. We had to keep taking foreign language, regardless of which degree program we were pursuing. Liberal arts students also had to take what we considered advanced science and math, statistics, and so on. We always thought the requirements were strict.

Q: Did you think they were an imposition on you at the time?

N. Z.: Well, we thought they were certainly much more demanding than at other schools in the area. We assumed that it was essential to establish tough curriculum requirements for George Mason to break away from UVA.

Q: In retrospect, are you glad that . . .

N. Z.: I loved it. I'm glad. The tougher the better. The more we had to stretch, to research, to write, the more the challenge, the more the demand—you bet.

Q: Did you know when you went to college what you wanted to do later?

N. Z.: No, I didn't.

Q: What about when you left?

N. Z.: I certainly didn't think I would start a business, but if you look back on it, I had always been very focused on work and had a variety of jobs out of curiosity. I was a bank teller in many different bank branches, then I worked in libraries, and the different library branches, and retail stores, Woodward & Lothrop and Hecht's. I just wanted to see how these different stores or branches of banks or libraries worked in relation to each other. I did that all through college, and in retrospect I was really concentrating on the work environment. Checking out the market.

Q: Did you take any business courses?

N. Z.: Not a single one. It did not occur to me. In fact, until I started my company, I never had any exposure to business accounting. I did all my business reading—management books, planning and marketing—on the side.

Q: Have you regretted not focusing on business in your studies?

N. Z.: No. You can always learn these things if you have the interest.

Q: Did you have a hard time finding your first job after college with a B.A. in English?

N. Z.: No, because I had worked in so many places. I knew where to go. Actually, I formed the job, because they really did not have a definite position. It was in an engineering firm, and with an English degree they thought that I would be a writer or analyst of some type. I started creating and developing data bases, working with information systems, and that led to some marketing of those systems, hiring people to work on them and then training staff. In that job, I was there for five years and built a department. I learned to do most of it on the job, and I was going to graduate school at night. I think my work experience even prior to college helped. When I attended George Mason, the timing was perfect, because everyone had so many opportunities to start things, organize things, be a planner—good place for entrepreneurs!

Q: What kinds of opportunities?

N. Z.: When I was there, for example, I got involved in moving a local sorority to national, the first national sorority on the campus, Chi Omega. I was the president and believed that it would be a permanent organization if it could become national. The school offered a lot of opportunities for people who had ideas. George Mason fostered the direction I was already motivated to pursue.

Q: Once you had been in that job for five years, you obviously accumulated a lot of technical knowledge. You learned the field, you were going to graduate school and getting your information sciences degree. What kinds of new challenges did you then face in setting up Zimmerman Associates?

N. Z.: I started from scratch again when I started the firm. I started out from my apartment and went to ground zero again.

Q: What about some of the "running a business" aspects? You said you'd never learned accounting until you started the firm.

N. Z.: I had to. Everything. I had never studied marketing, business, strategic planning, accounting, personnel issues. I may have had a natural inclination because of an interest in people, but there are so many personnel laws and considerations and things concerning recruitment and motivation. I started alone, and in the first two years we grew to eight people. And now we're about 150 people, after eight years.

Q: What kinds of things do you do now as CEO of Zimmerman Associates? What's a day in the life of Nancy Zimmerman?

N. Z.: A big part of it, and this is where the liberal arts degree is so helpful, is adapting. Being open-minded about new markets, ideas, approaches, and focusing on the changes occurring economically in the country and internationally, as well as business opportunities and liabilities. The liberal arts degree, I believe, keeps your mind open to change. Most CEOs are probably spending a great deal of their time, as I am, in planning, which is focusing on the near-term changes as well as the future and being flexible enough to move with change, what you anticipate, or expect.

Q: What kinds of clients do you have now at Zimmerman Associates?

N. Z.: Government contracting is a major portion, and within that there is variety in the clients and services. The Department of Defense is the primary client, and we work for the Department of Agriculture, Library of Congress, Government Printing Office, National Library of Medicine, Department of Interior, State Department—we've had some international projects. We work for private companies—big firms, small firms, and individuals.

Q: Would adaptability fit in there also?

N. Z.: It sure does. Because servicing a DOD contract

that is directly responding either to an air force or navy customer is very different from servicing an individual, a law firm, or a small business who comes to us for some type of management help.

Q: So you think that having a broad foundation both in college and in your work experiences, having a diverse kind of education, helps you now.

N. Z.: Absolutely. It makes it possible to integrate a diversified work force. I have a staff that is a mixture of people who have backgrounds and degrees in electrical engineering, mechanical engineering, computer science, software systems, hardware systems, physics, chemistry, the liberal arts, and those with foreign language capabilities. Bringing together, integrating, and maximizing the talent, for either a product or a service—a liberal arts background is enormously helpful—perfect.

Q: And you're not shy about hiring liberal arts graduates.

N. Z.: They can take any subject and analyze it. They are adaptable to new challenges. They are usually good researchers. They can organize, they can write. They can communicate. I think adapting is the key to business, to doing good business, to jobs and to productivity in the future. Some of the best people we have have a liberal education.

John Gidding
President
Ex Cellars, Ltd.

Q: How did you get interested in wine importing?

J. G.: I was a professional basketball player in France for ten years. I was involved somewhat in banking there and spent a lot of time in restaurants, drinking wine. These things are all related. Several of the best restaurants in France are in towns that have basketball teams, Paul Bocuse's in Ansières and Pierre Troisgros's in Roanne, for example. Also, as a player traveling around France with the team, there's not a lot to do except eat. So I got to know some of the restaurant owners and some of the people in the vineyards. My involvement in banking also brought me into contact with the wine industry, where there is a lot of financing going on. The Protestant banks are fairly close with the Bordelaise, for example, and the people in Champagne, and the Catholic banks are fairly tied in with the Burgundians.

Q: What were you doing in banking?

J. G.: Well, I married a Turkish woman while I was in France. Her family had a stake in the Third World banking that goes on in France and Germany in order to secure funds for Turkey and Greece, and since I was a math major in college and knew something about Turkey and Greece, I was the one who would do this for them.

Q: How did the math help you?

J. G.: It's a fairly complicated transaction hedging Third World currencies into stable currencies. A lot of time, when a country would want something in francs, but the only real currency that was available was marks, that had to be secured with Turkish lira. It was a fairly involved transaction to make sure that the numbers came out right and that you don't lose all your money on the transaction on each date. There were a lot of rather peculiar restrictions involving hard currency coming to soft currency countries like Turkey. It was all numbers. Basically, it was a piece of paper with a lot of numbers on it. And so you had to reconcile these numbers with what you felt would be the eventual reality, and then you had to make transactions.

Q: Would you describe the kinds of math courses you took in college as business related?

J. G.: Actually, at the University of Virginia, it was pure math.

Q: And did that turn out to have any value to you?

J. G.: Yes. You had to have a clear theoretical model to perform any transaction. The business models provided in economics are macroeconomic models and aren't that helpful, because you have to accumulate your variables, if you will. There are a lot of potential variables, and some variables you don't need. You have to rearrange the ones you do into some sort of model. All of the exercise in pure math is to arrange variables into some sort of working model. So, as opposed to the business math, the job of pure math is to teach you to construct models. It is much more helpful, if you will, than business math, which is really how to relate external phenomena to models someone else has already devised. I think pure math is much more helpful than business math. That's how I use it today, for that matter.

Q: In what sense?

J. G.: I'm in the wine business. I have to purchase wine, finance it, ship it, sell it. It's mostly classed Bordeaux and *grand cru* Burgundies, and there's not so much of it. It's a very evolved commodity. It's an appreciating commodity in some years and a depreciating commodity in other years. The market demand fluctuates wildly. There are several currencies involved —it's called "the snake"—the pound, the dollar, the mark, and the franc. The Germans, the English, and the Americans all purchase French wines in varying amounts depending on what the demand is and what the strength of their currency is. So you get very involved in hedging. These are the nuts and bolts of my business today. I mean, the fact that I can taste wine and see it now is almost incidental. I'm happy that it exists, and I'm sure that some people eventually do drink it.

Q: I assure you they do.

J. G.: But mostly, it's trading, and it's trading with very fine markets. It's a fairly exposed market. You only get a relative advantage by buying all of it or varying the same stances on currency positions. So you try and hedge yourself by your selling ability more than your currency ability.

Q: When you were in college, and you decided to major in math, you didn't have wine importing in mind, did you?

J. G.: No, at six feet seven inches, I had professional basketball in mind. I started out as a history major, but as my basketball became slightly better, it just took too much time. There were papers to write. I was always fairly fluent in math, so I went into math because it was less homework.

Q: What was it that interested you about history originally?

J. G.: I had always been interested in history. I spent most of my life overseas. I simply continued the study of history. I am not *that* interested in math as a subject. I had a fairly good working knowledge of the Northern Hemisphere's geography, so history was much more accessible in a way.

Q: Were there any particular courses in either math or history, or in any other subject, that you think back to now that you enjoyed a lot or that mean a lot to you?

J. G.: I don't know. Most of the things in Virginia seemed to take this vague Civil War stance. Algebra and the reconstruction of the South. Topology and monetary reforms during the Civil War. It was hard to get away from the Civil War down there. Actually, I really liked all the survey courses more than anything in Virginia. The first two years, there were a lot of survey courses in economics, in math, in history, in English. And they were taught by full professors, and the scope of them was excellent. They really opened up a lot of paths of study. Then, the last two years, they were taught mostly by graduate assistants teaching the next level of courses, and they didn't have the breadth that those early courses had. I remember all the early survey courses because they sort of displayed the subject for you in a really coherent manner, and then it was sort of disappointing when you're getting near the end of your time to have these teachers who only wanted to get their graduate degree and get out. It became paper grading and tests. I have a bad memory of that part and a pleasant memory of all these wonderful survey courses in these big amphitheaters. They were in a range of fields.

Q: Did you go to Europe right after you left UVA?

J. G.: Yes.

Q: And that was for basketball?

J. G.: I was a professional basketball player for ten years. I went to the Sorbonne in Paris and the university in Caen, and I taught English and math to French people for four years.

Q: Did you enjoy doing that?

J. G.: Sure, it was fun.

Q: This was while you were playing pro ball.

J. G.: Yes, but that would only take a couple of hours a

week. It's not like over here. I took courses at the Sorbonne in Paris and the university in Caen. I taught English at a French college and math at an English high school. I worked in banking. I was a national coach for some time also.

Q: Was it while you were in Europe that you started to get into wine importing?

J. G.: No, I got into wine importing when I came back. I was divorced in Istanbul about five years ago, and I couldn't keep playing basketball, and I didn't want to teach school, and I knew a little bit about everything, and when I came back to America, I was not employable.

Q: Why not?

J. G.: I didn't have a teaching certificate, so I couldn't teach, and the NBA didn't want to take my option in basketball. But I spoke French, I knew something about banking and a little bit about shipping, so I got into the wine business. I went back to France for about six to eight months and sort of schlepped around all the vineyards, trying to find something that (1) I could buy and (2) I could sell and (3) I could finance, which is more difficult. And then—I know something about wine—I found a few that I could represent. I came over here and got all the corporate forms taken care of, the importing license, and then went out and ordered it and tried to sell it. In the failure of doing all three of those things—ordering it, selling it, and financing it—I learned a little bit more and then went back and tried it again, and eventually I got better at it, and now I control quite a lot.

Q: What does the business look like today?

J. G.: About four million dollars.

Q: Is there any particular aspect of it that you enjoy more or less than another?

J. G.: Oh, heavens, yes, I like to actually consume the wine the best. No, I'm leaving for Europe tonight. I get to tour around all the vineyards, taste the varying vintages, and the people are all quite lovely. That's nice, certainly. America's not so bad, either. Wine is usually sold in nicer, rather than not nicer, places. San Francisco, Chicago, Dallas, Miami, Boston, Washington, New York. These are nice places. And most of your big resorts have it. Aspen, Vermont. It's a civilized sort of a thing, because where you have to go to have trade shows and tastings and sell it are quite pleasant.

Q: What about the business aspects of your job right now? Aside from traveling, what presents a challenge to you or keeps your interest?

J. G.: There are channels of distribution that are very, very important, as there are channels of supply. It's a really interesting part of the business aligning the channels of supply with the channels of distribution. These nuts and bolts of the business, how to make it functional, how to make a profit, make it viable. The systems of distribution of wine are very serious mathematical and historical models. Wine is traded in a peculiar way in Europe and in a very peculiar way in America. They're not rational ways, they're historical ways. There is a three-tiered system in America—of importers, wholesalers, and retailers—which the law protects. There are rather strange ways that Bordeaux Chateaux are traded, quite irrationally. I find those sorts of things very interesting. And I have to do the accounting, the sales, and financing and capital and growth, but that could be any business. I could be in the business of selling frozen hog bellies, for that matter. You'd have to do the exact same thing. What's interesting in the wine business are these historical models and how they are related to one another. I think that's the most interesting thing, other than sipping vintage champagne, if you want to know the truth.

Q: As you think about what you do and how you got into the business, do you think there's anything about your education, other than the math, that helps you now?

J. G.: Sure. We studied languages. I'm fluent in three or four languages. The history is important because of the development of these historical models. European history is terribly important in terms of understanding how the product is traded. A lot of people get out of the business because they're not really interested in these things. There's a reason to be Protestant in Bordeaux, there's a reason to be Catholic in Burgundy. It's not obvious, and so the education that I received at Virginia didn't close down any of these doors. It opened them. It opened up the particular aims of studying, so in that sense, it was very valuable.

Q: Is there anything you would have done differently in your education?

J. G.:   Yes. I shied away from writing classes. I find that that was a big mistake. I would have taken more writing. And I was unsuccessful in languages, which I blamed on the school, but now that I'm fluent in three languages, I can see that it wasn't the school's fault. The fault was mine. I just didn't want to break down my resistance to learning a foreign language at that time. So I would have been happier if I had been involved more in writing and in the languages that I could have learned. I certainly took math to its illogical extreme.

Q: Its illogical extreme?

J. G.:   There comes a point where you shouldn't be taking math any more unless you're prepared to . . . oh, I don't know . . . I don't know what people are supposed to do with it. The people who know it don't study it, they know it all at once. It's like being a trapezist without having a real good sense of balance. People with a sense of balance are up there on the trapeze. They don't want to be hanging around learning it. But it's certainly better than business math, because the ability to formulate models is very important, and that's what you can learn from math besides mathematics itself.

Charlotte Kuenan
Director of Database Publishing
Bureau of National Affairs, Inc.

Q: What does BNA do?

C. K.:   BNA is a for-profit information company headquartered in Washington, D.C. We publish notification and reference-information services to businesses and professionals in law, labor relations, business and economics, environment and safety, tax, and other areas. We publish about seventy information services that are sold on a subscription basis, including dailies, weeklies, biweeklies, monthlies. I'm talking now about our traditional print business. BNA began publishing in 1929 with the *United States Patents Quarterly*. *United States Law Week* is one of our flagship publications. We have about two thousand employees, ten subsidiaries, and regional sales offices throughout the country and abroad.

Q: As director of Database Publishing, what are you responsible for?

C. K.: I'm responsible for conceiving, producing, and distributing electronic versions of BNA's information resources. BNA is committed to producing and providing information to its customers in whatever media they need. Whether it's print, or on-line, or fiche, or film, or laser disks, or what have you, we want to take advantage of whatever technology adds value to the *information* that is our bread and butter. Our strength really is in the information gathering and analysis. We report on developments in Congress, activities in the various federal agencies, and rulings of the courts. We keep people informed of what's going on in Washington that affects their organization, as well as selected state and industry developments.

Q: Within that aspect of BNA's activities, what is it that you yourself do? Are you gathering information, or doing product development? What is it exactly?

C. K.: I do product development, project management, contract negotiations, and some promotional activities. The Database Publishing section that I manage is responsible for business and product development. We redesign the "raw" information resources of BNA and convert those into electronic products for direct access by customers. We license the electronic information products through third-party "vendors," like LEXIS, WESTLAW, DIALOG, and others, as well as through electronic information subsidiaries of BNA. In addition to product development and vendor relations, we update and maintain about forty on-line products. Our group also provides many kinds of customer support, training, and marketing.

Q: When you talk about product development—in other words, taking the so-called raw material from BNA and turning it into an electronic package that's going to be of service to your clients—what's involved?

C. K.:   Several steps. First of all, you have to determine what it is that your customers need—and whether they would benefit from having the information available in an electronic format. For example, we have a product that makes it that much easier for a user to do research in our labor information services by being able to find in a matter of seconds, for example, all of the comparable-worth cases decided in New York since 1984. From references found "on line," the user can go directly to the print product to see the full text of cases that match the search criteria.

Q: So it's saving clients a lot of library work.

C. K.:   It's saving them a lot of time, and in many cases they can do research that they couldn't do manually, by combining multiple research criteria in one search statement.

Q: What's the next step after you've determined that the technology would enhance the product?

C. K.:   After that, you take a look in detail at the information itself, as it's available in your company. My staff looks at the in-house system on which the information is produced, sees how that information is organized, and determines how it needs to be modified to serve the user's need in an electronic product. We then come up with the design and convert the raw information. That process doesn't require technical knowledge in the sense that you might think. You don't have to be a computer programmer to develop or use on-line data bases. I tend to employ people who have a background in information, have used information extensively. Frequently, they're librarians. But they don't have to have a technical background at all, and the users of our products don't have a technical background. We work with programmers and systems analysts in the implementation, but our work really is more in the design and assessment of the product's value, working with potential users and getting their advice and feedback about how to best design these products for their use.

Q: What do you think are some of the skills that you draw on to do this kind of work?

C. K.:   I think analytical thinking is really a key. You have to be able to look at a problem and identify all its component parts, identify all of the issues that need to be resolved surrounding an information need, before you can come up with an end product that's going to make sense. So in the product-design area, a strong analytical bent is very important. On the business side, where I spend more and more of my time—drawing up contracts and negotiating business agreements with other companies—I think you have to be pretty strong in planning and human relations skills. You have to have a sense of what it is that your market needs and how your product is going to bring that to them. You have to explain the value of your product to other companies through whom you're distributing your information. You also need to explain and promote your activities in house. You work with many departments and coordinate with many different people with various backgrounds to bring these electronic products to fruition. You have to talk to editorial people, production people, marketing people, technical people, customers, and outside vendors.

So there are analytical skills, human relations skills, planning and organizing skills. And there's certainly a sense of curiosity and enthusiasm that you bring to any new effort, and I think that's something that I draw on from my college days. I took a great variety of courses and was exposed to enough disciplines that the curiosity that I've always had was fueled. It's something that I find really essential in business and in people who work for me—a constant interest in the new opportunities, new problems, and issues that we face every day.

Q: You majored in philosophy at George Washington University. Why did you decide to go there in the first place?

C. K.: I grew up on a mink farm, and I wanted to get as far away from it as possible. I wanted to come to an urban environment, and GW had many of the things I was looking for. It's a large university with a broad offering of courses, and it's located right in the heart of the nation's capital, not a blade of grass in sight. It was perfect, it was just what I wanted.

Q: When you got there, did you have a particular kind of education in mind?

C. K.: I did, and it's totally different from what I ended up pursuing. I wanted to be a physicist. I was always encouraged as a child and in my high school years to major in the sciences, in physics or chemistry or math. I was always very good in those subjects, and I had sort of a Faustian curiosity—I wanted to know where things came from, how they originated, what made the world tick. I had good science courses at GW, and I'm glad I took them. But—because I wanted more than the kinds of answers those fields provided—I found myself, after a couple of years in the sciences, moving over into the humanities. I found philosophy particularly intriguing and ended up majoring in it.

Philosophy was just very broadening for me, that and the literature courses that I also took. It provided such a good picture of other times, other cultures, other ways of thinking. Somebody said—it might have been Weber—that every generation rewrites history using its own perspective, its own experience. Seeing how different cultures at different times saw life and reality, and what issues they saw as important, and different ways they had of looking at problems and the condition of mankind was just fascinating. I think what it makes you aware of is that you as an individual in the 1980s are a part of a very particular culture in a very specific time slice that affects, if not determines, much of your perspective on social issues, political issues, business issues. If you have enough background from a liberal education to borrow approaches from other cultures and other times and other disciplines, then I think you have gained some of the flexibility that you need, certainly in business, to be able to look at things in different ways, and not to get tunnel vision about a particular project or problem.

That kind of flexibility and breadth helps in other ways. As a manager, you have a staff that you are responsible for hiring and developing. The broader perspective you have, the better you can understand the differences among your staff members, and that makes it easier for you to deal with them on an individual basis and draw on their strengths and develop them in a way that makes the most of their potential. Seeing how you can bring the expertise of various people together on a project and have this confluence of different backgrounds bring a project to fruition—that's invaluable.

Q: Some people might come back to you and say, well, some people are simply innately better able to work with and through their staff in the ways that you've suggested. What exactly is it about a liberal education that you think helps you to do that well?

C. K.: I think that there may be some innate ability in that regard, but it's an ability that can definitely be cultivated and developed. A liberal education may give you more general flexibility and adaptability and openness to a variety of approaches than a more specific, more rigid discipline would. I think the actual skills that you use in managing people are something that you gain through experience. There are also courses you can take in developing or making you aware of certain management techniques. And you have role models in your own business environment that you can either choose to emulate or ignore. So I think a lot of it is something that you develop and get better at as you gain more experience.

But I think that the breadth of the liberal education just makes you a more open and receptive person in a way that helps in business. That's not to say that people trained, say, in engineering or business aren't receptive and open, but I think that they are often trained at an early age to think in a specific way that a liberal arts graduate isn't. For example, I went to law school for a year, to get some background in the law that I was using in one of my jobs at BNA, and I can see how it is that the law schools train people to think like lawyers. It's a very definite process that they take you through. And you do learn to think in a particular kind of way, which is very important to that discipline. But if you learn that kind of very specific orientation and mode of thinking at a stage before you've really been exposed to the variety of fields available, I think you may get locked in too early and not be able to take advantage of the broad array of perspectives and approaches to problems that are out there.

Q: When you left GW, did you know what you wanted to do?

C. K.: No, I really didn't. People would ask me that during my college years. My father would say, "what are you going to do with a degree in philosophy, how are you going to make your way in the world?" I really didn't concern myself much with it, and I got a lot of encouragement to study philosophy and not to really worry about where it was going to take me in the business world or elsewhere until I was ready to decide how I wanted to work. It was that '60s "get that sheepskin" philosophy.

Q: Did you know you wanted to go into business?

C. K.:   No, I didn't. My first job after college I sort of fell into. A professor at GW asked me if I would work on a grant funded by the Law Enforcement Assistance Administration. It was a six-month research project to study how young people in Washington, D.C., who got into various social and legal problems were being processed by the institutions designed to handle them. That included studying the schools, the police, the correctional institutions, and the courts. It was a systems-theory kind of approach to the handling of these kids and their problems. We found that many of the institutional mechanisms designed to handle truancy, discipline, and drug problems actually worked to perpetuate the problems. I spent a lot of time interviewing people and doing literature research and writing up summaries of our findings.

When that project ended, I moved to my hometown, Canandaigua, in upstate New York, and I worked as a social worker for about a year and a half, on the food stamp program. That was very revealing, too. I burned out on that very quickly. I found it very difficult and depressing to see the kinds of conditions under which certain people have to live, and sometimes you find yourself in the position of playing God—making pro and con decisions about people's entitlements to things that are supposed to be very objective, but there are some subjective considerations involved in that as well.

Q: By that point, did you have any clearer idea of moving in a particular direction?

C. K.:   Well, as it turned out, while I was a social worker, I was asked to take over a public-service radio program in a nearby town, and I did that for about six months. I conducted various interviews with local community leaders and talked about various social issues, and I found working in radio very exciting. I wanted to come back to Washington to live—it's a much larger community with more variety of work opportunities—and I wanted to get into radio or some sort of broadcasting. I had heard about BNA from a friend and came here to talk to some people, and when they learned that I had a background in research, writing, and interviewing, they asked me to come to work at BNA.

I started out in the editorial department, where I indexed and abstracted, at some point in my career, probably half of the BNA publications, and got involved in a project to automate the indexing process. In 1978, we began to look at the electronic publishing business and began some experiments. Someone hired me to begin looking into that area, and I took to it like a duck to water. I just found it incredibly interesting. It was kind of like playing with a new toy—the technology was really fascinating to me. We began working with some product-development concepts in electronic publishing, and we've been growing very rapidly in that area. I built a team of strong people, and we have about forty electronic products to date.

I guess it was during my career at BNA that I became much more interested in business and began taking some courses, again at GW. Some in law, some in business—marketing, finance, economics—some more technically related to my field, which I found very helpful. But I think that the broader education in the liberal arts was a foundation that will always stand me in good stead, because of the flexibility and the adaptability that it encouraged. As opposed to a narrow specialty, a liberal education doesn't really focus you so specifically on one area, and you have the flexibility and the option of moving around in your career. The breadth of your education often gives you an interest in a variety of areas, which you can then develop and specialize as you get onto a particular career path. But I think no matter what career path, what type of business you get into, a liberal education helps give you the perspective and the curiosity and the analytical skills to solve any number of problems.

Q: You've spoken very positively of the liberal education that you got and of the ways in which you've used it. Is there anything that you would change?

C. K.: If there's one thing about liberal arts that I

would change, that would be that I would introduce it much earlier in a student's life. I would have a stronger emphasis on the liberal arts during high school. In my own case, I went to a small rural high school, where the budget and the number of students were limited, so that we had a very skeletal curriculum, and by the time I was a senior in high school, there were no courses left for me to take. I'm sure it's very different in big-city high schools, but, nevertheless, I think if there were a more uniform focus on bringing the liberal arts to students of high school age, that would be valuable. Specialization could then be included as part of the liberal arts education at the college level, but I don't think that you can go straight from high school into a specialized area without losing a great deal.

Patrick Coady
Chief Financial Officer
Acacia Mutual Life Insurance Company

Q: Why don't we start by talking about your undergraduate college, a leading school of engineering, and what caused you to go to school there?

P. C.:   I was valedictorian of my high school class and good in sciences, and my chemistry teacher said I should consider it. My high school was in Springfield, Illinois, and I had never even seen the campus before registration day. In fact, the brochure shows trees and a grassy lawn, which is the only lawn they have. It was quite a shock when I actually got there. From day one, you were on the firing line as an engineering student, but they also had wonderful departments in other subjects— economics, political science, architecture, languages, and a "great books" core program in the humanities. These were considered "nonsubjects," but the courses and the faculty were excellent.

Q: You went there because of the chemistry?

P. C.:   Yes, but by my own personal nature, I was just always drawn to the humanities subjects. You usually got a full professor teaching humanities; in other areas, you always got grad students. If you failed in the humanities, that was never really held against you. The last thing you did at the end of the day, after you did physics, chemistry, and math, was the humanities. And if you didn't get to it, you didn't get to it. That was kind of the norm. But I always took a dose. I had a course in the history of the Russian revolution, which was an excellent course, and I took German, a couple of art and architecture courses and economics. One summer I studied American literature. The irony was, if you'd just taken away the engineering courses, you'd have one of the best liberal arts colleges in the country—except nobody knew that or cared. I guess the turning point for me came in my junior year when I interviewed for a job. It was very hard to get a job. What I discovered was that just being a junior really didn't qualify me to do much in engineering science. In fact, some interviewers said, "come back when you get your Ph.D."

Q: It was really a thin field, then, a thin market?

P. C.: At the time, the country was saying it wanted a lot of scientists and engineers, but what it was really saying was, "we want only the really bright ones, only the very best ones. And we want a lot of drones who are willing to sit at drafting boards and walk around turning valves in sulphuric acid plants." But there was virtually no intermediate role that was challenging. When I left college, the engineering job I was offered at a consulting firm brought with it a draft deferral. I didn't feel comfortable with that. So I went into the navy, but a large part of the decision was feeling that I wanted to leave engineering behind.

Q: You knew you didn't want to push for the Ph.D.?

P. C.: I knew I'd already missed the cut on that. I was not in the top 10 percent of my college class, so I was already behind the eight ball. The alternative careers in engineering didn't look very challenging—secure but not very challenging. My father had been a small-town banker, kind of a businessman, and I enjoyed taking some finance courses during my last year at college. Even then, I knew that I wanted to go to business school, but I wanted to get some experience first. That's why I joined the navy. I left school with a semi-sense of failure. The

other part, the nontechnical part, of my education was not
something that I thought qualified me for anything. The idea of
going to business school, which I pretty much had decided to
do after college, was to get credentials, to qualify myself to go
do something. I had no sense that what I'd done was something
valuable.

Q: When did you start feeling that some of that was valuable?

P. C.: Well, with my technical education, I was successful in the navy as an intelligence briefing officer. In terms of
planning missions and understanding my job, I was way ahead,
because I had a better understanding of the reality around me.
Later, when I got to business school and then to Wall Street, I
found that investment banking increasingly required a lot of
analysis. The markets were getting more complicated. I was able
to take cost-of-capital models and discounted-cash-flow models
and other technical skills and really use them to advantage. And
I usually got assigned to work with the technical companies because of my background. Venture capital was flourishing in the
early '60s, and I found that my technical education had great
value.

It is when you get into areas of leadership that you begin
to truly appreciate a liberal education. You get to wrestle with
issues that no longer have automatic answers. Until you start
getting to positions of responsibility that deal with human issues, philosophical issues, judgment issues—things that cause
you to take a look at why you do what you do—you probably
don't appreciate a liberal education. Especially if you never
thought it was worth anything to begin with.

One of the things that struck me as I walked up the educational ladder is that people mature intellectually and educa-
tionally at different times. In Sweden, where I worked for
about five months, they really don't start formal school until
age seven or eight. In Japan, they can't start teaching children
soon enough. My observation about the education system in the
United States is that it throws away people too fast and slams
the door after them. Many of my friends in high school, people
who were pretty smart, dropped out or did something else and

then went back to school and rediscovered themselves. Our system takes itself so seriously and grades people so seriously that it keeps putting them in boxes. If you don't make it to the next box, you're a bad person. As a result, your discovery of a sense of self and of your particular strengths gets lost. And I'm not sure that that process isn't getting worse rather than better.

The fact that I can sit down and talk intelligently about the history of architecture or the social sciences or the Russian revolution and that such material can give me a new perspective on things—there was a time I didn't think it was worth anything. I'm lucky, because most people who aren't excited about what they're doing kind of get thrown away or discouraged. To me, the beauty of a liberal education is its value as a thought process, a development process, a growth process. Ignoring that can really destroy a lot of talent for a lot of years. Who is to say what success or failure is? Was Grandma Moses a failure at some earlier stage in her life?

Q: We read and talk fairly glibly about child development and physical development and about what happens to your body when you turn thirty and forty and fifty, but we think less about the intellectual maturation process. If what you're saying is that liberal education facilitates a more broadly defined maturation process, it strikes me that it would permit you to go in different directions because it offers more avenues. You may discover at a later date a strength that at an earlier date you had rejected or someone had rejected on your behalf.

P. C.: The system is geared up to get people to physical maturity and into a job, period. You have to get from grade school to high school to college, and you have to take some tests. If you don't fit neatly into that system, you have to be pretty resourceful to figure out that there's still plenty of time to grow, time to do something else. A truly liberal education shouldn't have any boundaries on it. What we usually call an education has a degree at the end of it or a series of degrees. You've got to write a thesis, and you've got to take so many courses in this area and so many courses in that area to get really good at history, to be a history professor. It's as if there's no other way you can be good at history. I don't believe that's true. A liberal education ought to assist people in making choices for themselves, not be a degree/scholarship/job process that leads you down some particular path. We need to get out of the credential process and more into the discovery process, self-discovery. The best period for turning out engineers was after the Second World War, the Korean War. People had been out in the world for a while, and they really *chose* engineering as a career. Whenever I take courses at the New School in New York, they're always much more fun than I remember courses in college being, because people choose, really choose to be in the classroom. They are interested in that course rather than fulfilling some requirement.

Q: Let's go back to something you talked about a minute ago. You started talking a little bit about leadership and about how getting into leadership roles of one kind or another makes you feel the value of the liberal education that you've had.

P. C.:   Well, this realization came home to me in a certain sense at business school. We went through the process of asking for more information, more market research, more cost data, more of this and that. Ultimately, though, you had to say chocolate or vanilla, but the issue between chocolate or vanilla wasn't the only issue involved. You had corporate values and personal values, personal goals, trade-offs between your career and your family. As you go up an organization, the issues just aren't answered by more facts. You make judgments based upon something that you think is going to happen in the future or happen a certain way or happen just because you say it's going to happen. You know that you're playing a role in creating the consequences. You start looking at facts, and then you begin to discover what shaky ground you're on. What is your goal? What is your willingness to be right or wrong? What do you want out of a decision for yourself? You become better grounded in the diversity of human experience.

Q: When you start talking about relying on your intuition and your judgment, you need to have a firm grip on yourself to know that, more often than not, your intuition is accurate. And you have to be aware that a lot of things will happen just because you say so.

P. C.:   That's why I worry that the educational system is drifting more toward its own self-interest than to the interest of the students it purports to serve. At our twenty-fifth reunion, the bioengineering faculty made a presentation to the visiting alumni about what the cutting edge of this technology was. I think they just had tremendous disdain for their audience. It was very clear to me they had written three zillion research papers, and they were doing more research. Out of their two hours, I would say half an hour was given to trying out their resumés. They used a quarter of their time to tell us their resumés rather than what they were doing or why they were excited about it. So, deep down in my heart, I wonder if the school isn't, ultimately, more worried about its reputation than about the students marching in the door. In high school, I had the kind of teachers that, ten years later, you're still writing Christmas cards to, and on the way home you go see them. You didn't know what influence they'd had on your life except you knew they had one. But I don't think that was the case at college.

4   *Michael Useem*

❖ ❖ ❖ ❖ ❖ ❖ ❖ ❖ ❖ ❖ ❖ ❖

What the Research Shows

Higher education and business face a seeming paradox. On the one hand, as Chapter Two, by Roger Smith, suggests, concern with the complex challenges facing corporations has led more and more of our most thoughtful executives to view liberal education as a near prerequisite for effective management. On the other hand, more and more undergraduates, spurred by a security-oriented culture on campus, have become skeptical of the value of the liberal arts.

It is important to understand, as general background, the current distribution of employment opportunities for college graduates between the public and private sectors. During the 1970s, job growth for college graduates shifted from the public sector to the private sector. Young college graduates in 1970 found civilian employment in approximately equal numbers in the public and private sectors; 47 percent entered government service that year, and 51 percent entered industry. By 1980, however, the balance had shifted sharply toward business employment: only 25 percent of the college graduates with less than five years' work experience in 1980 were employed by local, state, or federal government agencies, while 72 percent had entered the private sector.

Of necessity, then, many college students have turned

their attention to preparing themselves for successful entry into the private sector. Their career anxieties have also been fueled by a drop in opportunities for challenging white-collar jobs, whatever the sector. In 1970, 76 percent of new college graduates found employment as professionals or managers; by 1980, only 62 percent were able to enter such positions (Rumberger, 1984). It is in order to compete for entry-level jobs in business, then, that many undergraduate students have moved toward more practically oriented college curricula. Their response to changing market conditions has not been illogical. But it has often been shortsighted, limiting both for them and for their employing corporations.

Liberal arts graduates may be initially disadvantaged by their less specialized and less career-oriented training. But, as we shall see from a range of studies discussed here, as liberal arts graduates climb the corporate ladder, they often become advantaged. The immediate employment gains of a practical course of study may come at the sacrifice of ultimate career gains. Companies lose as well. Executives are devoting increasing effort to managing the company's environment. Yet, just at a moment when broadly educated executives are more needed than ever to manage the turbulent world of the corporation, fewer and fewer university students are in a position to learn about it.

This chapter begins by noting that liberal arts graduates do face more difficult entry-level problems than graduates who have concentrated on acquiring job-relevant skills for the private sector. We then consider a range of studies that confirm the longer-term value of a liberal education for ascent in the corporation. Finally, we turn to the impact of managers' liberal learning on the behavior of the firm.

Two points should be clarified at the outset. First, the studies we will review often focus on the managerial experience of liberal arts graduates, frequently comparing their experience with that of graduates of preprofessional curricula, such as business and engineering. This permits broad comparative assessment. It is important to recognize, however, that when liberal arts graduates are shown to have performed well in relation to their peers, it is often their liberal learning, rather than their graduation from a liberal arts program, that has made the difference. Clearly, liberal learning is achieved as often as it is through the liberal arts largely because it is traditionally sought as an aim of liberal arts programs. Were liberal arts learning a more central aim of business and engineering programs, their graduates might well demonstrate competencies more similar to those of liberal arts graduates. In subsequent pages, we sometimes follow the examples of studies we cite in focusing on liberal arts graduates; but the conclusions should be viewed as applying to all liberally educated managers, regardless of their course of study.

Secondly, many of these studies must be interpreted cautiously. The determinants of effective managerial performance and career advancement are many, and education is only one among such influential elements as motivation, intelligence, networks of contacts, family background, and personal wealth. Yet few studies of the educational backgrounds of managers that we review include more than one or two of the other factors, if any. Thus, while liberally educated managers appear advantaged in some studies, we may not know the extent to which the apparent advantage reflects their educations or other correlated factors. Similarly, caution is always in order as we interpret the current relevance of data from the past. The range of educational options offered college students has greatly increased in recent decades. The average ability levels and other characteristics of graduates from various programs all change with time, as do the requirements of managerial practice.

Problems of Entry for Liberal Arts Graduates

When employers recruit graduating college seniors, they screen for grade-point average, work attitude, extracurricular activities, communication skills, and, above all, academic major. Individual experiences vary widely, but, on average, those with liberal arts majors fare less well when first entering the private sector than do those with undergraduate degrees in directly job-related subjects. The salience of academic major for getting started in business and industry is evident in the annual survey of employer recruiting trends conducted by Michigan State University's placement services (Shingleton and Scheetz, 1984). In the fall of 1984, the survey obtained responses from 648 sampled employers, 80 percent in the private sector. Employers were asked to rank the importance of ten factors in prescreening candidates for campus interviews and eighteen factors in inviting candidates to visit the company after the initial interview. Rankings fell in five categories, ranging from no importance to "extremely high" importance. The proportion of the 648 firms giving the highest ranking to the top five factors in prescreening students for campus interviews and in subsequent invitation to visit the employer are reported in Table 4-1. At both of these two decision points, academic major emerges as the first consideration.

Table 4-1. Leading Criteria in Employer Selection
of Job Candidates, 1984.

Prescreening Criteria	Percentage Reporting Extremely High Importance
Campus interview	
Academic major	67
Degree levels	21
Major grade-point average	16
Previous work experience	16
Expected date of graduation	14
Invitation to visit employer	
Academic major	45
Attitude toward work ethic	44
Oral communication skills	43
Enthusiasm and confidence	34
Motivation to achieve	34

Source: Shingleton and Sheetz, 1984, pp. 34-35.

With employers considering academic majors more than any other single factor, those with different majors have very different experiences in entering the labor market. Compared to those in several fields, particularly engineering, liberal arts graduates face fewer prospective openings and lower salaries when

they do find a position. This is again evident in the 1984 survey of recruitment of new college graduates, in which the
surveyed employers, 80 percent located in the private sector,
rated the job "outlook" for new college graduates by major. On
the whole, engineering fields received far more optimistic assess-
ments than did liberal arts fields (Table 4-2). The estimated

Table 4-2. Estimated Employment Outlook and Starting Salaries
for 1985 College Graduates, by Major.

Academic Major	Outlook Rated Very Good or Excellent	Estimated Starting Salaries
Non-liberal arts majors		
Electrical engineering	66%	$28,086
Chemical engineering	30	27,827
Civil engineering	16	20,630
Accounting	36	19,262
General business administration	20	17,782
Liberal arts majors		
Computer science	69	26,690
Physics	25	25,411
Mathematics	30	20,630
Social sciences	5	17,640
Liberal arts and letters	5	15,124

Source: Shingleton and Scheetz, 1984, pp. 27, 42.

starting salaries of new bachelor's degree holders in leading engineering fields were about 10 percent higher than for physics
majors, more than a third higher than for mathematics majors,
and nearly double those of other "liberal arts and letters" majors. Employment opportunities facing bachelor's degree holders are thus on the whole less remunerative for liberal arts graduates than engineering graduates. It should be kept in mind,
however, that relative prospects vary considerably from major
to major. Liberal arts graduates in physics, for example, do
nearly as well as graduates in chemical engineering and better
than those in the social sciences and civil engineering. The experience of college graduates on entering the job market is
strongly shaped, then, by their undergraduate major. Career-
oriented majors tend to fare better, though some liberal arts

majors do equally well, a conclusion corroborated by numerous studies (for example, Parrish and Duff, 1975; Bisconti and Gomberg, 1975).

Career Advantages of a Liberal Education

Once liberally educated graduates gain a foothold in the private sector, their special abilities serve them increasingly well along the path of rising responsibilities. As a group, they perform at least as effectively as those with more practical but less liberal education. Because the value of a liberal education varies by managerial level, we divide the managerial career of the college graduate into four stages: (1) entry-level management positions; (2) lower-middle management ranks, usually reached after a decade of work; (3) upper-middle management ranks, achieved by some after two decades; and (4) the senior ranks, attained by a handful after three decades of managerial experience.

Entry-Level Management Positions. Liberal arts graduates generally do as well in lower managerial ranks as the graduates of career-oriented baccalaureate programs. What they lack in technical knowledge they often make up for even here in breadth of knowledge. This can be seen, for instance, in an in-depth study of new recruits at Chase Manhattan Bank (Burns, 1983). The major features of the study are worth reviewing, for they usefully illustrate how research in this area is structured.

Chase Manhattan Bank, the nation's third-largest commercial bank, hires large numbers of new college graduates every year, its U.S. offices bringing in 343 graduates in 1982. Two-thirds enter positions as "relationship managers," responsible for overseeing the bank's work with customers. Both recent B.A. and M.B.A. recipients are hired, with the bulk of the B.A.s earned in the liberal arts. In recruiting, Chase searches for individuals who bring specialized managerial skills or who have the right mental abilities and work motivations. In Chase's view, it can be difficult to inculcate reasoning abilities in those who lack them, but many technical business skills can be transferred through employer training and on-the-job experience. "For the most part," observes Stanley Burns, who as a vice-president once oversaw the program, "our people are able to acquire specialized characteristics for successful job performance if they have the right mental abilities and motivation for work" (Burns, 1983, p. 5). Thus, if effective job training can be provided at reasonable cost, hiring smart, well-motivated B.A.s can be a good bet. Chase Manhattan's own studies confirm the hypothesis.

New relationship managers at Chase receive specialized training at the outset in the bank's "Credit Development Program." The B.A. and M.B.A. recruits alike are steeped in risk analysis and its application to markets in which the bank operates. To evaluate the value of the program, Chase reviewed the experience of seventy-nine trainees who completed the program between 1977 and 1980. Credit supervisors were asked to evaluate the relationship managers' performance one to four years after the course, focusing on the managers' "application of credit skills on the job with emphasis on quantitative analytical ability" (Burns, 1983, p. 12). The evaluation was concerned only with the technical aspects of the job, neglecting communication and related skills, where liberal arts graduates might have been expected to shine. Dividing the relationship managers into groups of low performers and high performers according to their supervisor ratings, the Chase study found that 60 percent of the low performers held M.B.A.s, while 60 percent of the high performers held B.A.s. Thus, from virtually the start, liberally educated new managers without prior business training may in some circumstances perform as well as those with extensive formal training in business administration.

Lower-Middle Management Positions. After a decade of work experience, many aspiring graduates have moved into the lower-middle ranks of corporate management. The evidence here also reveals that the liberally educated do as well as any. One national cross-sectional study (Bisconti, 1978), for instance, focused on a sample of 419 men who had entered college in 1961, earned a bachelor's degree but no subsequent degree, and became business executives by 1974. The research, conducted for the National Institute of Education and the College Placement Council, found that only a quarter of the managers had decided on their occupational direction while in college, another quarter had so resolved at the time of graduation, and fully half finally settled on a business career only after leaving the university. Not surprisingly, then, many of the business executives had taken no business courses of any kind in college.

Follow-up interviews with the B.A.-holding business executives a decade after graduation acquired information on one measure of managerial success, their annual income. The high-salary managers—that one-quarter of the men whose income exceeded $25,000 in the mid 1970s, when the study was conducted—were found to have majored in undergraduate subjects little different from those of the lesser-paid executives. Thus, 38 percent of the high-income managers, 32 percent of the middle-income managers, and 34 percent of the lower-income managers had concentrated on business administration. Moreover, the study also found no correlation of managerial salary with college study in other fields, including mathematics, the natural sciences, and engineering. High earnings, however, were strongly predicted by other factors in the managers' biographies. Foremost among these were attendance at a selective college, intellectual and personal self-confidence, and a drive to achieve. But studying business as an undergraduate did not advantage—nor did the liberal arts disadvantage—those seeking managerial advancement a decade later (Bisconti, 1978).

Upper-Middle Management Positions. The corporate pyramid becomes increasingly narrow in the upper range of middle management. Responsibilities enlarge, however, with division and plant chiefs coming to oversee the work of hundreds or even thousands of employees. The value of a liberal education here can be seen in a study of managers with American Telephone and Telegraph (AT&T; Beck, 1981). Until its breakup in 1983, AT&T was America's largest corporation, with nearly a million people on the payroll. The yearly demand for new managerial personnel was enormous, and more than six thousand college graduates were hired into the Bell system annually, about a third with degrees in the liberal arts. When new managerial recruits arrived, they began their career in the first of seven managerial grades. After two decades, a substantial fraction reached the third grade, the lower rung of middle management, and a smaller number reached the fourth, upper-middle management grade.

In 1956, a group of 274 fresh college graduates entered the Bell system, and a research group at AT&T has been tracking them ever since. All men, they were viewed as a general management group for whom expectations were high. And, more specifically, expectations for the liberally educated were as high as for any. Early evaluations of the cohort revealed that humanities and social science majors were similar to business majors in their administrative skills and motivation for advancement; they lagged in their quantitative skills, but they excelled in their interpersonal skills. On the basis of these evaluations, the managers were rated on their overall potential for advancement into middle management, and AT&T forecast that the humanities and social science majors were most likely to make the grade into upper-middle management.

The early research-based predictions were borne out. At first, the differences were modest, with the humanities and social science graduates moving into the second managerial level about as fast as the business graduates, though somewhat more quickly than engineering graduates (Table 4-3). After eight

Table 4-3. Managerial Level of College Graduates in AT&T
After Twenty Years, by College Major.

Measure of Managerial Level	Major Field of College Study		
	Engineering	Business	Humanities and Social Sciences
Years to reach second managerial level	5.4	3.9	4.0
Average managerial level after eight years	2.2	2.4	2.6
Percentage of managers at fourth level or higher after 20 years	23%	32%	43%

Source: Beck, 1981, p. 12.

years, however, the liberal arts graduates' average managerial level came to exceed that of both other groups. After twenty years with the Bell system, even larger proportions of the liberal arts majors had moved well up the middle-management ladder. While 23 percent of the engineering graduates and 32 percent of the business graduates had reached the fourth grade after two decades, 43 percent of the humanities and social science majors had moved to this level. Moreover, within each managerial grade, the humanities and social science majors were rated by their bosses as having brighter prospects for further upward movement than their peers from engineering and business (Beck, 1981; Howard, 1984).

This study is particularly important, for it is one of the few to have systematically tracked the careers of a group of managers in a large corporation over a long period of time, using a variety of carefully constructed measures. As a regulated company, however, AT&T's environment is not typical of many firms, and we do not know the extent to which these advancement patterns would be seen in other companies as well. Still, many of the problems faced by AT&T managers are generic to large-firm management, and the general experience of the AT&T group is probably similar to that found in many firms. The experience suggests that a liberal education may provide some special assets and, even when not supplemented by pre-professional training, does not impair the effectiveness of managers.

The Senior Ranks. Top management is reached by only a tiny handful of executives, whose careers have typically been maturing for at least three decades since college. Top management is usually considered to encompass the highest-ranking five to ten officers of a corporation. These executives typically range in age from their mid and late fifties to early sixties. Their responsibilities can include oversight of work forces in the hundreds of thousands and annual budgets in the tens of billions (Shaeffer and Janger, 1982).

Virtually all senior managers of the nation's major corporations are college educated. Contemporary profiles of chief executives of large firms reveal that more than 90 percent hold college degrees. Yet, while higher education has become a near prerequisite for entry into the highest levels of management, no particular level or field of education has. A Conference Board survey (Bonfield, 1980) of 536 presidents and chairpersons of major companies in 1980, for instance, finds that half held only a bachelor's degree, while two-fifths had gone on to obtain a postgraduate degree. No single field of study predominated, either: liberal arts, engineering, law, and business degrees were all well represented among the executive biographies (Burck, 1976; Swinyard and Bond, 1980; Bonfield, 1980).

The continuing perception that collegiate origins are important for understanding a senior manager's career, even more than thirty years after the executive's graduation from college, is evident in press reports on top appointments. A profile of Donald Petersen in the *New York Times* (Holusha, 1984, p. D5) at the time of his elevation in 1984 to replace Philip Caldwell as chief executive of Ford Motor Company is illustrative. "He graduated from the University of Washington in 1946 with a bachelor's degree in mechanical engineering and a Phi Beta Kappa key," reported the *Times* writer. "After working on a farm to earn money, he enrolled in Stanford, earning his MBA in 1949 and joining Ford Motor Company upon graduation."

Whether the senior manager earned a master's degree in business administration or a bachelor's degree in the liberal arts is largely immaterial, provided that the degrees are conferred by ranking institutions. This conclusion emerges from a study of 2,700 senior managers of more than two hundred major corporations (Useem and Karabel, 1985). The study focused on the chief executives and ranking officers of the nation's leading manufacturing, financial, and service firms in the late 1970s. It found that, of those senior managers who had received no university education, 27 percent had reached the chief executiveship. The college educated did considerably better, but not uniformly so. Of those with only B.A. degrees, 36 percent had become chief executives. Of those who earned M.B.A. degrees from one of the nation's top eleven programs, 45 percent had reached the pinnacle of corporate achievement.

This would appear to indicate that M.B.A. recipients fare better than those with only B.A.s. Yet a closer look at the data revealed that a subgroup of the B.A. holders were actually *more* likely than the M.B.A. recipients to have reached the top of the corporate pyramid. The study separated out the B.A.-holding managers who had attended any of the nation's top eleven colleges and universities (the top eleven included such institutions as Yale, Williams, and Dartmouth). While 45 percent of the top M.B.A. holders had become chief executives, 52 percent of the top terminal B.A. holders had done so. It is certainly the case that many of the undergraduate alumni of institutions such as Yale, Williams, and Dartmouth carried the special advantage of old family wealth, an advantage less often shared by the M.B.A. holders. To test the possible significance of this advantage, the study compared managers of patrician origins with managers of more modest backgrounds. The basic differences still held: whether from wealthy families or not, the top B.A. holders were about 15 percent more likely to become chief executives than the top M.B.A. recipients.

It might also be argued that a fraction of the bachelor's degree holders obtained undergraduate degrees in business or engineering, and thus the comparison was not strictly between managers with liberal arts baccalaureates and managers with professional business training. Most of the top B.A.-granting institutions did not offer undergraduate degrees in business or engineering, however, and thus the comparison is largely apt. The point can be further sharpened if we compare the managerial careers of those who completed their formal education with B.A. degrees from Harvard, Yale, or Princeton, all three permitting the pursuit of only the liberal arts in their undergraduate colleges, with the careers of managers who completed their education with an M.B.A. degree from one of the nation's pre-eminent postgraduate business programs, Harvard's Graduate School of Business. The study reveals that the two groups were equally likely to rise to the top ranks of their company's leadership (Useem and Karabel, 1985).

Managerial Advancement Within the Firm. Drawn from the experience of managers in a range of companies, the evidence converges on a central conclusion: despite a sometimes wobbly start in corporate management, liberal arts graduates generally do as well as those trained in subjects more immediately related to business. Sometimes they do more poorly, but sometimes they also do better. In interpreting this experience, it is useful to draw on a distinction that economists make between external and internal labor markets. As applied here, the external labor market refers to competition among new college graduates for entry into company employment. The internal labor market refers to competition among older college graduates within a firm for upward movement into its better-paying and more responsible positions. The evidence suggests that some liberal arts graduates experience a modest disadvantage in the external labor market for entering a firm to start a management career. It also indicates that they are not disadvantaged in the internal labor markets for pursuing managerial careers within a corporation.

The distribution of liberal arts graduates among the managerial levels of one midwestern company illustrates the advantages that liberally educated managers occasionally have in a firm's internal labor market, even when the company is technologically oriented. Illinois Bell analyzed the educational background of its managers in 1984 according to their grade, following the same seven-level classification used by its former parent, AT&T. As shown in Table 4-4, the Illinois Bell managerial hierarchy rapidly constricts, dropping from 5,376 managers at the first level to a quarter of this number by the second level, only

Table 4-4. Proportion of Illinois Bell Managers
with a Liberal Arts Degree, 1984.

Management Level	Number of Managers	Average Age	Average Service	Percentage Holding Liberal Arts Degrees
1 (lowest)	5,376	41	19	6.2
2	1,330	46	23	13.6
3	255	49	25	18.4
4	67	50	26	26.9
5	19	53	26	31.6
6 and 7	10	51	27	60.0

Source: Wade, 1984, p. 13.

5 percent by the third level, and to just 19 people, or less than one-half of 1 percent, by the fifth level. The higher-level managers are somewhat older and have been with the company longer than lower-level managers, but the differences are not as great as one might expect. Level-one managers had been with the company nineteen years on average, while level-six and -seven managers had been there for twenty-seven years.

In examining the educational origins of the managers, the Illinois Bell study reveals that the higher the level of management, the greater were the proportions of managers holding liberal arts degrees. Of the first-level managers, 6 percent held liberal arts degrees; of the middle-level managers, 18 percent were liberal arts graduates; and of the top managers, 60 percent were recipients of baccalaureates in the liberal arts (Wade, 1984). Such studies and observations must be interpreted cautiously, however, for they may overstate the likelihood that today's liberally educated graduates will ascend into senior management. Most of the present-day top executives were educated during an era when undergraduate business and engineering programs were not nearly as widespread as today and when relatively few college graduates pursued postgraduate studies in management schools. Moreover, many graduates of well-known liberal arts colleges, such as Williams and Amherst, may have had successful business careers for reasons entirely unrelated to their liberal learning experiences in college. These colleges are highly selective, and they recruit individuals whose intellectual and motivational talents are exceptional. The disproportionate presence of their graduates among the top managerial echelons may reflect more the colleges' admission standards than what the colleges provided their graduates in the classroom.

Managerial Value of a Liberal Education

As mentioned in Chapter One, Charles Brown, the president of AT&T, sees the success of liberal arts graduates throughout the Bell system as the result of their being better suited than others to the rapidly changing environment of today's business world. Flexibility and adaptability may indeed be among the leading factors that generally explain the success of the liberally educated graduate. Critical thinking and decision-making skills are surely important as well, along with intelligence and personal skills. "Above all," asserts Judd Alexander, executive vice-president of James River Corporation, "business needs people who are smart, who know how to use their brains and how to work with others" (Alexander, 1981, p. 16). This section reviews what is known about why liberally educated company managers—whether the education is from a liberal arts or a preprofessional curriculum—often excel at their tasks. The assessment follows a standard distinction between the content of learning and the skills of learning. By the former is usually meant the knowledge and information imparted by formal course content; the latter include the capacity to think critically, conceptualize and communicate, obtain and integrate information, and act with initiative and self-confidence.

The information and facts acquired in most liberal education courses have little immediate bearing on the skills required of a graduate for an entry-level management position. This is the most frequent lament of liberal arts graduates and corporate recruiters alike as they consider what they have to offer one another. Yet this concern greatly overestimates the importance of facts and information for starting managerial work and underestimates the value of other skills for later managerial success.

The Content of Liberal Learning. Cognitive information has only a modest bearing on later managerial performance. This conclusion emerges from a range of studies of three separate types. The first type of study, on the correlation between academic achievement and later managerial achievement, typically investigates the relationship between an individual's course grades and later job performance. Course grades measure in part the extent to which a student has mastered the content of the field. If content matters, better grades should predict better performance.

Several studies do report positive correlations between college grades and valued elements of managerial performance. One investigation, for instance, found that college graduates with high grades were more engaged in their managerial work life and maintained more exacting standards for their own work performance (Howard, 1985). Yet most research yields negative conclusions. Thus, one study focused on the graduates of a university who were employed in managerial positions and who had graduated five to ten years before. It found that their college grade averages bore no relationship to eight types of supervisor-rated performance on the job. The absence of a relationship is not unique to management. Whether in business, law, medicine, or a range of other professions, the correlation of grades at both the undergraduate and postgraduate levels with later occupational performance is, according to dozens of studies, modest at best and most often nil (Hoyt, 1965).

The second line of research, on the relationship between specific cognitive information and managerial performance, focuses on the perceptions of college graduates some years after entering their business careers. The proportions of the graduates attributing high importance to course content are typically very low. One representative study (Bisconti and Kessler, 1980) asked graduates, most working in business, to rate the value of course content for their work a decade after leaving the campus. Only 29 percent stated that facts and information of their primary study area were the most important element in their ability to perform even their first job, and only 8 percent found them to be of singular value for their work a decade later.

A similar conclusion emerges from a mid-1970s study (Solmon, 1981, p. 636) of college graduates who had been in the labor force for three to nine years. A relatively high proportion—53 percent—of the recent graduates asserted that their college education gave them "knowledge and skills used in [their] current job," but this factor ranked fifth in importance, behind "increased general knowledge," "increased ability to think clearly," and other factors unrelated to specific course work. Moreover, the specific content further diminished in value over time: after nine years on the job, the proportion of the graduates still finding college "knowledge and skills" relevant had diminished by a third.

Still another investigation (Bisconti and Solmon, 1976) points to the same conclusion. Focusing a decade after graduation on some four thousand men and women who obtained no postgraduate training and who were working in company management, this study asked how the graduates had acquired the managerial skills needed for their present work. Of the English majors, 81 percent reported that they acquired their administrative skills through on-the-job training; 85 percent of the arts and humanities majors reported the same; and, among the social science majors, 86 percent stressed on-the-job training. Yet, even among the business majors, the proportion stressing work experience was just as high, at 87 percent.

A third line of research, on the value of specialized knowledge for managerial promotion, focuses on managers' evaluation of promotion criteria within their own firm. Cognitive competence ranks first on no list, and it invariably comes distantly behind communication skills, interpersonal abilities, and a capacity to assume responsibility, particularly as the manager moves up the corporate ladder. Although cognitive capacity is often an important predictor of career advancement among lower-level managers, one study of fourteen hundred corporate executives (Randle, 1956) finds that the primary predictor for higher-level managers is personality style. Another study (Gordon and Howell, 1959), based on interviews with top executives at ninety large firms, concludes that, except for certain types of jobs, possession of specialized knowledge and technical skills was considered of only moderate or minor importance compared with various character elements. Still another investigation (Rawlins and Ulman, 1974), a survey of professional and managerial employees for two companies, found that specific skills were less important for promotion than such traits as self-confidence and willingness to make decisions.

A 1982 survey of 113 officers of large American companies illustrates the rankings of managerial traits commonly found in such studies. Drawing on a list of thirty-two traits, the officers were asked to identify the five that "become more important to success as a college graduate employee progresses to middle or top positions in your company" (Warren, 1983, p. 11). The eight traits most frequently singled out were the following (with the percentage of the officers who included each trait among the top five): verbal communications skills (51 percent); ability to identify and formulate problems (45 percent); willingness to assume responsibility (43 percent); interpersonal skills (42 percent); reasoning ability (38 percent); creativity (27 percent); writing skills (24 percent); and ability to function independently (24 percent). It is seen that communication, decision making, and interpersonal abilities, rather than technical knowledge, lead the list. For the internal labor market of the corporation, then, the specific content of college learning typically plays little role in the manager's performance or advancement (Warren, 1983).

Specialized knowledge plays a larger role in helping a new manager obtain an entry-level position. This is shown in the survey of 113 company officers referred to previously. When asked what advice they would give to a college student preparing for a career in business, many stressed the acquisition of analytical abilities and communication skills. But they also stressed the acquisition of depth of knowledge in a specialized field of immediate applicability, such as management, finance, or economics.

The same emphasis is shown in the 1984 placement survey of 648 firms described above. It revealed that an applicant's college major (that is, the content area) was the single most important criterion in company recruitment of new graduates (Table 4-1). Moreover, when employers were asked what courses would "make liberal arts graduates more employable" in their organizations, business-related courses were among the top recommendations. The courses that employers asserted would always or almost always help the liberal arts graduate find the first job, with percentages of employers listing them, are as follows (Shingleton and Scheetz, 1984): writing and communication (58 percent); business administration (55 percent); accounting and finance (55 percent); data processing (44 percent); and public speaking (35 percent).

Yet even the apparent emphasis on specialized training in business-related courses requires careful interpretation. Employers may look at the inclusion of such courses as much for an indication of a graduate's motivation as for evidence of the acquisition of specialized business knowledge. Corroborating evidence comes from a comparative study of liberal arts graduates from schools that offer an undergraduate business major and graduates from liberal arts colleges that do not. As perceived by employers, liberal arts students attending an institution without a business concentration had no choice but to major in the liberal arts, while liberal arts students at a college with a business major could have chosen it but opted not to do so. The latter are riskier hires than the former, company recruiters infer, since the latter appear to have rejected business values. This is one reason that many colleges and universities have added a minor in business administration for majors in liberal arts (Collins, 1971; Garis, Hess, and Marron, 1985; Unger, 1985).

There is a suggestion in some of the above that employer preferences can at times be subjective. When successful managers are asked what courses of study they would recommend for others and would prefer to see among new recruits, for instance, they generally recommend the courses that they themselves have taken, whether they include preprofessional training or not. This can be seen in a survey of recently promoted executives who were asked not only their own undergraduate major but also what college field of study they recommended for future executives. The study compared male and female executives. Of the men, a third had majored in business administration, a third in engineering, and a third in the liberal arts (Table 4-5). Nearly identical proportions of the male managers recom-

Table 4-5. Undergraduate Major and Recommended Undergraduate Major of Newly Promoted Company Executives, by Gender.

	Male Executives		Female Executives	
Field of Study	Actual Major	Recommended Major	Actual Major	Recommended Major
Business administration	31.7%	31.8%	8.6%	32.7%
Engineering	27.9	33.5	1.7	5.5
Liberal arts	35.5	32.7	77.6	61.7

Source: Hildebrandt, 1985, pp. 11-12.

mend these three fields to the coming generation of managers. By contrast, only one in ten of the women had majored in business or engineering, and more than three-quarters had concentrated in the liberal arts. While a third of the female executives now urge a business major, two-thirds still would recommend the liberal arts course.

Similar conclusions emerge from a study of managers in three middle-sized companies (Ward, 1959). "What subject, course of study, or area of interest during college," they were asked, "has done you the most good in getting ahead?" Of those who had majored in business administration, 69 percent answered that business courses had, while only 24 percent reported liberal arts courses. By contrast, 13 percent of those who had *not* majored in business singled out business subjects, and 73 percent answered with the liberal arts. By implication, there is no single best path to top company management. Into this ambiguity successful managers tend to project their own course of study as the one most appropriate for future managers (Hildebrandt, 1985).

Learning to Learn and to Lead. Technical knowledge acquired in college is important for entry-level management positions. Its value, however, is a declining function of career ascent. The value of other kinds of college learning, on the other hand, is an inclining function of career ascent. This is especially true of learning and leadership capacities, and available evidence indicates that liberal education can be particularly effective in fostering both.

Learning to learn connotes the acquisition of a capacity to search for needed information, to master new fields of endeavor, and to synthesize data from a range of sources. As corporate managers rise in their careers, the broadening of their responsibilities and the increasing diversity of constituencies with which they must deal place a premium on the capacity to learn effectively and quickly, to become a "fast study." Few college catalogue descriptions expressly focus on course effectiveness in engendering this ability, but well-taught courses in the liberal arts appear to be particularly good at doing so.

The point can be illustrated by a systematic study of students at three colleges: a private liberal arts college, a public college with a range of general and career programs, and a community college emphasizing career curricula (Winter, McClelland, and Stewart, 1981). Comparing freshmen and seniors, the research finds significant learning growth among students in all three settings. The greatest changes, however, are observed for students fully immersed in the liberal arts curriculum. Compared with the others, they made significantly greater gains in their (1) analytical and critical thinking, (2) independence of thought, (3) self-assurance and leadership abilities, and (4) maturity of judgment. (The study's authors are aware that the caliber of the students at the private liberal arts college is higher than that at the other two schools and that this could account for some of the difference. Detailed assessment of this possibility led them to conclude, however, that the differences are not reducible to the variant admissions standards of the colleges.)

The study found that these same qualities successfully forecast future performance in management and the professions. Students who graduated from the private liberal arts college in 1964 were approached a decade later for information on their career achievements. The great majority had entered a professional or business career, and the researchers found that the best college predictors of achievement were those capacities most often developed through the liberal arts. These capacities, moreover, were far more closely correlated with later career achievement than were a range of other factors, including the traditional measures of cognitive competence, such as grade-point average and academic honors. The former were three times more powerful predictors of occupational achievement than were the latter (Winter, McClelland, and Stewart, 1981).

In a final synthesis of these and other investigations, the study's authors, psychologists David Winter, David McClelland, and Abigail Stewart (1981), offer the following summary. Liberal education, they write, "increases students' capacity for mature adaptation to the environment when students encounter new experiences; critical thinking and conceptual skills by demanding that they integrate broad ranges of this novel experience; independence of thought . . . by setting them free from elaborate restraints on behavior and thought; and motivation for leadership by endowing them with a sense of being special" (pp. 177-178). Similar conclusions emerge from the twenty-year study of managers in American Telephone and Telegraph Company, which found that the liberally educated scored higher than preprofessional graduates in their creativity, leadership skills, communication, and solving of management problems. These differences held not only for managers who entered AT&T in the mid 1950s but also for a new group of managers who joined the company in the late 1970s (Howard, 1984, 1985).

The importance of a capacity to learn and to lead typically intensifies as the manager moves up. There is a kind of sleeper effect, according to various studies, with liberal education's benefits coming more to the fore over time. Following two cohorts of college graduates who had been working for three to nine years, for instance, one study (Solmon, 1981) reported that alumni who had taken English courses found more application of such course work with the passage of time, while those who took engineering courses reported less application for that specialty. Similarly, social science degrees were found to increase in value over time, as measured by the graduates' earnings, while engineering degrees, starting higher, lost some relative value. The latency effect is, however, not limited to liberal arts courses: the value of business courses and a business major were also found to grow with time.

A decade-later follow-up of a large sample of mid-1960s college graduates (Bisconti and Kessler, 1980) confirms the same. Graduates in business reported that, as their careers evolved, they relied less on specific training and more on their general management and communication abilities. As they moved up the corporate ladder and managerial responsibilities occupied more and more of their time, general administrative and leadership skills acquired increasing importance. Among those who began their careers as financial specialists, engineers, or accountants, fewer than one in five reported that the first job required administrative or managerial skills (Table 4-6). A decade later, however, 45 percent of the engineers, 73 percent

Table 4-6. Skills Performed in First Job After Graduation and in Job a Decade After Graduation.

								Skill			
	Management		Planning and Budgeting		Writing and Editing		Leading Meetings, Speaking to Groups	
Occupational Area	First Job	After Decade	First Job	After Decade	First Job	After Decade	First Job	After Decade
Finance	27%	73%	13%	40%	20%	53%	27%	73%
Marketing	22	78	7	56	26	63	22	59
Accounting	4	93	19	67	22	81	4	67
Personnel	20	85	2	46	34	78	32	78
Management of research and technology	18	93	17	86	43	71	25	77
Engineering	3	45	3	52	28	38	3	52

Source: Bisconti and Kessler, 1980, pp. 12–14.

of the financial specialists, and 93 percent of the accountants reported that general managerial skills were essential to their work (Bisconti and Kessler, 1980).

The importance of communication skills grows with career as well. In the same study, 26 percent of the marketing specialists reported that they were required to draw on writing skills in their first job, but 63 percent were required to do so a decade later (Table 4-6). Similarly, 3 percent of the engineers were required to speak before groups and meetings when they first began work, but more than 50 percent were doing so ten years later.

These studies may underestimate the initial and continuing importance of technical skills in the managerial career. A longitudinal study of the graduates in the late 1970s of the M.B.A. programs at Stanford University, the University of California at Los Angeles, the University of California at Berkeley, and the University of Southern California found that the technical content of the M.B.A. training was considered quite important. Two-thirds of the graduates stated that the technical skills and knowledge they had acquired were needed a great deal for effective performance in their first position after graduation, and half said that this was still true five years later. But again, as revealed by the previous studies, nontechnical skills increased in importance over time. Thus, 60 percent of the graduates asserted that the analytical skills acquired in their M.B.A. program were needed during the first year after the degree, but 75 percent said that this was so after five years. Similarly, 67 percent stated that interpersonal skills, such as communication and teamwork, were required for effective job performance at first, but 93 percent said they were essential after five years on the job (Louis, 1985).

Managing the Corporate Environment. While general managerial skills needed for the midcareer come to overshadow the technical skills required for the early career, still another set of skills is needed for successful movement into senior management. These are the skills of managing the company's environment. Among them is a comprehension of the legislative process and the key players in the nation's and states' capitals; of how public opinion is shaped and how it can affect the firm; and the role of environmental, labor, consumer, and other interest groups in American life. As managers move from middle to senior levels, they are increasingly called upon to read—and to shape—the company's social and political environment. Understanding that environment is largely a product of on-the-job experience. But a liberal education can facilitate and deepen that understanding (Useem, 1985).

Reflecting the growing concern with this issue at the highest levels of corporate management, a 1982 report of the Business Roundtable prods firms to improve managerial awareness. "Assess the ability of your company," the Roundtable urges, "to develop executives who are as adept in dealing with the public policy dimension of business as they are in managing its traditional functions" (Steckmest, 1982, p. 276). As Chapter Five demonstrates, corporations are experimenting with a range of programs to enhance the social and political awareness of their midcareer executives. Nearly half of 176 major companies responding to a 1979–80 survey by the Conference Board reported that they were running courses and workshops on public affairs for their managers, and two-thirds were planning to do so in the future (Lusterman, 1981; McGrath, 1980).

While not all middle-level managers are called upon to help manage the corporation's environment, for senior managers the call is universal. A Conference Board survey of nearly four hundred chief executives of large companies in 1979–80 reveals that more than nine in ten affirmed that they "should personally and actively express [their] views on public policy issues at senior government levels," and virtually all had done so. Nearly half had even taken time out for part-time service on a public commission or government advisory committee (Moore, 1980, p. 9).

Improving effectiveness in managing the environment has become a corporate priority. Half of the large companies surveyed in another Conference Board study, in 1981, report that top-management development for external affairs was among their most important goals. A majority of the chief executives of the 432 surveyed companies reported that a key challenge for the coming five years was "improving top management's grasp of emerging political, economic, and social issues." Half also assigned high priority to "building top-management effectiveness in dealing with governments and other external forces and groups" (Shaeffer, 1982, p. 11).

Among the liberal arts courses that can enhance one's ability to face these issues are political psychology, international relations, urban politics, and American history. While no studies to date have documented the special value of early courses in these subjects for top-executive effectiveness, they should provide a head start. Here, too, there is likely to be a sleeper effect. Most entry-level managers start with few responsibilities for managing the firm's environment. As a financial specialist or production supervisor, a typical manager climbs the lower rungs of the corporate ladder by mastering the company's internal world. Climbing the higher rungs, however, increasingly calls for mastery of the external world as well. While courses in the politics of regulation and the democratic process may have little immediate payoff, their eventual payoff may be significant.

The importance of a mastery of the external environment for managerial advancement can be seen in the compensation policies of one major firm, Eaton Company, where a senior manager's remuneration is based in part on his or her community involvement and public speaking appearances. Yet Eaton's approach is hardly unique, as nearly three in ten large companies surveyed in 1979–80 by the Conference Board report that public affairs performance is explicitly included in making annual assessment of managerial effectiveness. Moreover, in reviewing candidates to fill senior positions, most large corporations stress an understanding of the business environment. Significant weight is attached to this criterion in recruiting not only for the chief executive position but also for such positions as human resources officer, plant supervisor, and even manager of research and development (Lusterman, 1981).

Most of an executive's ability to manage an environment comes through the direct experience of doing so. Yet a solid foundation in history, political science, economics, and related subjects of the liberal curriculum, whether carried in a liberal arts college, business school, or engineering program, can provide the lens through which the experience is most fully interpreted and appreciated. For executives of companies whose operations or markets span national boundaries, an additional academic foundation in language, international relations, and cross-cultural understanding can be equally advantageous.

Behavior of the Firm

If a liberal education can make a manager more effective in the firm, can liberally educated managers also make the firm more effective? The educational *level* of managers is known to affect some areas of company behavior. Firms led by highly educated top managers, according to several studies, are, for example, more likely to innovate. There is little evidence, however, to say whether the *type* of higher education makes a difference. Studies of the management of other types of institutions suggest not. In one study of organizational innovations in hospitals, for instance, whether the hospital managers held degrees in administration was found to make no difference in their likelihood of innovation (Hambrick and Mason, 1984; Kimberly and Evanisko, 1981).

If change is defined more broadly to include corporate responsiveness to a range of organizational and marketing opportunities, however, it is arguable that a manager's foundation in liberal education can prove important. "The potential for an American corporate Renaissance would be enhanced by the kinds of people developed and rewarded in leading-edge innovating companies," concluded Rosabeth Kanter (1983, p. 368) after an extensive study of innovation in American industry. The key to competitive change, she argues, is "managers who are broader-gauged, more able to move across specialist boundaries, comfortable working in teams that may include many disciplines, knowledgeable about how to manage ambiguous assignments and webs of interdependencies" (p. 368). A liberal education cannot make a "Renaissance" manager, but it can lay an early foundation. If Kanter's hypothesis is correct, a broadly educated business leadership is essential for America's industrial future, and a liberal education may be the prerequisite.

Management's educational background will probably have little direct bearing on the general performance of a firm. Studies typically reveal little correlation between other traits of managers and standard financial measures of firm performance, such as profitability. One of the most extensively researched potential correlations, for example, is whether large corporations that are still managed by the original founders or their family descendants show higher rates of profit than companies now run by professional managers. Several dozen studies reveal virtually no difference in the profit performance of the firms run by the two kinds of managers (Berle and Means, [1932] 1967; Herman, 1981).

If the ownership stake of managers has little impact on the financial behavior of the firm, educational credentials are likely to have even less. The financial performance of companies is determined by market, sector, capitalization, and related factors, and it would be surprising, indeed, if the education of senior managers had much influence here. In areas less constrained by the iron discipline surrounding financial performance, however, the play in corporate behavior is greater, and the educational background of top management may come more to the fore. The area where this may be most likely is in the social performance of the firm. Corporate social performance is usually defined to encompass such social programs as philanthropic contributions, equal employment practices, employee assistance plans, and quality-of-work-life efforts. A central conclusion from a number of research studies of corporate social performance is that the role of senior management is critical.

One study, for example, examined the moving forces behind the establishment of special social programs by five major companies: General Electric's effort to increase minority representation among its managerial ranks; Raytheon's establishment of an inner-city job-training center; Cabot Corporation's expansion of its corporate contributions; Eastern Gas and Fuel's evolution of a system of social auditing and reporting; and Hancock's program to assist a metropolitan school system through a difficult period of compliance with court-ordered desegregation. In each instance, the researcher concluded, the chief executive is the "pivotal figure when it comes to the initiation of voluntary social programs" (Merenda, 1981, p. 39). While in each case the company's size, sector, and self-interest predisposed it to so act, the top officer was always the final catalyst. Similarly, in a study of why some firms give generously to charity and others do not, even when contributions programs are highly professionalized, the attitude of the chief executives remained decisive. In companies where they took an active interest, giving expanded; where they did not, it did not (Useem and Kutner, 1985).

The factors distinguishing executives who take an active interest from those who do not are reducible to neither economic nor organizational factors. It is often a product of personal connections; in other cases, it is a matter of personal biography. But one study does suggest that a distinguishing factor in the biography may be the executive's education. Two sets of large corporations were compared: one group of thirty-one companies was identified as "progressive" by a panel of senior human resource executives; a second group of nineteen "nonprogressive" companies was selected from the same industry and size class. Progressive companies were defined as those that had adopted practices intended to (1) improve work conditions through quality-of-work-life efforts, (2) assure equal employment opportunity, and (3) address the special problems of working parents. Direct study of the companies' practices reveals that the progressive companies lived up to their reputation: they had more often introduced such programs as quality circles, career development training, and flexible work schedules.

In explaining the differences, the study turned to, among other factors, the educational background of the senior executives. It found that the top twenty-five to thirty-five managers of nonprogressive companies were more likely than managers of progressive companies to have received a postgraduate education in business management. Thus, an average of 15 percent of the senior executives of progressive firms held M.B.A. degrees, while 25 percent of the senior executives of the nonprogressive firms had been so educated. This does not confirm the importance of a liberal education, but it does imply that educational background can affect firm social performance. Formal management training, the study's results suggest, may direct executive attention away from the human dimension of managing the work force. That this concentration on other concerns is not simply a product of hardheaded management thinking is evident in the economic performance of the two groups of companies: progressive corporations were on average more profitable than nonprogressive firms (Kanter, 1984).

The limited available research suggests, then, that a liberal education has no impact on a company's effectiveness if effectiveness is defined as financial performance. It may well have some impact, however, if effectiveness is defined as social responsiveness. If future research confirms an impact, it would mean that an emphasis on liberal learning is important not just for individual performance and career advancement. Liberally educated managers may be found to guide their firms in ways more responsive to the concerns of a range of corporate stakeholders. A broadly educated managerial cadre, therefore, may be as important for societal goals as for economic performance.

Moreover, it is arguable that liberal education may also have impact if effectiveness is defined as political responsiveness. Numerous studies have confirmed that a college education, and above all a liberal education, increases interest in political life, knowledge of the political process, and engagement in political activity (Feldman and Newcomb, 1969; Bowen, 1977). In recent years, corporations have themselves become increasingly active in American political life, and it may be that companies led by politically savvy managers are also those most effective in managing their political environment. A liberal education may be the most effective early way for managers to acquire the necessary political savoir faire (Steckmest, 1981; Useem, 1984).

Liberal Education for Management

Though sometimes lacking technical skills at the outset, liberally educated managers do well in part because they have acquired a range of other skills also important for corporate management. Foremost among these are the skills of communication, critical thinking, and leadership. Also important is the informed understanding of the complex social and political forces shaping the environment of the corporation. A disciplined broad-mindedness may be one of the special assets as well. "Companies are realizing," observed one seasoned executive, "that their problems may be due to technically qualified managers who see the trees but lack the wisdom imparted by the liberal arts to see the forest" (Rothberg, 1985, p. 7).

The research does not suggest that acquiring a liberal arts degree is a superior way to prepare for corporate management. As we have seen from available studies, the value of the liberal arts preparation is primarily in the most generic elements of learning how to learn and to lead. These elements can be, and often are, incorporated into undergraduate business and engineering programs as well as liberal arts programs. Some bachelor's programs in business administration have even come to stress liberal learning as a central part of the curriculum. Another contribution of liberal education, the preparation of managers to cope with the business environment, can also be achieved through preprofessional programs. On many campuses, courses on political history, social psychology, and international relations are as available to students enrolled in the business and engineering schools as to those in the liberal arts school. The research does suggest that undergraduate preprofessional programs that do not presently provide a full liberal learning experience should consider ways of doing so. Otherwise, they may be educating students for their first job but not their full career.

A liberally educated management cadre, however, contributes to more than just its own advancement. Firms with a broadly educated leadership are probably no more profitable than others. But they may be more innovative, more risk taking, and more socially responsive. If so, the impact of a liberal education goes far beyond giving some managers and some firms an advantage over others. Though indirect in effect, liberal education may be helping to facilitate industrial change, stimulate entrepreneurship, and improve the general quality of work life in America.

5   *Michael Useem*

New Opportunities
for Management Development
and Executive Education

Chapters One through Four of this book have reviewed the many reasons for giving liberal learning a more central place in the preparation of managers. We turn now to the environments in which that task needs to be accomplished. Chapters Six, Seven, and Eight focus on academic programs in business and in the arts and sciences. But just as important is business itself, the focus of the present chapter. Indeed, as more and more corporations themselves see it, liberal learning matters too much to be left to higher education.

　　With offerings that sometimes are little more than short seminars but occasionally are full-scale baccalaureate programs, companies have increasingly entered the business of managing their own liberal education programs—or, as the *New York Times* labeled it, "teaching arts instead of accounting" (Gutis,

　　Note: This chapter draws on interviews and discussions that the authors conducted with company managers and others familiar with corporate training programs. Unless otherwise indicated, direct quotations in the chapter are drawn from these interviews and discussions.

1985). The corporate classroom is no longer limited to management and technical training. Company employees can now pursue courses as well in physics, philosophy, and philology.

The rise of liberal learning within the corporation has been partly boosted by the growth of all corporate education programs, whatever the subject matter. "Education and training within large private sector corporations of the United States," observes a Carnegie Foundation study of the phenomenon, "has become a booming industry" (Eurich, 1985, p. 1). While the annual expenditures of American colleges and universities in the early 1980s had reached $60 billion, the training expenditures of corporations were exceeding $40 billion and climbing. "America's workers and managers have been going back to school for a long time," the Carnegie report concludes, "but in the last decade their numbers have increased, the variety of subjects has broadened and, most strikingly, America's business has become its own educational provider" (p. 1).

While liberal education has risen with the tide of corporate training, it has been driven as well by an intensifying involvement of companies in community and national life. Though never shrinking violets, companies have nonetheless usually preferred the comfortable seclusion of the private sector. Managers were encouraged in past decades to follow a fourfold path to corporate success: "stick to business, stay out of trouble, join the right clubs, and don't talk to reporters." The formula, however, failed. In sticking strictly to business, corporations by the mid 1970s lost public confidence, and their profits were in general decline (Shapiro, 1979; Lipset and Schneider, 1981; Feldstein, Poterba, and Dicks-Mireaux, 1982).

A more socially responsive and politically active strategy was seen as the sine qua non for corporate recovery, and in the late 1970s and early 1980s, most large firms expanded their programs on both fronts. Corporate gifts, political action committees, Washington affairs, media relations, and community partnerships were moved high on the company agenda. To manage the new activism and the corporate environment it was intended to shape, a new breed of managers was required as well. "Large corporations are highly vulnerable targets for public criticism and government control," warned the Business Roundtable, an association of the chief executives of the nation's two hundred largest firms. Company officers must, the Roundtable urged, "make certain that their successors and the oncoming generation of executives develop the ability to participate in the public policy process and to manage the evolving role of the large corporation as effectively as executives must manage other aspects of their work" (Steckmest, 1982, p. 265).

Managerial appreciation for the public policy process can be cultivated. So, too, can executive skills in managing employees who are as concerned about the quality of their work life as their wages; community groups as worried about environmental preservation as job expansion; and media reporters as eager to cover corporate failings as achievements. Liberal learning has an important part to play here, in helping managers deal with the often bruising environment in which they must operate.

Liberal learning within the corporation, the subject of this chapter, takes diverse forms. For nonexempt employees (those outside the professional and managerial ranks) aspiring to be more exempt, it may be a full-blown baccalaureate program under company contract with a local university. For middle managers with broadening responsibilities, it may be a three-day seminar on public affairs at corporate headquarters. For senior executives, it may be informal reading and direct participation in the affairs of government and the nonprofit world. Whatever the form, the objective is generally not so much technique as breadth of understanding—especially the capacity to grasp issues bearing on decisions and reflect broadly on their implications.

Companies devise varying forms of liberal learning opportunities for varying levels of employees. This chapter focuses on programs first for nonexempt employees, then for middle managers, and finally for senior-level executives. Our purpose is to describe the primary features of such programs, drawing on a diverse sampling of programs as illustrations.

Nonexempt Employees:
Liberal Arts Baccalaureate Programs

Among corporations with five hundred or more employees, nonexempt employees typically constitute the bulk of the work force. Approximately two-thirds of the employees of the typical large firm are nonexempt, while the remainder of the work force is about equally divided among professional and technical staff, sales and marketing, and general management (Lusterman, 1977). Virtually all major corporations provide educational benefits to their employees, most typically as tuition assistance. They have become a near-universal personnel benefit, expected by employees in almost all large firms. A 1979 Conference Board survey (Gorlin, 1981) of 346 large companies reveals, for instance, that 88 percent furnish tuition aid to production workers pursuing college or university courses, and 97 percent provide such assistance to office workers. Whether in manufacturing, banking, insurance, or utilities, almost all major companies offer these benefits. The one exception, according to a 1975 Conference Board survey (Lusterman, 1977), of 610 firms, is the wholesale and retail industry: only two-thirds of these companies offered tuition-aid plans.

The employee participation rate varies widely among firms but averages about 3 percent among production employees and 5 percent among office workers. Most companies with tuition plans cover the entire tuition cost, typically reimbursing the employee upon completion of the course with a passing grade. Company tuition-assistance plans are encouraged under national tax law. Since 1978, employer-paid educational aid has been excluded from the taxable income of employees up to a maximum of $5,000 per year, even for training that has no direct bearing on the employee's present job (Gorlin, 1981; Craig and Evers, 1981).

Corporations report that the leading purpose of the tuition aid is to support study in areas that are immediately related to the employee's current job. But almost equally important is preparation for the next job, and closely behind that is "preparation for a more distant career goal." Half of the participating companies see their programs as furthering the employee's broader career aspirations. Whatever the purpose, nearly all large companies express a continuing commitment to the further learning of their employees by carrying the considerable cost of the tuition-assistance programs (Gorlin, 1981).

The career aspiration of many nonexempt employees is

to move into professional and managerial positions, and substantial numbers enroll in baccalaureate degree programs to facilitate such movement. Not surprisingly, the programs typically have a technical cast. But their curricula are not without a substantial dose of liberal studies. This is illustrated by an off-site cooperative education program of Digital Equipment Corporation, the major Massachusetts-based maker of minicomputers and related computer products.

Many of Digital's 85,000 employees join the firm without a college education but come to regret its absence from their resume. Losing none of their livelihood and enjoying full tuition benefits, nonexempt Digital employees can enter a bachelor of science program administered by Boston University. While the program is "designed to develop ... an in-depth understanding of [employees'] chosen profession," according to the university catalogue, it also builds "upon a firm foundation in the liberal arts and sciences." Employees may major in either computer science or business administration, both disciplines in which a broad array of courses are available. But the liberal arts foundation is there as well, resembling that found in any undergraduate liberal arts program. Students must complete courses in English composition, and they are required to carry several classes each in the humanities, natural sciences, and social sciences.

Chase Manhattan Bank, the nation's third-largest commercial bank with 44,000 employees, maintains an arrangement with Cornell University for its clerical and administrative employees. Chase workers may begin a bachelor's degree program in liberal studies upon recommendation of their manager, with classes offered at the bank. The program was the product of a settlement of a legal suit by clerical employees against the bank and expressed a Chase commitment to expand the career opportunities of its largely female clerical ranks. The program is now open to both women and men and is intended to provide a bridge through the first year of college work for people who did not attend college after high school. The participants have usually had from five to twenty years of work experience and are selected for both their academic and work potential. Seventy-three employees graduated from the program in 1985.

The CIGNA Corporation, a large Philadelphia insurance firm, contracts for a similar program for similar reasons with the University of Pennsylvania. Initiated in 1981, this program enrolls approximately a hundred clerical and operations employees annually in courses offered at the company's headquarters. The convenience of the course site is considered critical to the program's success. Choosing from among a range of courses, including history, psychology, economics, Italian, English, and philosophy, nonexempt CIGNA employees pursue majors leading to a bachelor's degree in the liberal arts. The company covers all expenses associated with the course work, for an annual total cost of approximately $150,000. The program's first baccalaureate degrees were awarded in 1984.

Like the Chase program, the CIGNA arrangement with the University of Pennsylvania was initiated in part as a response to a class-action suit by minority employees against the company's hiring practices (Brown, 1985). Despite the origins, the company now actively promotes the program, and it is viewed as improving employee morale and reducing turnover. "A liberal arts degree develops critical skills and gives a better perspective on work," offered a company vice-president at the time of the program's launching (Williams and King, 1981, p. 74). Participants are not necessarily, however, being groomed for entry into management. Rather, the liberal arts experience is seen as enriching an essential knowledge base of the company's staff. "As a multinational company doing business in 145 countries around the world," concludes chairperson Ralph S. Saul, CIGNA "recognizes the need to understand not only our own business, but also the diverse and complex social, political, economic, and cultural environments we work in" (Mohrman, 1983b, p. 60).

About one major firm in three now offers employees an educational program developed in direct collaboration with a local college and university. A 1980 survey of 217 industrial firms with more than five thousand employees found that nearly one-third had contractual relations with local schools to offer degree programs. Some programs include a liberal learning option, but many are largely technical in nature. Company contracts with specific colleges and universities to provide a liberal education to nonexempt employees are thus far from the rule. Far more common are tuition-aid plans that permit employees to enroll in any accredited institution in any course of study, including the liberal arts. Nearly all major companies have instituted such assistance plans. While tuition programs foster more diversity and flexibility, the logistics are usually less appealing. Employees must compete with other applicants for admission, commute some distance to campus, and select from courses not always suited to their substantive needs or time constraints (Baker, 1983).

Liberal Learning for Managers Within the Corporation

By training and temperament, most new managers commence their careers with little interest in the broader issues of corporate organization or the company's environment. Nor are they normally expected to concern themselves with either. As a marketing specialist or financial analyst, the new manager climbs the early ranks by mastering the narrowly defined functions of early assignments. Career development for the manager, however, increasingly comes to depend on the application of other abilities. The importance of new skills can be seen, for example, in a study mentioned in Chapter Four of a large national sample of mid-1960s college graduates working in business. When surveyed a decade after entering their careers, the managers reported that communication and group leadership abilities had become far more important than when they started work. Thus, 20 percent of the financial analysts reported that they drew upon writing and editing skills in their first job, but 53 percent were doing so a decade later. Among those managing technology, 25 percent needed skills in leading meetings and speaking before groups when first employed, but 77 percent required such abilities ten years later (Bisconti and Kessler, 1980).

Movement into middle management is contingent on mastery not only of the company's internal world but of its social and political environment as well. For a plant manager, familiarity with local political traditions, union sensitivities, and environmental concerns can be essential. For a marketing or financial manager, the job description can include a general knowledge of international investment risks and of the political climates for trade restrictions. To ensure that upwardly moving middle managers acquire an enlarged perspective commensurate with their broadening responsibilities, many firms foster midcareer liberal learning.

Virtually all major companies make tuition-assistance programs available to managers. A 1979 Conference Board survey of 346 companies (Gorlin, 1981) revealed that 97 percent covered managers' costs in attending local colleges and universities. Of those managers eligible to participate, only 5 percent do so in the typical company, and many of these are enrolled in technical curricula. Nonetheless, managers wishing to pursue courses in English literature or political behavior can usually find a company subsidy to do so.

For enhancing the environmental awareness and political adeptness of middle managers, formal schooling in public affairs and contemporary issues is provided by company-sponsored seminars and courses, some held within the company, others offered by colleges and universities. Half of the large corporations surveyed by the Conference Board in 1979–80 enrolled managers in these programs, and two-thirds intended to do so in the near future. Companies rate these formal offerings as the most effective means available for enlarging managers' understanding of the company's social and political environment (Lusterman, 1981).

The company-sponsored seminar held within the corporation can be illustrated by a program of Shell Oil Company, the Houston-based petroleum firm with sales exceeding $20 billion and a work force of more than 35,000. Shell sponsors an annual "faculty forum" near its home office, bringing rising middle managers together with university faculty for an intensive give-and-take on current social and political affairs. A dozen Shell managers and an equal number of university faculty members are cloistered in a Houston conference center for three days of structured dialogue. The Shell forum topics are not technical but focus, rather, on issues that midcareer managers must come to master if they are to lead the company in the future. Among the subjects discussed at the 1985 Shell program were national industrial policy, affirmative action, and the international competitive position of the United States. While the formal topics were never too far from the pragmatic concerns of the corporation, informal discussion frequently drifted far afield, the expansive give-and-take resembling that of any college seminar.

Generally in their mid thirties, the Shell participants in 1985 included a manager of international supply who held a B.S. degree in business administration; a manager of plans at a manufacturing complex who possessed a B.S. degree in chemical engineering; and a budget coordinator for exploration and production who had earned a B.S. degree in civil engineering. As intended by Shell, the interests of the faculty participants could hardly have been more contrasting. Also largely in their thirties, the faculty included professors of economics, law, biology, psychology, history, and journalism.

The manager of Shell's Deer Park Manufacturing Complex, William Thompson, attended the faculty forum in 1974. Shell Oil Company hires hundreds of new engineering and business graduates every year, and Thompson reflected on why some of the engineers eventually assume broader responsibilities for the company, while others do not. "A most important element in top management is the capacity to speak with a variety of groups, those who agree with our position and policies and those who would like to see changes—unions, environmental groups, and so on. To communicate effectively, you have to be open and nondefensive, and to listen." But often, he concluded, "engineers who know the technical side can't deal with the nonmeasurable elements required for top management. Those who can, make it; the others probably won't." The faculty forum was one of Shell's ways of enhancing their appreciation of the unmeasurable.

Companies also contract with local colleges and universities to operate similar seminars within the academic setting. Hallmark Cards, Inc., the greeting card manufacturer based in

Kansas City, has long stressed the need for executive familiarity with the arts and humanities. Since many of its managers have had little exposure to either in college, Hallmark arranges for a select set of managers to participate in an annual "Hallmark Executive Seminar in the Humanities," organized and hosted by the nearby University of Kansas. Hallmark's managers receive a week's immersion in such topics as creativity, liberty and criticism, literature, and the uses and misuses of history. Participants use self-study guides, view films, and complete reading from classics ranging from Thomas Kuhn's *The Structure of Scientific Revolutions* to John Stuart Mill's *On Liberty,* Joseph Conrad's *Heart of Darkness,* and Thucydides' *The Peloponnesian War* (Randall, 1981).

Another approach employed by many corporations is to foster liberal learning among managers through internal seminars led by company executives themselves. Rather than relying on academic faculty as facilitators, companies draw on the talents of their own senior managers. The executive faculty's time is scarce and costly, but their presence in the program conveys a special message to the participants about the importance attached to the learning. Koppers Company, a large Pittsburgh-based manufacturing, engineering, and construction firm, conducted such a program for more than a decade during the 1970s and early 1980s. Some twenty middle managers were selected annually to participate in a year-long seminar focused on major contemporary books of social and political significance. Participants gathered for three hours every month to discuss such works as Charles Silberman's *Crisis in Black and White,* Michael Novak's *The Spirit of Democratic Capitalism,* and James Q. Wilson's *Thinking About Crime.* In Koppers's view, many of the most promising engineers, managers, and other professionals who came into the company were too specialized and limited in their ability to communicate. "We were interested in exposing people who might end up in [top] management" to current issues of widespread concern, recalls the program's creator, Otto B. Wheeley. "Like it or not, these are the issues that are going to influence the environment that [the managers] will be making decisions within, and they have to understand it."

Koppers's special approach was to put three of its officers in the classroom as teachers. In addition to Otto Wheeley, then deputy chairperson of the company, the monthly seminars were jointly led by the chairperson of the board and a senior vice-president. The seminars were initially held at the company's headquarters in Pittsburgh, but to broaden their reach, they were also convened in Baltimore and other locales with major concentrations of Koppers employees. Even then, the seminars were still conducted by the three senior officers of the company, despite the special travel burden placed upon them. This stress on liberal learning was not lost on aspiring engineers and managers. The regular opportunity for informal discussion with the company's top people never failed to attract a full complement of participants.

College and University Programs in Liberal Learning for Managers

While the Shell, Hallmark, and Koppers programs are examples of the short-term seminar programs run exclusively for managers of a single company, colleges and universities also provide a variety of seminars open to all business executives. Seminars not concerned primarily with business and technical topics, while growing in number, still constitute only a tiny minority of the executive education programs operated by business schools and universities around the country. Yet their expansion reflects a growing belief that executive education must reach beyond traditional topics.

For managers whose job descriptions call for involvement in community affairs but whose backgrounds include little knowledge of city politics, Boston College offers a three-day institute on "Corporate Community Relations." The seminar is designed, according to its announcement, for "the general or plant manager who is being called upon to analyze community issues and to develop the corporate response." To this end, in 1984 Boston College offered managers an intensive introduction to local leadership structures; working with the print and broadcast media; employment training, affirmative action, and public education; community expectations of the corporation; and strategic management of local threats to the firm. One of the major users of the seminar, Polaroid Corporation, selects managers who have just been appointed to head a plant or major office away from its Cambridge, Massachusetts, headquarters. As with the Shell forum, a manager's invitation to join this program is both an early sign of recognition and a grooming for even greater responsibilities in the firm. Ten Polaroid managers each year are selected for the institute, and, because of the diverse mix of corporate participants, they learn from fellow students and faculty alike. In one recent seminar, for instance, the Polaroid managers of plants in New Jersey and Illinois were joined by counterparts from Bank of America, IBM, and Texaco. Their faculty included not only Boston College professors but also the public affairs director for Raytheon Corporation, the top state official for employment training in Massachusetts, an editor of *The Boston Globe,* the director of the local United Way, and two city mayors.

Several colleges and universities offer corporate managers more sustained study in the liberal arts. Perhaps best known are the programs of two of the nation's pre-eminent liberal arts colleges, Williams and Dartmouth. Each year for several decades, both have been offering intensive summer courses for advanced midcareer executives. The Williams College Executive Program dates to 1956, when American Telephone and Telegraph persuaded the college to offer its most promising executives a quick introduction to the liberal arts. "They were concerned that the people they wanted to promote to top level positions had too narrow and technical an outlook," reports Vincent Barnett, the program's first director. "Most of the people had been educated as engineers and in technical fields and had little liberal arts background. They were uncomfortable dealing with the kinds of people they would have to deal with in the next level up" (Brown, 1985, p. 9).

The Williams program was opened to executives of other companies in the early 1960s. It annually draws about twenty participants for a five-week summer session costing, in 1985, $6,000. Largely in their early forties, the participants encountered a broad range of liberal arts subjects, which include American economic development; American foreign policy; American politics; art and architecture; the computer and society; determinants of behavior; drama; film; literature in America; music theory and history; and philosophical ethics. "The program gives you the ability to talk about things a lot more interesting than technical subjects," recalls Darwin Clark, an assistant general sales manager for General Motors, who completed the program in 1980. "But it was not only a broadening of myself, it gave me a different perspective on the business world and enhanced my ability to make decisions" (Brown, 1985, pp. 2-3). An executive vice-president for South Central Bell and alumnus of the 1970 program, John C. McPherson, Jr., corroborates the value of the liberal arts experience at Williams. "It helps one deal with the intangible or more subjective things in decision making," he found. "As one moves up the corporate ladder this becomes more and more important."

Dartmouth College annually offers a larger but otherwise analogous summer program in the liberal arts for corporate managers. Founded in 1972, the program draws approximately fifty-five participants annually from diverse companies for a four-week experience in liberal learning. Company executives carry three courses, whose titles and themes resemble those found in the core curricula of many liberal arts colleges. For a fee of $6,300 (and $3,600 for accompanying spouses), participants in 1985 completed three courses drawing on classic readings: Culture in Perspective (*An Economic History of Medieval Europe,* by N. J. G. Pounds, *The Worldly Philosophers,* by Robert Heilbroner, and *Three-Penny Opera,* by Berthol Brecht); Science and Society (*Ever Since Darwin,* by Stephen Jay Gould, *The Double Helix,* by James D. Watson, and *The Earth and Planetary Sciences,* by G. W. Wetherhill and C. L. Drake); and the Idea and the Reality of America (*On the Road,* by Jack Kerouac, *The Protestant Ethic and the Spirit of Capitalism,* by Max Weber, and *The Federalist Papers,* by James Madison). The average age of the executives is forty-five. Many of the participants come only reluctantly at the urging of their company, personally preferring a more traditional management development program. But they are sent precisely because they are being groomed for broader responsibilities, and the firm views an enlarged perspective as a prerequisite (Grantham, 1985; Dartmouth Institute, 1985). In the summary of Larry Biederman, a regional director of Merrill Lynch and 1984 graduate of the institute, it is "an opportunity to recharge the battery on totally new fuel" (Brown, 1985, p. 3).

One of the oldest and lengthiest liberal arts programs for managers is operated by Wabash College (1985) in Indiana. Dating to 1955, the Wabash Executive Program annually recruits about fifteen managers for summer exposure to the arts and sciences. The participants' commitment, however, is for seven weeks, spread over three summer sessions, with three weeks of seminars during the "freshman" summer and two weeks during each of the two following summers. The typical student is in his or her early forties and has moved or is about to move from a technical to a managerial function in the firm. Indeed, the program is explicitly designed to facilitate that transition. "The program," states the Wabash program announcement, "best serves the mature person, perhaps with a technical specialty, who is about to enter general management."

The three Wabash summers have distinct focuses, with a diverse set of lectures and discussions fashioned around each; in 1985, they included Western Culture (first summer)—ancient history, theater in the ancient world, scientific thought to Newton, Nietzsche, and Kierkegaard, foundations of chemistry, and religion and the state; American Genius (second summer)—public policy and dissent, nuclear physics, the Jew and Israel, the colonial period, monetary policy, and the American novel; and Contemporary Society (third summer)—modern theater, race in the United States, the Muslim world, genetics and reproduction, urban problems, and cosmology. The roster of faculty assembled for the program is a cross section of a liberal arts faculty. Lectures and discussions are led by professors of theater, psychology, history, biology, chemistry, political science, religion, economics, physics, philosophy, speech, and Greek.

Consistent with a fundamental purpose of liberal learning, the Wabash program places particular stress on effective communication. During the first summer, the managers receive daily instruction in public speaking. Their instruction is capped by a weekly speech that they deliver on a topic of their own choice, followed by a private videotape review of the delivery with a speech teacher. Writing skills are stressed during the second summer. Each morning of the two-week session begins with a session on writing style. Participants bring samples of writing from their firms, and they prepare daily reports on the main themes of the program's lectures and seminars. Again, as in any strong liberal arts program, private tutorial assistance accompanies classroom learning. The Wabash Executive Program and the other campus-based liberal learning programs serve largely the nation's major corporations. While a few smaller firms send an occasional executive, the bulk of the participants come from major firms. Among the companies sending managers to the Wabash seminar are Caterpillar Tractor Company, IBM, Whirlpool Corporation, Indiana Bell Telephone Company, and Citibank.

The Williams, Dartmouth, and Wabash programs concentrate almost exclusively on liberal learning, avoiding explicit connection with the managers' work world. Others programs go halfway, combining liberal education with traditional management training. Virginia's Washington and Lee University, for example, has sponsored a summer institute for executives each year since 1981. Termed a Program in the Humanities: Business Ethics and Decisions, the two-week, $3,000 seminar devotes mornings to literary and philosophical works and afternoons to case studies in business ethical dilemmas. Thus, morning lecture-discussions have concerned themselves with the writings of figures from Plato to Ralph Waldo Emerson, while afternoon discussions have focused on case studies ranging from investing in South Africa to whistle blowing in the face of corporate wrongdoing. "Today's business leader must understand not only rapidly expanding technologies but also increasingly complex social issues," observes Ross R. Millhiser, vice-chairperson of the board of Phillip Morris, Inc., and adviser to the Washington and Lee Institute. "I know of no better preparation for such responsibilities than that provided by a sound education in the humanities" (Washington and Lee University, 1985, p. i).

Washington and Lee's program draws from a familiar constituency. The participants are upper-middle managers of large firms who have recently been promoted or will soon move into more responsible posts. Most come from major regional and national firms. Among the fourteen participants in 1984 were a district manager of Virginia Electric and Power Company, a senior associate counsel of John Hancock Mutual Life Insurance Company, a manager of international product marketing for IBM, and a project manager for engineering for Newport News Shipbuilding. "For those of us without liberal arts backgrounds, the in-depth introduction to the humanities has been quite an 'eye opener,' " concluded Joseph Vengrouskie, the director of corporate personnel for Gulf States Paper Corporation and a 1981 institute participant. "I have a deeper appreciation for a liberal arts education," and "it will benefit me both in business and personal life" (Washington and Lee University, 1985, p. 16).

The oldest and best-known program in the humanities for executives is operated not by a college or university but by a separately incorporated organization in Aspen, Colorado. Since 1950, the Aspen Institute for Humanistic Studies (1985) has offered a broad array of short-term summer seminars for executives. The seminars focus on questions of "justice, power, equity, and the roles of the individual, the corporation, and the state." Participants receive seminar readings prior to attending, with selections taken from both classic and contemporary works, including those of Plato, Locke, Marx, Dostoevski, Freud, and Martin Luther King, Jr. In 1985, some thirteen executive seminars of two weeks' duration each enrolled a total of more than three hundred executives, most drawn from the nation's major firms. More than five thousand corporate executives have passed through the program since its inception (Eurich, 1985).

Senior Managers: Sustaining Liberal Learning

As managers move into the seniormost ranks of a corporation after several decades of experience, the breadth of understanding engendered by liberal learning becomes essential. Corporate officers must continually confront diverse internal and external constituencies, and a capacity to comprehend the culture and currents that animate these groups is an integral facet of the job description. It is largely for this reason that liberally educated managers more often rise into top company posts. Half or more of the officers of many major firms, as seen in the previous chapter, hold undergraduate degrees in the liberal arts. Yet, because many corporations quite rightly view liberal education as a continuing experience, a variety of means have been devised for sustaining that learning among those whose responsibilities and time pressures put a premium on informal learning.

One common practice is for a corporation to select and circulate articles and books of contemporary interest among its top managers. Gillette Company's program is typical of many. The staff of Gillette's public relations department scans new books and dozens of periodicals for articles of particular salience. Selecting about ten every two months, the staff prepares summaries and circulates a final digest among key management throughout the company, some thirty top managers in all. Articles are drawn from business periodicals such as *Barron's,* but they are also taken from the *New York Times, Public Opinion,* and *Foreign Policy.*

At the seniormost levels of a corporation, however, there can be no substitute for the learning that comes from direct experience. Most companies encourage forms of experiential liberal learning whereby senior managers directly involve themselves in a variety of external affairs that will broaden their appreciation for the diverse forces shaping the environment in which their firms operate. Half of the large companies surveyed by the Conference Board in 1981 report that the further development of top management's capacity in this area was a leading priority. The chief executives of the 432 surveyed companies were asked: "When it comes to the top-management group, . . . what are the key challenges you believe your company will face during the next five years?" Developing a "strategic business-planning perspective" ranked first, with 85 percent of the CEOs identifying it as a top priority. This itself takes the kind of broad global insight that comes from a liberal education. But external affairs were also close behind; 49 percent specified that "improving top management's grasp of emerging political, economic, and social issues" was a key challenge, and 52 percent assigned high priority to "building top-management effectiveness in dealing with governments and other external forces and groups" (Shaeffer, 1982, p. 11).

The direct involvement of managers in external settings is generally viewed as the best single means of schooling. Top executives are thus encouraged to participate in the governance and affairs of outside organizations. Most major corporations stimulate involvement in the life of four kinds of organizations: (1) other corporations, through service on their boards of directors; (2) major business and trade associations; (3) nonprofit organizations, through participation in their governance; and (4) public agencies, through service on advisory committees and commissions.

Company officers generally take up such roles not only as a matter of individual choice but as a product of corporate preference as well. In serving on the board of another major company, the executive learns how other firms are responding to federal regulation and public opinion. By taking an active role in the Committee for Economic Development, Council on Foreign Relations, and other key associations, the executive acquires a refined sense of the formulation of economic and foreign policy in Washington. Through participation in the governance of hospitals, universities, and civic agencies, the executive is exposed to the concerns of the local community and the nonprofit world. And in serving on government advisory boards, the executive acquires a direct knowledge of the inner workings of local and national government. While much of the information assimilated is of direct professional relevance, the learning experience goes far beyond, building an enriched understanding of the institutions and society in which the firm operates.

Indicative of the importance that they attach to knowledge of external affairs, most companies stress it in making senior appointments. In a 1979–80 survey of major companies by the Conference Board, more than three-quarters of the firms affirmed that external-affairs competence was important not only in selecting a chief executive but also in choosing an executive vice-president, plant manager, human resources manager, planning manager, general counsel, or division manager. Consistent with this, direct study of senior managers of two hundred large firms reveals that large numbers had external involvements: a quarter served on two or more corporate boards; more than two-fifths had been active in a business or trade association; nearly half held a seat on the governing board of a nonprofit organization; and one in seven had served on a local or national government advisory committee (Lusterman, 1981; Useem, 1985).

Corporations that are active in promoting liberal learning at this level are often active at all levels. The Aluminum Company of America (Alcoa), for instance, assists liberal learning among nonexempt employees through tuition support of those pursuing a bachelor's degree in liberal studies at Evansville University and elsewhere. For middle managers, it encourages participation in the University of Pittsburgh's special program in "The American Experience," a six-day program on government affairs operated by the Brookings Institution in Washington, D.C., and in Alcoa's own management program, "The Pittsburgh Management Conference." Special educational programs are also available on topics ranging from business ethics to minority-group dynamics and women's issues in the workplace.

Alcoa's "Advanced Management Program" brings more senior executives together with company officers, other corporate leaders, political figures—a former prime minister of Jamaica, for example—and leading scholars to explore contemporary social and economic issues. Direct management participation in outside affairs is encouraged by Alcoa as well. A half dozen rising middle managers have been "loaned" for a year to work in offices of the federal government. And managers are encouraged to take active part in civic and national affairs. The diverse individual programs constitute a single learning strategy by the firm, according to George Anderson, Alcoa's manager of corporate education. The pragmatic approach to liberal learning promotes "the notion that the corporation really cares," he reported, and is central to Alcoa's "long-term development process, while at the same time addressing very real problems."

Conclusion

While liberal education is an important asset for a career in management, like all learning, it does not end with the end of formal training. Effective managers remain effective by continually enlarging their store of experience and knowledge. Virtually all major corporations sponsor traditional management development programs; increasingly, they are reaching beyond as well.

"In addition to possessing certain professional skills, business leaders must be able to motivate people and organizations," concluded a special study of business education by the Business–Higher Education Forum (1985, p. 7), a blue-ribbon panel of corporate chief executives and university presidents. Managers "must be flexible, and able to tolerate ambiguity and uncertainty," the study declared. Moreover, as urged by many observers of management education, "effective business leadership requires an understanding of the evolving role of business enterprise within our society." To this end, formal schooling is only a first step, for "lifelong learning," the analysis concluded, "is of critical importance to the development of future business leaders" (Business–Higher Education Forum, 1985, p. 7; see also Branscomb and Gilmore, 1975; Lynton, 1981a, 1981b, 1984; Behrman and Levin, 1984).

Companies now sponsor programs in lifelong liberal learning for employees at all levels. Tuition-assistance plans encourage nonexempt employees to pursue the bachelor's degree in liberal studies that they were unable to earn before joining the firm. Company seminars and college institutes allow middle managers to study the forces that shape the culture of the firm and the business climate. And senior managers are encouraged to deepen their understanding of those forces through experiential learning, participating directly in other organizations that play a part in generating them.

The diversity and depth of such company efforts is of recent origin, for corporate-sponsored liberal learning is almost entirely a postwar phenomenon. The first sustained programs appeared in the early 1950s, led by the founding of the Aspen Institute for Humanistic Studies and the executive programs at

Dartmouth and Williams Colleges. The pioneering of the early programs came from large corporations and visionary leaders within them, American Telephone and Telegraph in the case of the Williams program and Walter Paepcke of the Container Corporation of America in the case of the Aspen Institute.

Most internal programs were developed somewhat later, many during the 1970s, when numerous companies abandoned their posture of privacy and seclusion for one of social and political activism. A broadly informed management came to be seen as a prerequisite for effective management of a far more turbulent business environment. The creation of many of the special management seminars can be traced to vigorous promotion by one or two educational "intrapreneurs" within the firm. In this area, as in so many areas of corporate innovation, individual leadership played a critical role. By the mid 1980s, innovation had nearly become corporate convention, and virtually all major firms sponsored at least one program, however limited in scope, to expand the liberal learning of its management (Kanter, 1983).

Still, corporate-sponsored programs in liberal learning continue to expand in number and scope. "More and more companies are teaching analytical skills and critical thinking," found a Carnegie Foundation study of corporate education in 1985, providing "conceptual bases for transferable knowledge" through offerings in "foreign languages, psychology and sociology, economics, college algebra, physics, and other courses in science and technology" (Eurich, 1985, p. 77). The growth curve for such programs is certain to flatten as saturation occurs, but, as it does so, the early experimental efforts will have been transformed into tradition, a fixed feature of contemporary corporate practice.

While the personal testimony of individual participants almost uniformly confirms the value of liberal learning for management, less certain is the value for overall corporate performance. We do know, however, that companies that spend more on research and development efforts also spend more on the continuing education of their employees and that companies whose R&D staffs more extensively avail themselves of educational opportunities are also those companies whose scientists and engineers perform better (Johnson and Tornatzky, 1981). The jury is still out on the issue of whether companies whose managers have taken advantage of company-sponsored opportunities for liberal learning become better-managed companies. As with most management education programs, there is virtually no evaluation of the lasting impact on either the participants or the sponsoring corporation. When the jury comes in, however, a positive verdict can be expected. Corporate experience with lifelong liberal learning is now too widespread and too highly valued for the judgment to be otherwise.

6   *Thomas B. Jones*

Liberal Learning and Undergraduate Business Study

Liberal learning and undergraduate business study are contrary partners in an uneasy alliance. In theory, the two should be compatible, collaborating in the education of future managers; in practice, liberal learning and business study have seldom co-existed happily in the undergraduate curriculum. Despite encouragement and pressure from several sources—accrediting associations, reform-minded faculty, administrators, academic organizations, educational commissions, and business leadership —liberal learning and business study remain at odds. The undergraduate business school curriculum, in all but a handful of cases, seldom makes room for liberal learning and consigns it to required general education courses. The curriculum models that integrate liberal learning and business study are isolated alternatives. Some optimism, however, is justified by recent developments.

First, as the contents of this volume strongly suggest, the importance of liberal learning for successful management practices and careers is sustained by research studies, management

124

analysts, conference recommendations, grant projects, and well-reasoned testimony from business leaders. Second, business schools are under some pressure to update their programs as a means of boosting economic competitiveness and productivity in the United States. Finally, more precise definitions of the skills and understandings that constitute liberal learning, improved teaching strategies, new curricular developments, and revived interest within the academic community make the traditional gap between liberal learning and undergraduate business study less formidable now—and, perhaps, easier to bridge with genuine reforms.

If past experience is any guide, though, reforms will be hard to attain. Today's plans and models for integrating liberal learning and business study in the undergraduate curriculum are exciting, but they face an uphill battle against several historical factors: negative American attitudes toward liberal learning and intellectual pursuits; the enrollment success of undergraduate business study in higher education; the tactical and intellectual failures of liberal education since World War II; and the vocationalism and skepticism of business students. Each of these historical factors remains a barrier to change. This chapter explores these historical factors as important background for a review of current programs in some business schools and an agenda that reform might follow in the next few years.

Roots of the Problem

Liberal learning has always been but grudgingly accepted in the American view of education. Historians remind us that what Americans "imagine themselves to be" as individuals and as a nation quite often excludes certain qualities of intellect and the reflective, philosophical pursuits that liberal learning encompasses. Liberal learning has rubbed against a "suspicion of intellect itself" that is "part of the extensive American devotion to practicality and direct experience" (Hofstadter, 1963, p. 236). Americans prefer to look at individual success and the national experience as anything but the product of scholarship and book learning.

Indeed, because of prejudice against most types of formal

education, the study of business in postsecondary schools could expect little popular support before the 1890s. The idea that business success had anything to do with college study would have struck early-nineteenth-century businesspeople as complete nonsense. Most thought that a college education "delayed the start in business life, taught what was useless, and gave students bad habits and bad attitudes, the worst of which was to live by wit rather than work" (Kirkland, 1956, p. 87). Even high school education smacked of foolishness unless it included heavy doses of practical application and stressed "virtue" and "character." Experience, not classwork, gave aspiring youths their edge in business careers. It would take dramatic changes in the American economy for the business world to find any use for formal college-level study.

But fundamental changes in the pre–Civil War American economy, which accelerated rapidly after 1865, transformed business attitudes about formal education. Because of these changes, business study would soon outgrow the constraints of the cultural imagination and blend easily with the pragmatic, entrepreneurial, and individualistic character of American society.

The emerging urban-industrial economy had at its core large-scale business organizations devoted to goals of efficiency and continued growth. Success in business no longer hinged primarily on the achievement of individual ownership; instead, young men and women prepared themselves for careers as specialists and bureaucrats within big business and government. The ideal of the "uneducated self-made man, especially in the most desirable business positions," contradicted the real world of early-twentieth-century business (Hofstadter, 1963, pp. 260–261). An education that prepared individuals for the climb to managerial positions or entry on the new employment ladder now had considerable currency.

Business called for more education and for more literature on management and marketing. Although business still rhetorically championed the self-made man and practical experience, undergraduate schools of business gained sizable support. And, of course, their curricula leaned heavily on practical training, such as accounting, real estate, and office management. Even the first collegiate school of business—the Wharton School of Finance and Economy, founded in 1881—had, by World War I, abandoned its original goals of liberal education for more specialized business study (Sass, 1982; Cheit, 1975).

As business schools increased their numbers and graduate schools of business made their debut, the gap between liberal learning and business study grew. Growing numbers of middle-class Americans sent their children to study at the schools of business. These new students wanted practical, vocational education for business careers as a guarantee for postgraduation employment. The growth of the elective system weakened efforts to promote broad-based study for business students by leaving the issue of liberal learning to college graduation requirements of so many hours of studies in the liberal arts.

Hard times in the 1930s pressured students more directly toward vocationalism. The Depression taught its lesson well: employers looked for entry-level skills; students used their time at business schools to prepare for specific job openings. After World War II, the large numbers of returning veterans trooped to the business schools. Still mindful of the 1930s and alert to personal issues of economic security, veterans and their fellow students favored specialized, entry-level business education.

Throughout this first half-century of climbing enrollments and increased vocationalism, the business schools used requirements of liberal arts courses, offered elsewhere in the university, to uphold the ideal of liberal learning. Of course, liberal learning requirements took up few of the total credits that business students had to work with in their undergraduate years. The nonbusiness requirements at the business schools also tended to be a "hodgepodge of courses" that students "took more because they had to than because they were a vital part of the work" (Pierson and others, 1959, p. 45).

By the late 1950s and the early 1960s, undergraduate business study felt the sting of criticism from business and higher education leaders because of its overspecialization and vocationalism. Despite its success in attracting students, one source portrayed business education at the college level as "an uncer-

tain giant, gnawed by doubt and harassed by the barbs of un-
friendly critics" (Gordon and Howell, 1959, p. 4). Another
prominent authority on higher education reported that schools
of business across the nation were "trying, sometimes desperately, to find their souls" (Kerr, 1958, p. 63). Problems in the
business schools at this time stemmed mainly from roots other
than the issue of liberal learning. But, in the published reports
and internal discussions taking place during this period, the
relationship between liberal learning and business study always
surfaced.

In 1959, two major studies, funded by the Carnegie Corporation and the Ford Foundation, challenged the goals, methods, curricula, and purposes of business study at the collegiate
level. Robert Aaron Gordon and James Edwin Howell's *Higher
Education for Business* (Gordon and Howell, 1959) and Frank
C. Pierson's *The Education of American Businessmen* (Pierson
and others, 1959) agreed on most fundamental matters related
to business study. The two reports also made a strong case for
liberal learning within the business program. The Pierson report
promoted close ties between business study and certain liberal
arts disciplines, "notably literature, psychology, history, political science, and mathematics-science" (Pierson and others,
1959, p. 203). It concluded that required business courses
should help students transfer liberal arts learning to "career interests and, ultimately, to . . . daily work, showing wherever
possible how the insights and methods of the humanities, social
sciences, and sciences can be used to analyze and illuminate
problems of business" (p. xii). Both the Pierson and Gordon-
Howell reports recognized the value of liberal learning in preparing competent managers, and both reports recommended
that 50 percent of undergraduate business study should be in
general education. In practice, this proportion of nonbusiness
study would have exceeded the standards of the time by 10 to
15 percent. Pierson pointed out that most business schools
never required students to go much beyond freshman-sopho-
more courses in the liberal arts.

In 1964, the Committee on Economic Development followed up on the Pierson and Gordon-Howell reports. Their report, *Educating Tomorrow's Managers* (Committee on Eco-

nomic Development, 1964), identified several qualities that business study ought to develop in students as undergraduates. These qualities closely paralleled understandings and skills claimed by the liberal arts disciplines. The committee also emphasized that undergraduate business study should prepare students for "the long pull," not just a first job.

Despite what critics assumed, most business faculty backed liberal learning in the 1950s. In one survey, over 80 percent of business faculty thought that liberal learning, joined with appropriate professional education, gave students an edge in future careers. Business faculty also supported the idea that study in the liberal arts should spread over a four-year period. They expressed a preference for broad surveys in liberal arts courses and a common core rather than free electives or liberal arts courses geared to business programs. A surprising 50 percent surveyed thought that business students needed more liberal learning, even if the curriculum had to be expanded (Dressel and Lorimer, 1959, pp. 45–52). In a matter of years, though, business faculty would lose their enthusiasm for liberal learning.

The national reports on business study and the friendly mood of business faculty had little impact on liberal learning; however, the business schools "liberalized" their approaches by stepping up support for social sciences and appointing faculty members based in those disciplines who applied them to business matters. Skeptics wondered "whether or not a new specialization" had been "substituted for an old one" (Hugstad, 1983). This response to the 1950s reports had a certain predictability and several interrelated causes. The new generation of business students and the business schools faced the rising influence of American corporations. Gaining access to corporate careers required men and women to fashion an education that pleased the recruiters. These recruiters had short-term needs to fill; they also had specialized entry-level positions that demanded employees "ready to run the minute their feet touched the floor." American corporations wanted practical business skills and specialized management approaches. No matter what corporate higher-ups said in public speeches about liberal learning, they did not hire personnel, especially at the entry level.

Undergraduate programs in business felt the pressure on

all sides: students wanted a pragmatic, made-to-order education without frills; American businesses needed specialists to fine tune their rapid expansion and growing complexity; and corporate recruiters had employment quotas to cover without delay. The new generation of business faculty—specialists themselves— welcomed the pressures on their institutions. Business faculty discovered that, by specializing, they could overcome suspicions about academic respectability and, at the same time, attract students and funding. Leaning heavily on the social sciences and the growth of quantitative approaches, business faculty worked hard to create specialized "disciplines" in business schools. Functional areas now had "career tracks," such as advertising management within marketing. New faculty increased the research emphasis of their programs and pressed for graduate study in business. Led by young Ph.D.s intent on achieving a new respectability through research and publication, the business schools did grow in size and prestige (Hugstad, 1983). At the same time, the fragile basis of liberal learning in business study weakened substantially.

By the early 1970s, business faculty occupied high ground on campus. More undergraduates majored in business than in any other field. Administrators supported what made business schools successful. And American corporations filled their ranks with business school graduates. Issues of liberal learning got lost in the blush of prosperity. Business school faculty surveyed in this decade preferred a smaller liberal arts component in business study. Two-thirds of these faculty thought that administrators and liberal arts disciplines pushed liberal learning at the expense of business courses. For the liberal learning core, business faculty favored subjects that had immediate application to business and mentioned the arts and humanities only infrequently (Vandermeer and Lyons, 1979). Business faculty adopted the social sciences, increased emphasis on quantitative and policy studies, and squeezed out the older vocational training and practical skill development in business study. Most still claimed respect for liberal learning, but their curricula failed to prove it.

The liberal arts establishment did little throughout this period to make its issues demand attention—only plummeting enrollments and threatened cutbacks in staff and budget could do that. It missed its chance to influence undergraduate business study when the opportunity arose in the late 1950s and early 1960s. The majority of liberal arts faculty always had a dim view of business education and business students. In the 1950s and 1960s, few wanted to "water down" the quality of their own courses to fit the needs of professional students. They considered their courses more as preparation for majors than as vehicles of general education for everyone. Most liberal arts faculty doubted that their courses served as prerequisites for success in the professions, including business management (Dressel and Lorimer, 1959). To the need for liberal learning in business study, liberal arts faculty were, for the most part, simply indifferent.

In the late 1950s, liberal arts faculty had little conception of the scope and purposes of the undergraduate business school; they had considerable enthusiasm themselves for "specialization in a narrow discipline" (Dressel and Lorimer, 1959, p. 54). Indeed, liberal arts faculty made "their function in the university no different from that of the overtly professional faculties" (p. 2). Each group—business and liberal arts—"equally engaged in . . . specialties" (p. 52; compare Gamson and Associates, 1984, pp. 1-10). Faculty members from the business schools, who might have looked for help from the liberal arts campus, would meet with disappointment. As Dressel and Lorimer concluded: "Much of the failure to give adequate attention to the liberal arts in professional and technical education . . . stems directly from the attitudes and the deficiencies of the liberal arts colleges and their faculties" (1959, p. 54).

The 1959 Pierson report had predicted that it would be difficult to lure undergraduate business students to liberal learning without a revitalization of the liberal arts disciplines. (Correctly, the Pierson report had not limited liberal learning skills and understandings solely to the liberal arts.) Merely "requiring courses in nonbusiness areas taught in a perfunctory manner by instructors whose main interest lies elsewhere," the Pierson report advised, "will not meet the situation and, in fact, do much harm" (Pierson and others, 1959, p. xii, fn. 22). Most general education courses featured junior faculty or graduate students as instructors. Liberal arts faculty wanted to teach in specialized areas that followed their individual research and publication trails. They cared little about teaching strategies, interdisciplinary courses, and concepts of liberal learning; they had little time for students, except those who majored in the disciplines and filled budding graduate programs.

As the good times of higher education in the 1960s encouraged isolation and more elitism in the liberal arts, faculty in these fields had little motivation to extend themselves on the issue of liberal learning and business study. Through all this period, the rhetoric in favor of liberal learning sounded repeatedly in the executive pulpits. But, these verbal bouquets notwithstanding, business leaders had little time for such idealism in everyday operations. In the period from 1950 to 1970, business's ideas on what kind of an education best suited its managers changed significantly. Business management ranks filled up with graduates of business schools and the now-notorious M.B.A.s. These modern business managers reflected the social science and quantitative specialization of modern business study. They had little understanding and appreciation of liberal learning in connection with business practice. William Whyte observed that business leaders of the 1950s "graduated while the straight A.B. was still in fashion, and many have at least a sentimental attachment to the humanities" (Whyte, 1956, p. 79). Their successors in management and personnel diverged sharply from that prototype. A growing commitment to technology, systems, decision science, and an array of quantitative management techniques decreased the perceived importance of liberal learning as preparation for business careers. This direction in business had its effects on the business curriculum and encouraged its isolation from liberal learning.

Undergraduate business study in the 1970s remained just as specialized as before the critical reports of the late 1950s (although the new specialization had a much classier academic veneer). Business faculty could dismiss attacks on specialization with wide support from students, administration, and corporate recruiters. Advocates of liberal learning, after years of neglecting the issues, had precious little ground for reform. Besides, critics could charge with justification that such reform was largely a matter of disingenuous self-interest by liberal arts faculty whose enrollments suffered badly in the 1970s. And the charge would be correct in most cases.

To sum up this brief history, the split between liberal learning and undergraduate business study admits to no easy solutions. Reform will be difficult, because students, business, and business faculty have inherited a deep-rooted skepticism in American life against liberal learning. Also, the failure of liberal arts faculty throughout recent history to claim a role in business education and their penchant for elitism and self-destructiveness preclude any easy optimism about reform. The success of undergraduate business study—if measured by student enrollments, administrative support, and public approval—now makes it hard for liberal learning even to get a hearing. Finally, the legions of business school graduates in management positions now comprise a tough audience for liberal learning advocates.

Models for Reform

Nevertheless, challenges to the status quo have sounded recently with surprising clarity and enthusiasm. These challenges have issued from several sources, not the least of which is the Business–Higher Education Forum. That group, affiliated with the American Council on Education, has published a report urging the nation's business schools to update their curricula (Business–Higher Education Forum, 1985). The report suggests, specifically, that the business schools provide broader political, technological, and ethical frameworks for the application of business skills, stimulate more interdisciplinary teaching and research, and place more emphasis on communication skills. The Association of American Colleges has sponsored several conferences and projects that have resulted in similar calls for a broad-based undergraduate business school curriculum. It appears that the specialized nature of business study is once again under examination, and the call for integrated programs of liberal learning and professional education has gained a wider audience.

But why the revived interest? First, business leaders are

not uniformly satisfied with the new generation of business students they have employed. Among the many entering the business world, fewer come prepared with the necessary levels of communication skills, cognitive abilities, and human understandings that are requisite for success beyond the entry level. The technical bent of business study can equip students with narrow problem-solving approaches destined for an early obsolescence. The underlying rationale of business study at many colleges is also flawed: it assumes that business "is populated by rational executives who operate in a systematic results-oriented fashion." Of course, those who have spent "even a brief time in the business world know that this is rarely true" (Mandt, 1982, p. 49). By 9:00 A.M. in many business schools, calculators are running on full battery; classic reflections on human nature and human behavior take a back seat to the latest models on decision making or conflict resolution. "Number crunching" is the thing to do, and students attack the "multidimensional, consequential problems of enterprise with largely unidimensional, inconsequential mathematical models and similarly limited paradigms of human behavior" (Behrman and Levin, 1984, p. 141).

Second, the liberal arts faculty at long last have started action on the liberal learning and business study connection—though it took several enrollment scares and declining on-campus status to get them started. Despite tardy beginnings, new programs designed to bridge the gap between liberal learning and business study have appeared. Foundations, businesses, and academic associations—including the American Assembly of Collegiate Schools of Business itself—have supported and fueled these initiatives, so that faculty throughout the campus are perhaps more receptive to changes and experiments. The 1980s might yet be a period of consequential reform.

But where does such reform begin? What are the models for curriculum reform that bridge the gap between liberal learning and business study? What is necessary for change? Several undergraduate business schools already supply some answers to these questions. For example, the School of Business at the University of Kansas used a multiyear grant from the National Endowment for the Humanities (NEH) to construct several model programs at the undergraduate level. During that grant period, liberal arts and business school faculty taught courses that combined the humanities and business. Several of these courses have found a permanent place in the curriculum. (These include courses with such titles as Moral Issues in Business; Business and the Humanities in the Hispanic World; Justice and Economic Systems; Literature and Management; and Topics in U.S. Business History.) A professor-in-residence project, which saw humanists and business faculty auditing courses, lecturing, meeting in seminars, and serving as consultants for each other, survived on an informal basis. Some faculty have initiated joint research projects and have coauthored papers.

Faculty development projects at Kansas, deemed a critical first step in integration, stress issues of business ethics. The training in ethics for business faculty is then incorporated into business courses taught on a regular basis. New faculty seminars are planned that will expand earlier philosophical inquiry to focus on questions of economic justice. Students at the Kansas School of Business are encouraged to add concentrations in the liberal arts to their business majors. The School of Business has also stressed communication skills, and the NEH grant included the establishment of a communications clinic for business majors.

At Bentley College, an independent school of business in Waltham, Massachusetts, several projects have matured into permanent fixtures of the curriculum. Bentley aims purposefully at developing "liberally educated professionals"—students with technical and business skills who can think clearly, communicate easily, and make decisions on the basis of defensible ethical principles. In support of these objectives (which most business schools and liberal arts colleges would claim), Bentley has created a course sequence under the heading of Values and Choices. This course sequence links the humanities with business disciplines and concentrates on values and value choices. Eight departments at the college—including both humanities and business disciplines—share responsibility for teaching the courses and work in partnership with a Humanities Committee. The Center for Business Ethics at Bentley sponsors a major national conference each year and supports research in that area of concern. Bentley also has developed several courses that combine humanities and business in the area of ethics (such as Private Property, Public Policy, Multinational Corporations in the Third World, and Philosophy of Work).

The Ohio State University School of Business has worked with several liberal arts departments on campus to frame required courses for business students. Ohio State also offers a double degree program combining business administration and foreign languages that calls for students to complete forty credits more than the total normally required for graduation. Business students are also limited in the number of credits they can take in a specialized business field, a policy that promotes a broader range of undergraduate study over four years.

The University of Florida has developed interdisciplinary courses that "help students discover some of the essential relationships between the humanities, their vocationally oriented courses, and the demands placed upon them in today's society as practicing professionals" (Brown, 1982, p. 10). The multidisciplinary course for business students deals with values, work environment, individual responsibility, discrimination and affirmative action, and technology and the future.

In the late 1960s, Babson College (Wellesley, Massachusetts)—a four-year undergraduate school of management—adopted a curriculum that included a 40 percent required base of liberal arts. Babson now offers its undergraduate business students liberal arts majors in society and technology, communications, and American studies. The Babson College approach stresses the value of liberal learning and management through interdisciplinary study and special cocurricular programs that feature, among other visitors, poets in residence. The mission of the college is thus founded on the bond between liberal learning and management education.

Despite the innovative approaches briefly sampled so far that combine business study with liberal learning, the majority of business schools pass the matter by without serious thought. Most prefer to leave the provision of liberal learning to general education requirements and a small percentage of elective courses. Reform and innovation by the business schools generally take the form of sideline applause for new general education requirements and core curricula. (Heavy handclaps sound for increased emphasis on communication skills and subjects most directly related to business functions.) So the question remains: What other strategies and models—beyond the few examples reviewed here—could be used by business schools to better mix liberal learning and business study?

Recent projects in liberal arts colleges, many of which are reviewed at length in Chapter Eight, provide several possibilities for the business schools. Some liberal arts colleges, for example, actively promote contacts between students and working professionals in business fields. These professional businesspeople, often alumni of the sponsoring institutions, consult with students about future business careers. Several of the consultation projects emphasize the relationship between liberal learning and business. More often than not, the advice of these consultants carries considerable weight with students, because it brings to life the values of liberal learning for business decision making and business success. The consultation strategy seems made to order for business students, who, on the whole, are skeptical and suspicious of liberal learning. Their skepticism is not easily addressed, but working business professionals make a compelling case for liberal learning by their example and experience. They can also explain exactly how it is of value in a business setting.

Internship programs at liberal arts colleges help build frameworks that join liberal learning with the acquisition of on-the-job skills. As part of internships, many college programs include seminars and readings from the humanities and social sciences that deal with marketplace issues (for example, business ethics, economic history, equal opportunity). In programs such as this, students can learn firsthand what liberal learning adds to everyday work situations. Business students might find such seminars an exciting introduction to liberal learning. It may be that Plato's *Republic,* Machiavelli's *The Prince,* and a number of similar classics of a liberal education are best introduced to students engaged in work experiences.

Liberal arts colleges have also examined their courses and

disciplines to determine the career-related competencies they develop. Written catalogues and guides pinpoint the skills and understandings that can be gained from liberal learning and then related to business careers. Often, business advisory committees help identify these competencies and develop written descriptions. Breaking down disciplines and course offerings into competencies offers business students another view of liberal learning and its connection to business careers; the process also promotes more informed and careful selection of liberal learning experiences by business students, who often have only college requirements and inflated catalogue copy as their guides.

Faculty advising at the liberal arts colleges has advanced rapidly to meet students' career needs. Recent faculty advising projects have application in the business schools as well. For example, liberal arts advisers have learned more about how their disciplines connect with the working world through a variety of seminars, residencies, internships, faculty development workshops, and written materials. Business faculty advisers can benefit from similar strategies that emphasize what liberal learning offers for business study and business careers.

Faculty in liberal arts colleges have done much in recent years to emphasize liberal learning both in their teaching and in their work on curriculum development. More and more faculty underscore the skills and understandings associated with liberal learning as they teach disciplinary subject matter. The development of writing across the curriculum and critical thinking projects is increasing. Success with these projects offers business faculty an important means by which to integrate liberal learning in their own courses. More precise descriptions of liberal learning, along with the teaching and curricular strategies current in the liberal arts disciplines, should be of great use to business schools. These definitions and strategies are not restricted to the liberal arts; they comprise an overall framework for liberal learning into which business faculty could easily integrate their curriculum. Without teaching excellence and a well-reasoned curriculum, however, liberal learning is difficult to achieve no matter what its source.

The bridging models and strategies now employed in the

business schools and liberal arts colleges can frame a unique approach to educating future managers. In addition, the emerging research on liberal learning and career success in management can strengthen the connection and give it enhanced currency. But, once again, given the history of liberal learning and business study, any new connections between the two depend on the considerations discussed in the following section.

Agenda for Reform

Cooperation between business faculty and liberal arts faculty is essential to reform. A repetition of the 1950s, that era of lost opportunities, would be unfortunate; business faculty need not repeat the mistakes of their liberal arts colleagues of that earlier period. Both sides will have to put students first. As teachers, business faculty and liberal arts faculty should strive to understand liberal learning in broad application; they should discover how the skills and understandings of liberal learning can be taught across the curriculum. The emphasis on specialized knowledge in both camps has to be re-examined in light of what business students need in an undergraduate education—and what future employers in management areas really want. What accounts for success in management positions over the long run of years? What skills and understandings are the substance of continued growth in management positions? Who are the most successful managers? What kind of managers does American business need for its future? These are critical questions for both business and liberal arts faculty.

In addition, business's attitude toward hiring bears heavily on any future connections between liberal learning and business study. The attitude and practices of business make a difference for what takes place in higher education, the curriculum not excluded. If business adopts as policy the rhetoric of its leaders, and personnel managers and middle managers approach hiring and development with a new appreciation for educational breadth, then the wheels of curricular change will turn more rapidly in schools of business.

Finally, the effective blend of liberal learning and business study depends on much more than general education and core requirements. Most business students are not willing candidates for liberal learning; they view it with skepticism, and requirements—no matter how thoughtfully constructed—have little effect on this skepticism except to deepen it. If this chapter's previous excursion into American cultural history has any point, it is to remind reformers that business students reflect suspicions in American culture about liberal learning. Or, perhaps more accurately, business students reflect general support for learning that can be easily identified as practical and directly tied to the marketplace. If business students are to gain anything from liberal learning, it must be better defined in its connection to future achievement and, to the degree possible, made an integral part of business school course work.

A successful curriculum mix for business students must combat their skepticism about liberal learning. This implies that faculty must come to understand liberal learning in connection with business study. Serious cross-campus discussion, support by administrators, and carefully planned faculty development are all important to success on this issue. Secondly, business students should learn the full story on liberal learning and what it means for them in the contexts of career, public decision making, and individual development. Straightforward introduction, eschewing the inflated copy of too many college catalogues, is required. The orientation workshops and degree-planning courses developed by several nontraditional programs for adults offer good models. For example, in Metropolitan State University's individualized degree-planning course, considerable time is spent examining liberal learning in relation to careers. The students, most of whom are in business positions or aiming at business careers, examine the question: What is an educated person? In doing so, the students deal with a variety of written materials on liberal learning, the professions, the humanities, and career planning. They draw on consultations with business professionals for links between liberal learning and experience.

The introductory approach used by Metropolitan State University and similar institutions could be used by the business schools. An introductory course or an orientation seminar could be planned with cooperation from liberal arts faculty. Liberal learning could be defined and examined *before* business students start their course work. Students and their faculty advisers could then plan individual courses of study with better results.

Of course, a little learning is a dangerous thing. If business students understood liberal learning as they began college study, they would expect their professors to understand it as well. Students might then ask for more than "knowledge-for-knowledge's-sake" teaching and production-line preparation of business majors. The cafeteria-style curriculum that so irks modern reformers in higher education would also fade from popularity—because students would have the background necessary to see its defects. Well-informed business students expecting certain skills and understandings in each course would force their professors, in turn, to consider which liberal learning outcomes their teaching should develop. Among these important objectives would be improved writing and speaking skills, critical-analysis skills, habits of reflective thought, multicultural perspectives, an understanding of ethical issues, a capacity for independent, lifelong learning, and an ability to make connections across disciplines and among sources of information.

Liberal learning should stretch across the entire undergraduate experience, not just the two years of general education requirements and introductory study. Upper-division study, in particular, should deepen and extend liberal learning for business students. These liberal learning outcomes can add much-needed perspective and depth to the specialized learning of undergraduate business study; providing these outcomes through upper-division study can help students prepare for more sophisticated applications in the business world.

No undergraduate program, whatever its quality, will develop students with mastery over the entire range of possible liberal learning outcomes. As the cliché has it, liberal learning is a lifetime pursuit. Obviously, business students have less time than most to pursue liberal learning in general education and elective courses. This fact, first and foremost, should encourage business schools to integrate liberal learning into their professional study through courses whenever appropriate. We know that liberal learning can contribute substantially to managerial performance and career success. Therefore, liberal learning should be a primary concern in a professional education.

In this last context, business students should have an advising system available to them that helps plot postgraduation education, including liberal learning. At the stage in a business career when specialized learning must yield gradually to a broader, more durable class of intellectual and personal competencies, business graduates too often are ill prepared. The compass of their business study has been too compressed to allow for the breadth of learning they need. Advising systems at the business schools have not yet met this issue. Business students would be well served, then, by advising systems that helped them, perhaps near the time of graduation, to logically plot postgraduation learning, whether formal or informal. A step in the advising process such as this, coming near the time of graduation, could help students to analyze the strengths and weaknesses of their studies and develop a tentative lifelong learning plan. This kind of assistance would be a valuable commencement of undergraduate study in any academic area, but perhaps especially valuable to the undertaking of management careers that will put a rising premium on broad skills and capacities.

Liberal learning still remains a missing element of undergraduate business study. Business students rarely understand what liberal learning is, where it is apt to be found in the curriculum, and why it has importance for career success beyond entry-level management. But, clearly defined and well taught, liberal learning has a unique place in business study, as in business life. Undergraduate business schools now have good reason and the opportunity to integrate professional and liberal education. If strong action is taken, liberal learning and business study may yet escape the legacies of cultural and academic isolation that limit both in the present day.

7

David W. Butler

The Humanities
and the M.B.A.

American graduate schools of business are in trouble. Over the last several years, they have been accused repeatedly of hastening and even of causing the decline in American competitiveness. An early and influential broadside was unloosed by Hayes and Abernathy (1980) in their article "Managing Our Way to Economic Decline." Guided by "the new managerial gospel," the professors argue, American managers have emphasized short-term results rather than long-term technological competitiveness and prized analytical detachment at the expense of hands-on experience in production (p. 68). These criticisms have since been widely echoed, elaborated, and oversimplified. In 1981, *Time* magazine detailed similar judgments in its cover story "The Money Chase." Declaring that "business school solutions may be part of the U.S. problem," *Time* added that to many of their critics the new M.B.A.s are arrogant, overly aggressive, and disloyal (Friedrich, 1981, p. 59).

For some, the short-term focus of M.B.A.s may be attributed not just to myopic analytical techniques but to ignorance of the history of business, management, and management education. A 1979 Wharton M.B.A. graduate laments in the *Ameri-*

143

can Scholar that "though business school trains professional managers, I learned nothing to put the profession into perspective until long after I graduated, when I began to be curious about the history of American business, the role of business in American life, the relation of education to success in business, and the history of American business education" (Baida, 1984, p. 41). M.B.A.s have been accused of geographical as well as chronological provincialism. The dean of the University of Washington's business school notes that, although the American Assembly of Collegiate Schools of Business calls for an international emphasis in its accreditation guidelines, "international topics are . . . covered only sporadically in many AACSB-accredited MBA programs" (Jacob, 1985, p. 4).

The excess of "analytical detachment" that Hayes and Abernathy noted is amplified in frequent allegations that M.B.A.s rely on reductive quantitative models at the expense of deep understanding of the human, political, and operational complexities of organizational life. With the lack of understanding goes a lack of communication and interpersonal skills and difficulty making decisions amid the flux and uncertainty that characterize the manager's life. A personnel instructor complains that management schools "concentrate on teaching people to count rather than teaching that people count" (Georgeson, 1982, p. 21). Two associate deans at a large graduate school of business couch the complaint in more academic language, asserting that the schools encourage students "to attack the multidimensional, consequential problems of enterprise with largely unidimensional, inconsequential mathematical models and similarly limited paradigms of human behavior" (Behrman and Levin, 1984, p. 141). And in a presidential address to the members of the Financial Management Association, a corporate executive stresses the need not for more refined techniques of financial analysis but for stronger operational skills: "We need more emphasis in business schools on areas that have come to be known as 'action skills,' 'noncognitive skills,' or 'competency skills.' They deal with such characteristics as leadership, decision making, creativity, communications, and the ability to deal with uncertainty" (Hastie, 1982, p. 61).

There are a number of responses to these criticisms, all of them with some merit. As Hayes and Abernathy would agree, the curricular reforms that engaged American business schools in the 1960s, partly in response to the widely read Gordon-Howell (Gordon and Howell, 1959) and Pierson reports (Pierson and others, 1959), have produced substantial positive results: techniques for financial analysis that favor the short term and methods of marketing research that tell us more about what is than what might be can sharpen decision making so long as their biases are understood. The quantitative models of the management scientist have proved their value in constrained situations, especially in such concrete areas as inventory control. And the explosion of computing power, the broad distribution of that power, and the development of increasingly sophisticated applications software have dramatically enhanced the potential for modeling managerial problems. Moreover, the decline of American competitiveness is linked to forces well beyond the control of the business school, to national economic policy, to the protectionist devices of other countries, to long-standing labor-management conflicts, and to shifts in the motivation of the work force that may have as much to do with relative affluence as with managerial technique. In addition, some of the weaknesses in the education of M.B.A.s derive from gaps in their elementary, secondary, and undergraduate educations that no two-year graduate program could fill. And, despite the outspoken criticisms of the past half-decade and dizzying growth in the production of the degree, the M.B.A. degree continues to be substantially more marketable at substantially higher salaries than most traditional master's degrees in the liberal arts and sciences.

But if there are responses to the criticisms of our graduate business schools, it would be foolish for those of us who manage them, teach in them, conduct research in them, or hire their products to dismiss such widespread and reiterated indictments. Too many of those judgments came and continue to come from the administrators and faculty of business schools themselves and from executives in the field for that position to be tenable for long. The problems of American business and

American management can be traced to many sources, but the graduate business school and the M.B.A. nevertheless remain in trouble. A recent survey of *Fortune* 500 presidents and directors of personnel, deans of business schools and business school faculty, and 1978 M.B.A. alumni confirms the fact (Jenkins, Reizenstein, and Rodgers, 1984, pp. 26–30). The survey data are by no means all negative, and in part they explain why industry continues to find the M.B.A.s desirable. Despite the criticisms of the M.B.A.s' "analytical detachment," the analytical skills of M.B.A.s receive relatively strong ratings from all groups; despite the concern with excesses of quantitative reasoning, the majority of all groups agree that the ideal M.B.A. program should "focus strongly on quantitative analysis"; and despite frequent references to their arrogance, M.B.A.s receive relatively good marks for their "poise and maturity" (p. 28). But all is not well. In what would seem to be a strong confirmation of the widely expressed dissatisfaction with the M.B.A.s' "action skills" or their ability to handle the complexities of day-to-day operations, all groups seem relatively displeased with the M.B.A.s' "administrative skills," their "written communication skills," their "interpersonal skills," and, perhaps most dismayingly, their "managerial skills" (p. 30).

Clearly, those aspects of the manager's job that require the most flexible intellectual and human relations skills are just those aspects that many current "masters of business administration" have not mastered. A part of the problem, of course, lies in the sheer complexity of what is being asked. Certainly, there are subtleties in the tangled human relations within organizations and in the complex web that ties them to multiple constituencies over time that are beyond the reach of fresh M.B.A. graduates in their mid twenties, whatever the content and method of their graduate education. The classroom cannot produce mature managers, full-blown, trailing clouds of chalk dust as they stride confidently out to grasp the reins of power. Perhaps the most telling observation in the spate of recent criticism of the M.B.A. is the most obvious one: at some point, managers must be apprenticed to experience. Still, graduate management education can do more than it does now to help management students profit from experience when they get it.

Accomplishing that goal will require a skeptical re-evaluation of what is still for some management educators a treasured dream. Surely somehow, the vision holds, we can transcend the messy notion that management practice is both art and science or, worse, a mixture of arts and sciences; surely we can fashion more than an eclectic discipline and discover a truly comprehensive "management science," as opposed to the disjointed quantitative subfield of management education that now bears that name. The vision is implicit in Herbert Simon's (1967) discussion of "The Business School," a discussion that reflects the still common view that the management school will win academic respectability by outgrowing the characterization of management as an art and by developing "an explicit, abstract, intellectual *theory* of the processes of synthesis and design, a theory that can be analyzed and taught in the same way that the laws of chemistry, physiology, and economics can be analyzed and taught" (p. 15). It is central to the vision that the practice of management be finally reducible to a coherent compendium of "scientific knowledge" and not simply to knowledge itself.

Simon's article reflects the enthusiasm with which business schools embraced the struggle for academic respectability in the 1960s and the tendency for many, then as now, to identify intellectual rigor with the scientific method. But the accumulating critiques of the business school that have characterized the 1980s have called into question the wisdom of the dream that we might soon establish a dependable science of management. It is too harsh to say, as does one commentator in *Business and Society,* that we have now achieved instead only "an ersatz 'physics' of business" (Thomas, 1983, p. 19). Empirical approaches to management study based in the social and behavioral sciences have proved and continue to prove their value in a variety of ways. But comprehensive theories that can long stand up against the manager's dynamic and amorphous experience have proved elusive indeed. In their calls for the development of the manager's action skills, intuitive abilities, and the like, critics of the graduate business school from within and without seem plainly to agree that more flexible and qualitative approaches are required. A science of managing seems to be as elusive as a science of living.

If we are at present unable to provide sufficient scientific knowledge to comprehend the manager's work, then it seems sensible to include knowledge derived from nonscientific disciplines in the M.B.A.'s curriculum. The very abilities that critics find underdeveloped in modern M.B.A.s—the abilities to respond sensitively to human relationships and ethical issues, to evaluate and judge in uncertain situations, to communicate clearly and compellingly, whether orally or in writing, to take the long view—are, of course, abilities that liberal education in general, and education in the humanities in particular, have long been thought to nurture. That observation has led some who have watched the flowering of graduate professional education with envy or horror or both to suggest that the time has come to close the business schools. One editorial contributor to the *Christian Science Monitor* expresses the glee with which many a tattered humanities graduate contemplates supplanting "our once proud-hearted management heroes, their glory smeared in dust and debt" and the ultimate return to a world of right reason where a "classical education must be the fundamental training for our nation's executives" (Weiner, 1984, p. 12). Surely, that turn of the wheel of fortune that had to come is here at last, and tweed and sherry can eclipse pinstripes and Perrier. The dark age is ending. You can go home again.

That dream, too, will founder. Education in the humanities will not supplant graduate professional education. But it can substantially enrich the life of the professional as well as that of the individual and the citizen. And the humanities can and should take a direct part in professional education. They can develop and fortify the graduate management curriculum in those very areas where it is now critically thin. Properly handled, their judicious application to the dilemmas of professional life might even provide one channel for renewal of the humanities disciplines themselves.

Successful synthesis of the humanities in the graduate management curriculum, however, requires a fuller understanding than many humanists now possess of how their content and methodologies complement those already established in the business school. As the many critiques of graduate business programs that have emerged from business school faculty members and administrators suggest, there is considerable debate within the schools themselves about the proper ends and design of their curriculum. The disciplinary diversity of the typical M.B.A. curriculum makes that debate complex indeed, but an important main theme is the opposition between entrenched specialization, on the one hand, and comprehensiveness and integration, on the other. The drive toward academic respectability in business schools has enhanced the emphasis on specialization as it has that on scientific knowledge. It is easier to demonstrate the sophistication of vertical requirements in a tightly defined field than the sophistication required to encompass multiple disciplinary perspectives. The tools of "Management Science VI" are by definition advanced and finely honed, whether or not they fit a given manager's hand or task.

And, of course, the natural tendency for academic specialties that have a base in any academic field is to extend themselves. If the M.B.A.'s conceptual toolbox contains an eight-point saw and a twelve-point saw, and there is room for just one more tool, the saw specialist will recommend a fifteen-point saw, arguing that a fine set of saws demands it. Although there may be no hammer, the sawyer is unlikely to notice. But if there are powerful drives toward specialization in the management curriculum, pressures for comprehensiveness and integration balance them. The professional school's purposes are the education of practicing professionals and the expansion of knowledge relevant to that practice. And those purposes demand close attention to the full complexity of management experience.

Improving the "Case"

One very common way in which business faculty try to capture and communicate the complexity of actual management experience is through the "case." The case might be a written study of a major business episode involving some evaluative interpretation and designed to be read by other scholars, much as a report of a laboratory experiment or field survey might be read. More frequently, however, cases are written to be used as teaching devices. Such cases attempt to recreate a business situation calling for managerial involvement. Students examine the case and are then asked what action, if any, the managers involved ought to take. Students might be required to offer their judgments in class discussions of the case, as members of small working groups who will prepare group reports, or as the authors of individual papers. Cases range widely in scope and complexity. But most cover only a single company or conglomerate within a limited time frame: often only a few weeks or months, rarely more than a few years. A broad strategic-management case might ask students to determine a competitive strategy for a small computer-manufacturing company struggling for survival amid an invasion of giants. A finance case might demand the selection of one of several optional machine tools. A case in personnel or human resources management might require that students decide how to deal with an accusation of sexual harassment.

In a few business schools, most notably Harvard's, the case method is the dominant instructional approach, and case instruction is practiced to some degree in virtually every business school. Some management faculty become extraordinarily skilled at leading case discussions, and students can indeed become deeply engaged in the managerial problems that cases pose. Still, despite Harvard's rhapsodic assertion that the case method is "often extolled as the most powerful pedagogic approach for developing a manager's judgment" (Harvard Business School, 1984, p. 6), rampant criticism of the judgment of fresh M.B.A.s suggests reasons for concern. Indeed, case studies, whether intended as contributions to management literature or as teaching devices, are the objects of some contempt on the part of many members of business school faculties themselves. In large part, that contempt reflects the difficulty that some members of professional faculties have acknowledging that professional schools must deal with the conceptual messiness of practice; no matter how well wrought, engaging, and factually accurate the case, and no matter how sophisticated the analysis that accompanies it, there will be those who will condemn it simply because it is "descriptive" and "unscientific." But the cases are, in fact, very uneven in quality. And, while their methodologies cannot be scientific and still accomplish the cases' purpose of reflecting the true complexity of management experience, the cases seem frequently to be devoid of any methodology at all. Dependent though business schools are on the case method, they rarely provide their faculty members with formal education in case writing. Strategic-management cases are typically written by professors of strategic management, finance cases by professors of finance, and human resource management cases by professors of personnel or organizational psychology.

But education in a management field or function is not the same as training in the rendering of qualitative experience. Indeed, extensive education in a functional business specialty frequently distorts the academician's ability to communicate the complexity of business experience. The finance professor who writes a case dealing with the acquisition of a tool-making machine is likely to emphasize depreciation, production capacity and related revenues, and the cost of financing. But that professor may totally disregard potential resistance to the new machine from established employees and their unions, relevant health and safety legislation, or competitive threats to the market for which the machine manufactures. Such narrowness is appropriate where the professor's stated intention is simply to present an exercise. The "word problem" has a place in drilling students in the application of specific techniques. But what is really little more than a narrow exercise is too often presented as a fully realized episode. Not surprisingly, the result is students who believe that they can manage by the numbers.

The humanities can play a role in improving the management case. Since the cases typically purport to be renderings of actual business situations, their authors might profit from some formal training in historical methods or from collaboration with skilled historians. Cases composed by accountants, economists, and professors of finance may be well founded in their presentation and interpretation of quantitative data. But they are less reliable when they depend on nonquantitative archives or on the gathering and reconciling of conflicting recollections, oral and

written, of past events. Professors of organizational psychology
and theory may be skilled in direct observation and in the gathering and interpretation of questionnaire and interview data.
But they are often less secure when dealing with the archival
and secondary accounts that are the historian's meat and more
comfortable with the statistical interpretation of aggregated
data than with compelling verbal accounts of specific occur-
rences.

The field of history, then, can supply the management
case study with some of the methodological underpinnings that
it typically lacks. But where the case is intended as a teaching
instrument, rather than as a contribution to our factual knowledge of the practice of management, there is a role for fiction
as well. Although the great majority of management cases designed for teaching purport to be factual, many are uneasy
blends of fact and awkward fiction. The motive behind the use
of fictional elements in the case is a solid one. The authors introduce dramatized scenes and snippets of dialogue to engage
students more deeply in the experience that the case describes. Dramatization is a powerful device for creating the feel
of managerial experience, for acquainting students not just
with the factual outlines of specific situations but with the sen-
sations and stresses of the executive's life. Northrop Frye's comments on art apply: "It does not quantify existence like science:
it qualifies it; it tries to express not what is there but what is
here, what is involved in consciousness and being themselves"
(Frye, 1966, p. 40). The comprehension of managerial experience through the case requires not just the analysis of a record
but emotional and intellectual identification with the situations
of the key managers involved. At its best, the teaching case
should heighten students' awareness of managerial consciousness itself, and that goal cries out for the devices of fiction.

But the effective use of fiction in the managerial case
calls for two things. It calls for conscious and sophisticated
understanding of the relationships between fact and fiction, art
and life, as they apply to case writing. And it calls for some
mastery of literary and dramatic technique. Teaching cases are
typically presented to students as factual, and the fictions, if

they are discussed at all, are blandly dismissed as devices to protect the privacy of the company managers involved. Students
are not informed of the trade-offs between art and life that have
gone into the creation of the case. And there is little evidence
that the great majority of the authors of business cases examine
those trade-offs deeply: certainly, few of them enjoy significant
exposure to the many discussions of these issues in literary criticism and elsewhere. Given the heavy emphasis that case instruction receives in graduate management schools, such naivete concerning its basic methods is dangerous. Similarly, case writers
are typically so poorly acquainted with basic dramatic and literary technique that their fictive efforts ring false. The dialogue
in today's typical business case has all the force and artistic
polish of that in a dime novel.

    Case writing might be improved, then, by fuller collabora-
tion not only between faculty members in business and those in
history but also between those in business and those in literature or creative writing. And present or prospective business faculty members who intend to write cases should themselves be
exposed to some formal grounding in the methodology of the
case method, a grounding to which the humanities should heavily contribute.

Broader Uses of the Humanities

    Historical and literary study and, indeed, the study of
other humanities disciplines can contribute more to graduate
management education than improvement of the management
case. If there is a need for fiction specifically adapted to the
purposes of the business school, there is also a place for selective and judicious use of works from the established literary
canon. Such use need not be limited to courses in "The Business
Novel" and the like. Many literary works could be effectively
used as substitutes for one or more standard cases in established
business school courses. A course in the currently popular field
of corporate culture might profit from the bemusing presence
of Melville's "Bartleby the Scrivener"; a course on motivation
might achieve added resonance from the quiet desperation of

Miller's Willie Loman; a course on business and society would be enriched by the conflicting views of the corporation dramatized in Norris's *The Octopus*.

And heavier use of history and historical methods in the business school can do much to describe the roots of management and management study, to enhance our understanding of the overall management process, to demonstrate the long-term relationships between the organization and society, and to provide vivid examples of effective leaders. The typical business case is too focused on specific situations to accomplish these ends. They are ends that require emphasis on eras rather than episodes, on lives rather than single moments of decision.

In these broader areas as well as with the case, management education is already far more dependent on historical approaches than many of its scientifically oriented faculty admit. Rigorous social-psychological research in management is insufficient in volume and perhaps even in kind to provide a comprehensive view of the management process. In developing that view, the field of management has relied heavily on the thoughtful, albeit unscientific, observation of managerial life. Some of the most influential shapers of our modern view of management —Fayol, Mooney, Alvin Brown, Sheldon, Barnard, and Urwick— were themselves experienced business managers struggling to order and generalize their experience (Koontz, O'Donnell, and Weihrich, 1976, p. 12). In this sense, they owe as much to the traditions of history and philosophy as to the methods of research based in the social and behavioral sciences that are most commonly cited as the basis for managerial knowledge. The efforts of these thoughtful practitioners have contributed substantially to the integrative fields in management studies, variously called "management," "strategic management," or "business policy." By contrast to the stereotypical view that business programs offer only specialized quantitative models, the integrative fields argue that management is a dynamic process that involves continual reassessment of the organization's purpose, assessment that requires careful analysis of trends in the organization's environment and of the enterprise's own human and material capabilities.

History can substantially amplify and complement the integrative insights of the practitioners: and management study desperately needs such amplification. Students devoid of a historical view of management have some difficulty comprehending, in their courses on strategic management, just how vulnerable the enterprise is to shifting social forces. Students whose sense of technological history reaches further back than the decline of Victor, Osborne, or the PCjr, who know what effect the railroad and the telegraph had on the character of the nineteenth century and the automobile and the airplane on the first half of the twentieth, will be far better equipped to comprehend the impacts of the information age on the organization than their timebound counterparts. Similarly, students truly in search of managerial excellence should know not just what companies seemed great from the perspective of 1982 but what organizations and institutions, political, religious, and military as well as commercial, seem great from the perspective of the twentieth century as a whole, and of centuries that have shaped it. Not only the study of strategic management and business policy but also the study of leadership, motivation, power, and authority can profit substantially from historical scholarship. Management students should not confine their knowledge of organizational and industrial leaders to that contained in the pages of Lee Iaccoca's autobiography or the biographical capsules in the popular business press: they should be exposed to at least some of the biographies and autobiographies of leaders and entrepreneurs of the past. They might read Plutarch and Benjamin Franklin or biographies of Richard Arkwright, Josiah Wedgwood, John Jacob Astor, the Rothschilds, the Rockefellers, Andrew Carnegie, and Alfred Sloan. The models of leadership and motivation that are routinely offered to M.B.A. students in their core courses in organizational behavior are useful. But in the absence of more fully fleshed portrayals of leadership and creativity in our M.B.A. programs, we are likely to continue to be disappointed in the leadership abilities of our M.B.A.s themselves.

The methods and content of historical and literary study, then, can make substantial contributions to the M.B.A.'s understanding of management experience. They can strengthen the traditional management case, and offer fictional enhancements to it, or alternatives to it that can heighten consciousness of managerial issues more intensely than fact itself. History provides methods of study that can enrich the thoughtful efforts of practitioners to provide generalized overviews of management. And it offers illuminating examples of the rise and fall of leaders and organizations and of the influence of sweeping social and economic changes on them both.

The humanities can also sharpen the written and oral communication abilities of M.B.A. students by sharpening the focus of the M.B.A. curriculum on language itself. Virtually every M.B.A. program already devotes considerable attention to communication. Courses in organizational behavior and organizational theory discuss the distortions that occur in the upward flows of communication, the patterns of communication in informal and formal organizations, and the importance of communication in obtaining employee commitment. Courses in organizational development and conflict resolution apply the techniques of clinical psychology to small-group relations. Courses in marketing and consumer behavior incorporate social-psychological theory and research describing individual attitude change and the processes through which new ideas are diffused through organizations, countries, and cultures.

There is much here that is of value to the communicator, and, indeed, the theories and the empirical data that psychological and social-psychological research provide deserve significantly more attention in college-level writing courses than they now receive. No rhetorician should be entirely innocent of them. But, while social-psychological study can help a student to understand the stages in which an individual, an organization, or a society processes a new idea, and while the simulations of the clinical psychologist can provide participants with important insights into their own personalities as persuaders or negotiators, these courses do not focus on the mastery of language itself. They provide few specific verbal skills.

Trying to teach communication without grappling with words is like trying to teach accounting without grappling with numbers. No M.B.A. program does the latter. Most do the former. M.B.A.s should be required to take a course in managerial rhetoric, a course focused on enriching their understanding of the options that the language offers for the communication of thought and feeling and, indeed, for the communication of their desired professional personae. M.B.A. programs are rife with discussions of alternative leadership styles, but they typically leave the prospective leader ignorant of the mastery of verbal technique essential to communicating those styles. Leadership style demands a stylist.

But M.B.A.s need to know more than how language can be used to effectively explain, direct, and motivate. They are paid not just to sell but to think, not just to persuade but to decide. M.B.A.s are usually educated extensively in courses in accounting, finance, managerial economics, and management science, all of which provide quantitative techniques for decision making. But although nearly every significant corporate decision involves extensive verbal as well as numerical analysis, M.B.A.s are rarely directly trained in the use of words to define, shape, and resolve managerial problems. Where the nonquantitative aspects of decision making are discussed, they are usually addressed, like communication issues, from the perspective of the organizational or clinical psychologist. These are valuable but not sufficient approaches. Masters of business administration should be masters of language for thought as well as expression.

Communication and decision making through language are too central to the manager's job to be relegated, as they often are in M.B.A. programs, to tangential, not-for-credit "communication skills" clinics or workshops. These facilities are useful, but primarily for purposes of remediation. They should be employed to develop students to the point where graduate-level work in rhetoric and argumentation is possible. If such graduate work is to become widely represented in the cores of M.B.A. programs, it is important that the case for it be communicated to the management faculty, especially those in the less verbal disciplines. While these scholars might view quantitative ability as being infinitely expandable, they often view the capacity to write as a basic skill. To them, mastery of the word is simply competency in elementary rules and devices. They confuse subtlety in expression with mere grammatical correctness, stylistic sophistication with mere economy of speech. The view is tantamount to the argument that students have mastered mathematics once they have mastered multiplication and division or have achieved the acme of motor development once they have learned to tie their shoes. M.B.A. programs should balance the development of verbal and quantitative analytical abilities, emphasizing subtlety in expression itself as well as general characteristics of organizational communication.

Professors of English interested in rhetoric, composition, stylistic criticism, and dramatic technique can, then, make critical contributions to the graduate management curriculum. The potential contributions of philosophy and religion are also substantial. Work in logic and dialectic can hone the student's ability to use language to grapple with managerial problems. Such work might be combined with work in managerial rhetoric to heighten the student's awareness of the fact that language shapes as well as communicates managerial tasks. Philosophy can contribute rigor to the manager's analysis of ethical choices, and religion can provide prospective managers the very terms in which they can discuss the moral choices in professional life. In a world of organizations, management has immense impact on the quality and the conditions of individual lives, substantially more impact, perhaps, than the traditional professions of law and medicine. Yet the curricula that prepare managers for professional life do not offer them even a vocabulary in terms of which to examine the moral or spiritual impacts of their decisions and practices on the organizational lives of those they supervise or the wider constituencies they affect: stockholders, customers, suppliers, and local communities and their ecologies, as well as society at large. The drive toward "scientific" management has encouraged avoidance of words that directly express value, so that we send prospective managers into the complex moral battleground of the modern organization naked of conceptual arms or ammunition. Words such as *pride, greed, envy, anger, lust, gluttony, sloth, charity, prudence, justice, temperance,* and *fortitude* are as rare in management literature as they are illuminating of managerial practice. The point is not that we should turn M.B.A. programs into programs in theology, nor is it realistic to believe that a few graduate professional programs can overcome the moral indifference of a secular age. But it might be useful for at least some courses, lectures, or case discussions to demonstrate the relevance of old typologies of good and evil to contemporary management problems.

The need is the greater since the purportedly neutral language in which so much management literature is written at times obscures rather than avoids moral assumptions. The literature in organizational behavior and development, for example, is not so much value free as reluctant to examine its values. To the specialist in "organizational development," "worker satisfaction," for all the admitted ambiguity of its links with worker productivity, is typically a presumed good. And the devices designed to nurture it are likewise benevolently viewed, though they are frequently condescending, manipulative, and oppressive.

Indeed, management studies have shown some considerable reluctance not only to examine assumptions of value but to examine the basic epistemological assumptions of the disciplines that dominate the field. It is critical to the success of managers that they understand how we know what we claim to know about management, that they comprehend what the eclectic array of disciplines that make up their subject can or cannot tell them about the shifting realities with which they deal. Students should understand with some sophistication both what is surrendered and what is gained as a result of the heavy dependence of management study on research in the social and behavioral sciences. They should understand what sorts of knowledge it is possible to attain through objective analysis of empirical data and what must come through the combined efforts of reason, emotion, and intuition—head, heart, and gut. They should understand what a word is and what a number is and how the two differ as analytical devices.

Every substantial graduate management program ought to devote at least some attention, then, to the epistemology of management study, even if in nothing more than an occasional guest lecture or assigned reading in required courses. The multi-disciplinary course focused on a specific theme might be another way of sensitizing students to the disciplinary biases and assumptions of their professors. The relationship between the individual and the organization, one of the central relationships with which managers must deal, might be profitably approached from more perspectives than that of the organizational psychologist, although that is a demonstrably useful one. Psychology can offer the results of extensive laboratory and field study indicating the strengths and limitations of money as a motivator, the value of other forms of reward, and the differential impacts of reward and punishment in winning commitment to the goals of the enterprise. History can suggest which social conditions have encouraged and which have discouraged that commitment and what its presence or absence has meant for the fates of countries or cultures. Philosophy and religion can raise the moral questions involved by the manager's efforts to absorb the individual in the group effort. Where must it stop? What professions of loyalty can justly be exacted? What are the appropriate claims of the organization, and what are those of the family? Literature can bring the issues alive, can enable the student to feel the tensions and synergies between individual aspiration and united effort.

Initiatives

The humanities, then, can make a substantial contribution to graduate education in management. That contribution, of course, must be weighed against all the other tasks that a graduate professional program must accomplish. The purpose of the M.B.A. is to produce effective practitioners. The degree will not and should not become a thinly disguised vehicle for traditional liberal arts education. The M.B.A. graduate should know the analytical techniques of managerial accounting, finance, and economics, will not be able to compete without comprehending the power of computer modeling, and could justly be accused of incompetency if released upon an unsuspecting organization innocent of proven techniques of employee selection. M.B.A.s are first and foremost being prepared as practitioners. I want to know first that my surgeon knows how and where to cut in removing my appendix and am only secondarily interested in whether she or he understands the history of surgery or can comment sensitively on the ethics of euthanasia. But over the longer view, I know that the primary and secondary interests overlap. A surgeon with some knowledge of the history of the field might be less likely to be operating out of passing fashion rather than necessity. And if the operation goes awry, I would hope that any decision to mercifully dismiss me would be thoughtfully taken. With management, where the issues are the conditions under which most of us spend our working lives, the competitiveness of our nation, and the economic, social, and political stability that depends upon that competitiveness, the breadth of vision that the humanities provide is just as important. The recent critiques of the M.B.A., reductive or intemperate though some of them are, point to real problems, problems that the humanities can help to resolve or examine. The issue is not, then, the reduction of the practical value of the degree but its enhancement. Given what many of the purchasers and even manufacturers of the M.B.A. are saying about the product, judicious investment in the humanities, even at the expense of some advanced work in established tools and functions, would seem to be wise.

To date, few graduate schools of management have made more than small and fragmented investments in this field. Responsiveness to the need for humanities-based skills and subjects has been strongest, perhaps, in managerial communication. Although core M.B.A. requirements in oral and written communication are still the exception rather than the rule, they are increasingly common in the strongest schools: Dartmouth, Harvard, and Wharton all have such requirements. Courses focused specifically on the history of business and capitalism or on ethics appear occasionally, but as electives, such as Stanford's offering on Management and Ethics and Harvard's on Ethical Aspects of Corporate Policy. Graduate-level management courses that focus specifically on historical methods of organization study and on epistemological questions that go to the core of the claims to knowledge in business curricula are relatively rare in the business schools themselves. And, although courses on business fiction appear relatively frequently in undergraduate programs, they are uncommon among graduate business offerings.

These restrictions are alleviated to some extent by the fact that many graduate schools of business allow their M.B.A. students to take some of their electives in other schools and programs, especially in the second year. In addition, it is now reasonably common for M.B.A. programs to require a broad survey course on business and its environment that will at least touch on questions of ethics and justice, perhaps with some historical referents. Stanford's required Business and the Changing Environment, which includes "concepts of equity and efficiency, market failure, social justice, social contracts, distributive politics, ethics, and the responsibilities of individuals, business, and the state" (Stanford University, 1984, p. 6), is representative both in its content and in its unrealistic ambition. These are laudable efforts. But more extensive integration of the humanities throughout the curriculum is needed if the humanities are to provide M.B.A. programs with a telling response to their critics.

A more extensive effort to tie the humanities into graduate management education than is typical nationally has been under way for over six years at the Claremont Graduate School. A close look at that effort reveals some approaches that others might wish to adapt. It also reveals the substantial difficulties involved in designing a humanities component truly fitted to the needs of management education; and it suggests some of the institutional, faculty, and administrative resources required to overcome those difficulties. Finally, it demonstrates the need for further creative experimentation if the potential contribution of the humanities to the graduate education of managers is to be fully realized.

The humanities offerings at Claremont involve two major management programs. The first, the Business Administration Program, annually enrolls approximately two hundred students who are anticipating careers in management. They average twenty-five years in age and are predominantly M.B.A. students, although some are seeking Ph.D. degrees. The second, the Executive Management Program, annually enrolls over three hundred midcareer managers from profit and nonprofit organizations. The midcareer group averages forty years in age. The largest number are seeking a master of arts in management degree or an advanced executive M.B.A. degree (which carries an M.B.A. prerequisite). A small number of accomplished executives with research interests are also admitted each year to a Ph.D. program in executive management.

Both programs offer courses based in history, philosophy, and English. Most of the courses are offered as "modules," half-semester-equivalent courses that carry two units of credit. Currently, about six of those modules are offered each year, including summers, in each program. History courses concentrate on business history, on American organizational and institutional history, on the history of Western attitudes toward capitalism and business, and, for Ph.D. students, on historical methods of organizational studies. Philosophy courses concentrate on the ethics of economic choices, on the interaction of institutions and personal morality, and on the concept of value, including the definition of value implied by the social and behavioral sciences. English courses stress the control of language for more effective problem solving, exposition, persuasion, and self-expression, with attention to conflicts and synergies among those purposes.

The Claremont humanities offerings are based on several important assumptions. First, the judgment of the faculties in management and the humanities, reinforced by early experience with the courses, has been that they are valuable enough to be allotted a cherished space in the M.B.A. core requirements. The traditional M.B.A. degree requires two two-unit humanities modules. The executive M.B.A. degree requires one. Second, it was assumed from the beginning that the humanities courses, if they were to have significant impact in the graduate management programs, should be designed specifically for those programs. The humanities modules that Claremont's graduate management students complete, then, are predominantly courses adapted specifically to the management curricula and offered as a regular part of those curricula. Finally, it was assumed that humanities subjects should be taught by faculty whose primary training was in the field in question. Most of the courses are taught by humanities faculty who retain their primary base in a humanities program, and all of them are taught by faculty whose primary academic base is in the subject area. While the ethics components of some graduate management programs, if they are available at all, might be taught by a faculty member trained in general business or economic policy, Claremont has relied upon a senior professor of philosophy to cover the subject.

Claremont's experience with the humanities component of its graduate management programs yields several generalizations that might be helpful to others considering similar experiments. First, careful reading of six years of written student evaluations of the humanities courses and conversations with students and faculty over that same period indicate that the experiment has been successful. Some students are overtly enthusiastic. One observes that "the humanities courses are a great idea. They provide breadth in a way no other courses can." Another refers to a course in the history of Western critiques of capitalism as "an awakening"; still another observes that a course on "the Idea of a Management Science," which dealt with the strengths and limitations of the epistemological base of much management literature, "should be mandatory for all graduate students." And the student evaluations generally demonstrate a respect for the depth of knowledge of the humanities faculty that confirms the wisdom of employing only faculty with substantial academic depth in the subjects taught. One student found a history professor's command of the subject "dazzling." Comments on the "thought-provoking" nature of the courses and the "lively" discussions are also common.

Still, some students are less enthusiastic. Although the majority seem at least as satisfied with the humanities requirements and professors as with the other courses and professors represented in the cores of the M.B.A. programs, there are negative responses. The minority question the value of the humani-

ties courses for management education and resent being required to take them. One critic praises the contribution of a
humanities module to "general knowledge" but asserts that it is
"irrelevant to the business administration program." Another
"could not find any relationship with management" in a module on management history. Even among students favorably dis-
posed toward the courses, there are frequent requests for heavier emphasis on practical applications. And while many students
prize the liveliness and breadth of humanistic discussion, some
long for more tightly programmed formats and tidier conclusions. Not surprisingly, given the pragmatic bias of most management students, some of the best-received subjects are those
that stress the acquisition of skills patently relevant to management, such as the ability to write and speak compellingly. A
higher proportion of students have difficulty understanding the
more abstract and at least equally valuable material: the relationship between the word and the thought, the indeterminacy
of interpretation of historical fact, the uncertainty of fact itself. Management students are most comfortable with the
hands-on task of smoothing out the verbal roughness of a
memo, less easy in a discussion of the linkages between transi-
tional language and conceptual clarity, and sometimes flatly ill
at ease in a philosophical discussion of the relationship between
the word and the world.

    These reactions suggest that, even with substantial effort
to adapt the humanities subjects to the needs of the management curriculum, some students remain unclear about the connections. And they suggest further that, without efforts to
adapt the courses at all, they would have met with substantial
resistance indeed. The great majority of graduate management
students at Claremont assess the courses in the terms in which
they are offered, as integral parts of their professional curricula. And in that they are thoroughly justified. But if the Claremont experience confirms the need to adapt the humanities to
the goals of graduate professional education, it also demonstrates that some of the strongest contributions that the humanities can make toward those goals are also among the toughest to communicate.

One does not, of course, surrender the toughest parts of the task. A potentially powerful way of helping management students to better understand the more sophisticated managerial applications of the humanities might be to combine the humanities more tightly with traditional business disciplines. The multidisciplinary course might serve as a particularly effective conceptual bridge between business school and humanities approaches to business subjects. I have suggested above that a multidisciplinary team of instructors could be used effectively to examine a central managerial theme, such as the oppositions and alliances between the rights and needs of the individual and those of the organization. A multidisciplinary approach also might be particularly appropriate to the standard "capstone" or "integrative" M.B.A. course, usually called "strategic management" or "business policy." This course, which is traditionally taught by a single professor who is responsible for the daunting task of incorporating in his or her vision all the primary functions and subjects to which the M.B.A. is exposed, might instead incorporate expert spokespersons for differing disciplinary approaches. The focal point might continue to be, as it is in most existing strategic-management courses, a challenging case or series of cases. One loses the coherence that the mind of a single professor might impose but might come closer to the true complexity of the task. Students would profit from noting the differing modes in which the accountant and the philosopher measure accountability, the differing approaches that the finance professor and the historian take to long-term yield, the differing approaches that the behaviorist and the teacher of literature might employ to define human conflict and work toward its resolution.

In the design of such courses, consideration needs to be given to tight coordination. The courses should be multifaceted but not fragmented. My own experience with prototypes of courses of this kind suggests that the designation of a strong coordinating professor is critical, as is extensive up-front design. Someone with administrative and theatrical flair, strong skills as a discussion leader, and academic depth in one of the important areas of the course is advisable. Ardent disciplinary sectarians should be shunned for this assignment, which is essentially that of dramatic director. The sectarians can be effectively typecast in the course itself: the key is to select them for balance in rhetorical and pedagogical skill. If the purpose of the course is to be realized, it must also include devices designed to force students to engage their own intellects and intuitions in the disciplinary interplay. They should not only be forced out in discussion but should also complete significant written assignments explicitly requiring comparative evaluations of the ability of the differing disciplines to grapple with the specific business themes or cases in question.

Multidisciplinary courses might powerfully dramatize the relative uses of humanities and other disciplines for the M.B.A. But fresh disciplinary perspectives can be added to many established courses with minimal effort through the use of guest lectures and more imaginatively selected case materials. A technological historian familiar with the history of the oil industry, for example, might have substantial contributions to make in an "economic forecasting" course concerned with the potential impacts of alternative energy policies. Such cross-disciplinary efforts should enrich not only students but also the faculty members from each of the disciplines involved. The finance professor who comes into closer contact with the professor of economic history than previously might become more sensitive to the long-term implications of certain investment strategies and valuation techniques. The psychologist who has closely read Melville's *Billy Budd* might never view worker satisfaction in quite the same way again.

Effective integration of the humanities in graduate management education will occur only if university faculty and administrators drive it forward and will endure only if the world of business can be persuaded that the humanities can indeed help prevent some of the current flaws in M.B.A.s. Claremont's extensive humanities experiment, for example, was begun through the considerable efforts of the graduate school's dean, who, with the assistance of key senior humanities faculty, was able to win a National Endowment for the Humanities pilot grant to support course development. The experiment has continued to thrive as a result of continuing commitment from the humanities faculty, commitment that has been carefully nurtured by a respected senior humanities faculty member who has taken a leadership role in coordinating the humanities resources and assuring their regular availability. On the management side, the program has been encouraged by sympathetic faculty and enthusiastic program chairs and directors. Members of the faculty and the administration alike have assumed responsibility for communicating the value of the humanities component to the business community and have achieved some success in establishing it as a distinct differential advantage. The key to future success will be whether the humanities experiment can be carried to the more elaborate levels of multidisciplinary exchange just discussed.

The purpose of this chapter has been to suggest that the humanities can play a significant role in curricular responses to widespread critiques of the M.B.A. and to briefly describe what has been attempted so far in developing this role and what might be next done. A central theme has been that the job of the manager is too complex and too closely tied to modern life as a whole to be effectively comprehended by the established business curriculum. The content and methodologies of the humanities are also needed, and urgently so. But if the humanities can make a significant contribution to graduate professional education in management, contact with management education can assist the humanities in return. If American graduate schools are in trouble, education in the humanities is in far more serious trouble; it is suffering now from two decades of decline. The answer is not to convert the humanities into commercial disciplines. That would be to surrender the very value that they hold for the businessperson as well as the individual and the citizen. But a part of the answer may lie in renewing the contact of scholarly study in the humanities with some of the salient issues of our time. In an age of complex organizations, the study of management encompasses, or should encompass, many of those issues. Humanistic study in many of our nation's colleges has fallen victim not so much to a barbarian or materialistic age as to its own specialization and disciplinary solipsism. Whether they do or do not share Roderick Usher's drive for the Ideal, some humanistic scholars have come to share his fastidious disdain for the world as it is and his incestuous taste for communion with his own kind. A house so isolated must collapse. For scholars in the humanities, some attention to the turbulent realities confronted by the manager need not represent a surrender of higher aims. It might, instead, provide some of the regeneration, some of the solid contact, support, and recognition, essential to the continued pursuit of those aims.

8

Kathryn Mohrman
Marcie Schorr Hirsch

Preparing
Liberal Arts Students
for Business

This chapter focuses on undergraduate programs offered by liberal arts colleges and by colleges of arts and sciences in multipurpose universities. No less than their peers in business programs, liberal arts students have a keen interest in the changing labor market. Arts and sciences faculty and administrators, moreover, have provided many special programs to assist those interested in management in the transition from college to career.

The climate in programs of liberal education is supportive of efforts to balance liberal education and career preparation. Attitudes among both students and faculty in the liberal arts have changed significantly from the hostility toward business prevalent at colleges and universities in the 1960s. There is now a new open-mindedness toward business careers and an interest in more cooperation between the business and academic sectors of society. Many of the programs described in this chapter are responses to justifiable criticisms. Most are conscious efforts of faculty and administrators in arts and sciences units to do more

170

to assist students in realizing their career aspirations while at the same time maintaining the integrity and strength of liberal education.

This chapter gives special emphasis to programs for young adults who are preparing to enter the world of work, because the links between college and career are most tenuous for these students. On the one hand, these inexperienced workers are "unknowns" to employers—their skills, abilities, and attitudes cannot be determined easily by firms seeking new managers. On the other, the business world is substantially unknown to college students who lack work experience in professional settings. Most older students, especially those studying part time while working, already have a track record as workers; the relationship between their studies and their professional goals is generally much clearer.

Across the country, colleges and universities have adopted a variety of approaches to link liberal learning and careers; this chapter gives specific examples of ways in which institutions have supplemented liberal arts programs or have integrated academic and experiential activities. While these examples are illustrative of recent innovations, they should by no means be viewed as an inclusive list of high-quality campus programs. Many other colleges and universities not mentioned in this volume are also engaged in such activities.

The implication of many of these programs is that change must occur at the campus level—students should be more self-conscious about their abilities and goals, academic programs should provide interested undergraduates with specific knowledge of business, and arts and sciences programs should offer more opportunities for internships or other direct experiences in business. The role of colleges and universities in these programs is to help students prepare for and adapt to the needs of their future employers.

Institutions have another responsibility, however: to speak aggressively about liberal education and its importance for work as well as for citizenship and individual satisfaction. The case for liberal education in management can be made effectively, we believe, by talking about liberal education in terms of the needs of businesses today. Colleges can help their students by examining the questions that managers face and then demonstrating the ways in which liberally educated graduates can answer these questions.

We are calling for a marketing strategy, if you will, but one that focuses on societal needs, not just the concerns of colleges and universities. The problems facing arts and sciences programs are very real—including the difficulties experienced by students entering the work world—but there is little reason for businesses to deal with these problems out of sympathy and charity alone. This chapter is structured around the premise developed throughout Part One, that a broad liberal arts education can be part of the solution to key corporate and national problems. The chapter poses and suggests answers to several questions faced by businesses that seek to recruit successful managers. In doing so, it also presents arts and sciences faculty and administrators with examples of institutions relating the liberal arts and career and corporate needs in ways that respect the inherent values of liberal education.

Evaluating Educational Programs

Today we cannot escape the demographic realities of more people seeking professional positions than there are jobs. Competition is fierce for entry-level positions among new college graduates without specific technical training; the salary statistics presented in Chapter Four suggest relative supply and demand. In the face of many potentially qualified candidates, employers must make a series of distinctions. The ways in which they evaluate these differences in college programs and the graduates they produce determine the opportunities for liberal arts graduates in the business world. Colleges and universities will assist themselves, their students, and employers by helping businesses make distinctions about students and positions in as accurate and sophisticated ways as possible.

Obviously, not all institutions provide comparable programs for their students; employers can distinguish on several grounds among the colleges and universities from which they will consider applicants, including the degree of emphasis on the liberal arts versus management and other subject areas. Often, however, the distinctions are not well correlated with the actual quality of programs and graduates. In such cases, colleges can provide a service by making clearer statements about their strengths in ways that are helpful to businesses seeking well-educated potential employees.

Some organizations screen by the reputation of the school, choosing to recruit only at Ivy League institutions or Big Ten universities. Perhaps they believe they are gaining a type of socialization or the future benefit of connections developed during the undergraduate years at such prestigious universities. Other organizations hire only from nearby colleges and universities. Such businesses may already have a number of productive employees from these institutions and therefore feel no reason to recruit more broadly. At the same time, the skills and understandings that business leaders say they want in their managers are developed in a much wider range of institutions. With the key distinctions developed below in mind, corporations will be in a better position to hire on the basis of actual quality of graduates rather than reputation, tradition, or proximity alone.

When and Where Should Management Training Occur?

The last thirty years, as we have seen, have brought tremendous growth in academic programs in management. The increasing complexity of business has called for more managers with sophisticated training in such fields as finance, information systems, and marketing. For many individuals aspiring to positions of leadership in business, undergraduate and graduate degrees in business subjects provide focused preparation for management careers.

Hiring business majors and M.B.A.s, however, is not the only way to recruit successful managers. Many companies are deciding that the most effective management training occurs on the job. Bright, motivated B.A.s can quickly develop business skills through formal training programs focused on the needs of the specific employer. Chase Manhattan Bank, as mentioned in

Chapter Four, found in an evaluation of its training programs
for both B.A.s and M.B.A.s that level of education was inversely
related to performance success—that is, a larger percentage of
the most successful managers had B.A.s only. In addition, these
bachelor's degree holders cost much less than their profession-
ally educated counterparts seeking returns on their investment
in graduate management training.

More top undergraduates are attracted to business careers
today than at any time in the recent past; employers with good
positions to offer can recruit the most able students finishing
college. These students often hold a different attitude from
that of management school graduates about entering the business world; not only do they demand less in salary, but they
have different expectations about career progress and pacing.
The "fast-track syndrome," the tendency to hop frequently
from job to job, the desire to run the company after only a
short time on the job—all common criticisms of M.B.A.s—are
characteristics less often found among B.A.s in business. Organizations seeking employee retention and loyalty often value liberally educated employees.

Some of the abilities essential for professional leadership
cannot be developed easily within the time that most organizations can allow for training programs. Among these skills are
written communication ability, analysis and decision-making
skills, and a long-term viewpoint—all central outcomes of a successful liberal education. Organizations seeking employees with
these skills may find their needs best met by hiring liberally
educated graduates who have already developed these abilities
in college.

At the same time, many jobs in business do not require
the specialized skills acquired through extensive technical training. Too often, companies hire specialists even when their expertise is unnecessary, passing up liberal arts graduates capable
of doing the job. If the need is essentially for persons with
generic abilities—people who can write, speak, think critically,
and handle numbers—then hiring liberally educated graduates
may be the best investment in human resources.

Small companies employ 80 percent of American workers; recent studies suggest that this is the most productive and innovative sector of the economy today. Because of their size, many small firms cannot afford to hire M.B.A.s or provide formal training programs, although they do need flexible, adaptable workers who can perform a wide range of tasks within the organization. Once again, generally trained graduates with a broad range of skills can be well suited to employment in such companies.

When and where should formal management training occur? There is no single answer. Often, employers use majors and degrees as a screening device to narrow the number of potential applicants with whom they must deal. However, more sophisticated distinctions about necessary skills, about on-the-job training, and about the necessary balance between general and professional education can suggest different matches between potential employees and firms seeking new professionals. Businesses should determine what they really want in terms of skills and knowledge in their workers for the long term. At the same time, colleges and universities should analyze carefully the training opportunities and the entry points in which a broad education in the arts and sciences can be an asset to the hiring company. If higher education institutions and individual students can help companies to make better distinctions, all parties will be well served.

Preparation for Careers in Business

How can employers distinguish among individual students? Once a firm has determined what combination of general and professional skills it needs for a particular job and where students develop those skills, the company must still choose among many applicants for the available positions. College and university programs offer differing levels of preparation for business careers. Liberally educated students present various combinations of awareness, training, and experience as they seek careers in management. This section describes initiatives undertaken by colleges and universities to prepare their students for careers in business through programs that develop self-awareness or that provide knowledge of business, academic preparation for management, or actual work experience for undergraduates.

Self-Knowledge. All successful workers need a clear understanding of personal values and needs, a sense of their strengths and interests. Students who have had no professional training as undergraduates often have a vague sense of what they can do in nonacademic settings, with little understanding of ways to employ classroom skills in business settings. Employers may perceive generally educated students as unfocused and uncommitted.

Many colleges and universities assist undergraduates in the process of self-assessment through testing, individual counseling, workshops, and credit courses. Students at Gettysburg College, for example, begin their career explorations with a "first-step" orientation session at which they learn how to gather information about themselves and about career options. These sessions are followed by opportunities for individual assistance and for research in occupational literature and self-assessment materials.

Vocational testing—and its new counterpart, computer-assisted guidance—are available at many career development offices. Undergraduates at Boston University, the State University of New York at Buffalo, and many other campuses use Discover, an interactive software program that assists students in identifying their interests, abilities, and values. Printouts bearing the results of student inputs are then reviewed individually with career counselors. Discover and a comparable program, SIGI, are so popular that their creators are providing second-generation software to meet student needs.

Alma College is one of many institutions that provide both credit courses and noncredit workshops on career and life planning. Alma's comprehensive program integrates these activities throughout the undergraduate years. The College of New Rochelle's School of New Resources has recently introduced a credit course in life planning. "Designing the Future" is tailored especially to the needs of a student population that is largely adult, female, and minority. Students read, for example, about discrimination in the labor market and learn from guest lecturers and assigned readings effective strategies for overcoming it. Working in small groups with supportive peers, they discover unsuspected connections between their prior experience and study and possible future careers. Tufts University and Whitman College offer career/life planning workshops, although not for academic credit. Students enroll in the workshops to increase their self-awareness and to learn to "know what they want when they see it." Participation in such programs has increased dramatically on campus; Whitman, for example, reported a 57 percent increase in the last year.

Noncredit workshops are also a component of the comprehensive placement activities of the University of Washington's Minority Job Placement Program. Established in 1974, this program offers career services specifically for Asian, black, Hispanic, and Native-American students and alumni. A recent study described in the program's newsletter exemplifies its efforts to determine the realities of the work world from a minority perspective. The media, the newsletter points out, continually warn students of a glut of M.B.A.s and attorneys. But the supply of *minority* M.B.A.s and lawyers, it continues, in no way begins to meet the demand. The same concern for minority students' needs shapes the program's considerable offerings in the areas of counseling and self-assessment.

Self-knowledge is the first step to effective careers in any field. For students with little experience outside the academic world, conscious attention to their own interests and abilities aids in the selection of courses, decisions about internships or other part-time work, and ultimately in the transition to professional life. But it is when self-assessment is combined with research in occupational literature and job possibilities that these students can best articulate the skills and knowledge they can offer prospective employers.

Learning from Alumni and Executives. In addition to knowledge of their own capabilities, students need to understand the general expectations of the business world and the opportunities available in specific industries and particular employers. Liberal arts colleges have used their alumni effectively to introduce students to the opportunities available in business. Many institutions invite alumni to return to campus to speak about their careers. In many instances, such workshops and programs include explicit attention to the use of liberal arts disciplines in business settings. Wheaton College (Massachusetts) is one of many institutions that brings graduates to campus; Wheaton Plus, a comprehensive career development program, supplements campus activities by involving alumnae as mentors for current undergraduates.

Some colleges have extended the concept of career workshops beyond the campus. For example, alumni of Grinnell College living in Washington, Chicago, Minneapolis, and New York have organized extensive programs for students focused on career opportunities in those cities. During breaks in the academic calendar, undergraduates travel to these cities to hear speakers, meet individually with graduates in career fields they are considering, and develop networks of contacts "on site."

Since travel to other cities is not possible for many undergraduates, some colleges and universities bring alumni expertise to campus via videotape. Lafayette College and Miami University of Ohio are two institutions that have developed systematic programs of video interviews of successful professionals. Interviewers pose the questions that students would be likely to ask in face-to-face conversations: How did you get your job? How did your college education prepare you? What is it like to work in your field? Students use these videotapes to explore career opportunities without leaving the campus.

Many colleges and universities maintain networks of graduates and friends who have agreed to advise undergraduates about careers. Brown University maintains a list of alumni who are willing to talk with students on the telephone or to meet with students at their work sites. Members of the alumni network serve as information resources on the details of career paths, entry points, job requirements, and so on; they also can provide connections to other professionals and make referrals to specific job openings. In addition to talking with students informally, many alumni participate in externships or "shadow" programs. A Swarthmore College student, for example, can spend several days or a week with a graduate of the college, following him or her in daily tasks. Although the student does not assume work responsibilities as would be the case in a typical internship, the experience of observing the work setting, asking questions, and talking with a successful executive provides a better understanding of a career field than can be obtained only through reading.

A related method of increasing students' knowledge of business is an executive-in-residence program, bringing corporate leaders to campus to participate more intensively in the life of the campus. Often these executives serve as guest lecturers in specific classes, informal advisers to students, and resources to faculty and career services professionals. Brandeis University has one such professional in residence every semester to meet with students in individual appointments or group meetings.

Birmingham-Southern College has invited managers from a variety of corporations in the Southeast to talk with students and faculty about business careers. Retirees from the Exxon Corporation receive facilities at Drew University in return for assisting undergraduates with their research. At Furman University, the executive-in-residence program has an explicitly two-way purpose. Since many business leaders in South Carolina have undergraduate degrees in technical subjects, they have not had extensive experience in the liberal arts. During their week at Furman, these executives attend regular classes in such subjects as history, literature, and philosophy; they also participate in extracurricular activities on campus. Several visiting executives have become sufficiently "hooked" that they have enrolled in regular courses in subsequent semesters.

Contacts with successful alumni and local executives are techniques employed by colleges and universities to give students some knowledge of professional opportunities in business. Especially at smaller institutions that do not have extensive on-campus recruiting programs, these methods are vital for assisting students in planning their future careers. Large numbers of students in arts and sciences programs acquire important insights through these largely noncredit, extracurricular activities.

Academic Preparation. Students with nontechnical backgrounds have long supplemented their studies with individual business courses. Some institutions, however, provide more structured opportunities for undergraduates with liberal arts majors to develop competencies in management topics.

At many universities, the business school is the fastest-growing unit on campus, often unable to hire enough faculty to serve its own students effectively. As a result, students outside the business program are often prohibited from enrolling in management courses because there is no room to accommodate them. Pennsylvania State University resolved this dilemma by devising a structured business minor requiring a minimum of twenty-seven credits for completion; students electing this option take it in addition to a regular liberal arts major. The business minor requires at least nine credits in accounting and economics and another nine in such subjects as business law, finance, insurance, management, and marketing. The remaining credits can come from a wider range of subjects, including computer science, journalism, psychology, and speech communications.

The University of Maryland adopted another approach. With the advice of a corporate advisory council, the division of arts and humanities instituted a new program, Liberal Arts in Business (LAB). Rather than providing a sampling from existing offerings in management, however, the program has developed new courses on such subjects as history of business and financial institutions, analytical problem solving, law and ethics of business, and computer literacy. The honors students selected for the program complete a regular humanities major plus a minimum of seven LAB courses; the goal is to preserve the integrity of the humanities while giving students a working knowledge of business.

Other institutions have developed new majors for students interested in combining study in liberal arts disciplines with preparation for business careers. One example is the arts and management major at Mount Vernon College. By drawing on the cultural resources of Washington, D.C., students combine internships, study in arts and humanities disciplines, and introductory management courses in their undergraduate major. Bradford College has restructured its entire undergraduate program to relate the liberal arts curriculum to life after college. General education requirements include such courses as the Individual and the Organization and Work and Productivity, as well as more typical offerings in writing, mathematics, and the humanities. Interdisciplinary majors, practical minors, internships, and projects for juniors and seniors round out the Bradford plan.

In developing such programs for academic credit, faculty and administrators can encounter real obstacles, from interschool jealousies to battles over resources. Initiating formal academic programs generally requires more political skill and administrative leadership than would be necessary to institute innovations in specific courses, advising, or career services activities.

In addition to creating new programs, some institutions are examining the present curriculum to determine the career-related skills they foster. Brandeis University has asked executives from various industries to examine curricular offerings with an eye to their usefulness for future careers. Seasoned professionals in banking, for example, looked at undergraduate courses in the arts and sciences and determined which ones might constitute useful preparation for a banking career. A master list of suggested courses, compiled from the opinions of many professionals, has become an important resource in career planning.

A more structured extension of this principle is the creation of course clusters around broad career interests of students. At the University of Massachusetts at Boston, students in the college of arts and sciences are encouraged to choose a set of related elective courses around such themes as law and justice, technical writing, and psychometrics. The University of Iowa devised a similar scheme for arts and sciences students, advising students about the match between existing courses in the arts and sciences curriculum and career interests. Similarly, students at Tougaloo College have completed clusters in career areas including civil service, communications, urban affairs, and business and finance.

A clusters program has the advantage of highlighting the

career values of liberal arts study without changing the institution's academic program; it is a strategic rather than a substantive approach. Students choose electives or minors from existing courses with an eye to transferable knowledge and skills, but individual courses remain the same. Faculty are not required to offer new courses, change teaching styles, or, as some might see it, capitulate to the growing vocationalism of students.

A different type of academic preparation for management careers is an intensive exposure to business subjects between semesters or in the summer. Approximately ten years ago, several universities began special business programs for Ph.D. candidates in the humanities seeking nonacademic careers. Summer institutes at New York University, the University of Virginia, the Wharton School, and other universities gave academic Ph.D. candidates exposure to basic principles of management as well as contacts with employers receptive to hiring nontraditional employees. Several colleges have now adapted the model for undergraduates. Vassar College offers an opportunity for sophomores and juniors to take a three-week introduction to management, followed by a paid internship for the remainder of the summer. Wellesley College offers a similar academic component, although no internship, during the January break between semesters. Management Basics at Wellesley, like other intensive programs, introduces students to fundamental business principles, helps them explore their interest in management, and develops an appreciation as well of the value of a liberal education in the business realm.

The University of Chicago business school has initiated a cooperative arrangement with twelve liberal arts colleges that allows selected students from those institutions to take the first quarter of M.B.A. study during the summer between the junior and senior years in college. Two students from each of the twelve colleges receive a full tuition grant, placement with a mentor from the executive ranks in the city, and guaranteed admission to Chicago's M.B.A. program within two years after successful completion of the summer quarter and of the senior year at their colleges. This opportunity allows students from liberal education programs to experience management education and explore career objectives while still undergraduates. The University of Chicago, on the other hand, invests in high-quality students with strong liberal arts backgrounds and also establishes links to colleges that may in time produce more good applicants than the summer program can support.

Business minors, summer institutes, and other supplementary academic programs help students develop an understanding of management principles, but not to the same extent as concentrated programs in business administration. However, students in the former kind of programs have better luck than other liberal arts majors in getting a foot in the door when seeking entry-level positions in business. The experience at Penn State, for example, has shown that liberal arts students with a business minor have a greater chance of being selected for an interview, because recruiters interpret the business minor as exposure to management principles and a commitment to a business-related career. The programs described in this section all serve as introductions to business and provide students with a focus for their professional aspirations while they secure as well the important advantages of a liberal education.

Work Experience. Nothing substitutes for the actual experience of working in a business setting. Increasingly, students seek opportunities to link their academic work with practical experience during their undergraduate years. In the eyes of many hiring organizations, the best indicator of a student's potential for success in business is past experience. For many students, however, the traditional source of such experience—the summer job—is not likely to provide career-related opportunities. Today, the top priority for many summer-job seekers is earning sufficient funds for the coming school year; students feel that they must accept the best-paying, not the most interesting, position they can locate. When they return to campus in the fall, they seek career-related opportunities in other ways.

Internships provide an important route to meaningful work experience; they give opportunities for relatively inexperienced students to do substantive work under the supervision of a professional in the field. At their best, internships allow students to learn new skills, make contacts, and test career objectives against reality. Employers, in turn, gain well-educated, highly motivated employees, often at no cost. Colleges and universities coordinate internship programs through career planning offices, academic advisers, deans' offices, academic departments, individual faculty members, and alumni networks. Even state governments can be involved; the Massachusetts Internship Office, for example, provides extensive listings of government internship opportunities to campus coordinators.

Some colleges have established direct links between internships and specific courses. Scripps College, for example, requires students participating in its humanities internship program to enroll in a special seminar that explores issues of work. While the syllabus varies from semester to semester depending upon the instructor, the purpose of the course remains the same —to study contemporary and traditional humanities texts and relate their content to students' internship experiences. Such seminars help to avoid the continuing dilemma surrounding internships—the granting of academic credit for work experience. Although most institutions require faculty sponsors for internships, in reality students are often left on their own to identify the relationship between their classroom studies and their internship experience. Concurrent or subsequent seminars can provide more faculty guidance, occasions for students to share experiences with one another, and more opportunities to think explicitly about the ways in which the work situation draws on one's liberal education.

Cooperative education is a special variation on the internship theme. Co-op students alternate terms of full-time work and full-time study to complete an undergraduate degree that links the practical and the theoretical; work and study in the liberal arts are equal components in the educational process. In addition to securing the obvious financial benefits of working, students in co-op programs gain substantive employment experience and training. Northeastern University and Antioch College, both of which have long-standing cooperative education programs, are only two of the many institutions providing programs of alternating periods in the classroom and in the work world.

By scheduling no classes on Tuesdays and Thursdays, World College West has structured its academic program to accommodate the daily integration of work experience with classroom learning. Lower-division students use these no-class days to complete a "lifework" requirement, which includes employment of their choice (plus a two-quarter course on work and personal development). Upper-division students work their major-related internship requirement into this schedule as well. The College Venture Program, a consortium of ten northeastern liberal arts institutions, places undergraduates in full-time paid positions while these students are on leaves of absence from their campuses. Many participants use the time off from college to develop skills and expertise in an area of long-term career interest, often through placements in business. Cornell University has developed a special program to ensure that students have summer work opportunities in the business world. Cornell alumni have raised funds specifically designated to provide stipends for undergraduates, so that students can in effect bring their own paychecks with them to their summer jobs. The employing organizations get free labor, and Cornell students get substantive work experiences that might otherwise be unavailable.

New Roles for Faculty

Not all college faculty subscribe to the idea that liberal education has vocational applicability as well as inherent value. Among some academics, there is a distrust of business and a stereotype of executives as unethical entrepreneurs driven solely by the profit motive. Since faculty serve as influential role models for students, such narrow perspectives can distort students' perceptions and career choices. Fortunately, such uninformed perspectives are less common on campuses today than in the past. Even the most supportive faculty member is limited, however, by the lack of personal experience in business. It is difficult for professors whose careers have been entirely on the campus to understand the ways in which skills developed through liberal education can be applied beyond the campus. At a number of colleges and universities across the country, faculty and administrators have initiated activities to address this problem.

Several colleges have involved faculty in examining individual courses to identify marketable skills developed by students as a by-product of the process of liberal education. At Gustavus Adolphus College, for example, faculty members analyzed the offerings in their own departments to identify transferable skills. Combined with information on the career histories of departmental majors in previous years, the lists of skills that these efforts produce are helpful advising tools for faculty and career services alike. Lafayette College piloted a successful program, Learning and Understanding, Not Choosing Haphazardly (LAUNCH), in which students answer questions about fundamental interests and goals for their education. With this information, faculty advisers and career counselors help students integrate their academic planning with long-term goals, assisting students in designing programs to develop desired skills.

Personal experience in the business world has helped faculty assist students in the transition from college to career. Carleton College has established a network of career advisers in each academic department; these faculty members have visited individual managers and corporate leaders to gather firsthand information on opportunities for majors in their disciplines. At Saint Olaf and Birmingham-Southern Colleges, some faculty members have worked as interns, consultants, and managers in the local community, developing personal understanding of the relationship between their classroom and the business world.

Team teaching is another way for faculty members and business executives to work closely together. While guest lecturers and instructors from industry are common in professional management programs, this form of exchange is less frequently found in liberal arts disciplines. At Memphis State University, a member of the philosophy department joined forces with a local business leader to teach a course structured around ethical issues arising in business. Students evaluated the course favorably, but the instructors reported that they themselves learned even more about one another's fields.

While individual faculty members can take personal initiatives to make contacts outside the academic sphere, efforts at the institutional level require collective action and administrative support. At Indiana University, the college of arts and sciences established its own placement office in 1976 at the urging of faculty members concerned about students' career prospects. Faculty in arts and sciences serve on an advisory council, and the dean of the college provides strong support for the office. The development of the Liberal Arts in Business program at the University of Maryland received similar support from the provost for arts and humanities; such political clout was essential for the successful inauguration of the program. Administrative support is not always enough, however; the clusters program at the University of Iowa was not endorsed by faculty despite outside grants and the enthusiasm of the dean. Faculty resistance centered on the concern that undue vocationalism would undermine the integrity of the liberal arts.

The faculty is not the villain in such stories; concerns about the integrity of undergraduate education are legitimate. At many institutions, moreover, the incentive system rewards publications and disciplinary specialization, not a concern about liberal education and its value for students' careers. The demographic realities of the baby boom, exacerbated by periods of sluggishness in the economy, have brought unprecedented pressures from students and parents for undergraduate programs that lead to good jobs. And business has not always done its part. Firms whose chief executive officers speak glowingly of the importance of liberal education too often limit their actual recruiting to students with technical and professional training. Faculty, students, parents, and executives alike have been guilty of taking a short-term perspective on the purposes of liberal education when the real value of such study comes through its application over a lifetime career.

As this chapter demonstrates, however, colleges and universities are providing many programs to assist students in making the transition from liberal education to careers in business. The focus is appropriately on students, the self-awareness they have, the content of their academic programs, the advice they receive. Institutions concerned about liberal education should do more than prepare students, however; they should speak directly with decision makers in the business world about the importance of liberal education in addressing corporate needs. Much of the conversation can be initiated by administrators in liberal arts programs through corporate advisory committees, executive-in-residence programs, and other means of communication described in this chapter.

Conclusion

This volume makes the case that business needs liberally educated managers. This chapter describes what liberal arts colleges and colleges of arts and sciences are doing to help prepare them. Faculty and administrators have weighed criticisms of traditional programs and have responded with effective new activities. On many campuses today, undergraduates seek—and obtain —both a strong liberal education and sound career preparation.

The many examples in this chapter also demonstrate the diversity among colleges and universities, not only in size and student profile but also in the ways in which they have addressed the growing concern for careers after college. Some institutions have maintained a traditional academic program enriched with noncredit activities and strong career advising; others have developed innovative courses, career minors, and work opportunities within the academic program.

Arts and sciences undergraduate programs are presenting a new type of candidate to employers seeking potential managers: graduates with a liberal education *plus* knowledge of, or experience with, business. These graduates are well equipped to tackle real problems in the business world. With increasing confidence, firms can look to liberal arts graduates to meet the challenges facing American business today and in the future.

9

Joseph S. Johnston, Jr.

Recommendations
for Business
and Academic Leaders

"Men are men before they are lawyers, physicians or business-men, and if you educate them to become capable and sensible men, they will make themselves capable and sensible lawyers and businessmen." The era in which John Stuart Mill spoke these words (in 1867, in an address at St. Andrews') has passed. With it has passed that supreme confidence—many would say wishful idealism—regarding a liberal education that they express. In its place, we have not a more tempered optimism about the role of liberal education in preparing men—*and* women—for work, but actual doubt about its efficacy. This doubt besets college faculty and administrators as well as business executives, and it has taken hold at an unfortunate time.

Preceding chapters have shown that the broad and rigorous education of managers serves business well. Current empirical evidence bears out the testimony of a range of business executives that the skills, abilities, and habits of mind fostered by a liberal education are of practical career value. Liberally educated managers, as a group, excel in business, and their firms reap the benefits of their excellence.

What makes a loss of confidence in the value of liberal education particularly untimely is the prospect of a future in which this kind of academic preparation will be more and more essential but in which the pressures militating against it will only increase. Change is, as the cliché has it, the one thing we can be sure of. As we have seen, the likely directions of change in business will put a premium on the liberally educated mind. Yet the short-term competitive pressures on business are intensifying. To meet its short-term goals, business may be under increasing pressure to act against its own long-term self-interest by preferring the narrowly over the broadly prepared in hiring and promotion. Students will be under pressures of their own. The job market for college graduates will remain tight. Many students will continue to feel that they need specialized education in order to compete. Their demands and educational choices will maintain the pressure on colleges and universities to offer programs that serve students' professional aspirations in as direct a way as possible. Clearly, efforts to preserve or reassert the centrality of liberal learning will run counter to powerful forces.

Mutual misunderstanding by business and the academy is inhibiting the vigorous collaboration needed to improve the situation. As Kathryn Mohrman (1983a, p. 3) has written elsewhere, "Many faculty members have spent most of their lives in academic settings; many business people have not been on a campus since their own graduation. Without some knowledge of the procedures and goals of the two sectors it is difficult to see relationships between business and liberal education." At present, few in academia and business see those relationships clearly; few have even tried. The old distortions and stereotypes—of faculty as, say, woolly-headed idealists and businesspeople as profit-mongering lowbrows—still enjoy considerable currency.

The effects of this estrangement of business from liberal education are increasingly costly. It is producing managers ever less prepared to advance in their careers or to help their employers compete, domestically or abroad, in tomorrow's highly dynamic marketplace. It is exacerbating recent enrollment declines in arts and sciences programs. It is eliminating a source of curricular enrichment there, in the business school, and in corporate management development programs. It is, finally, preventing more and more students from taking the time they need to explore broadly and discover and develop skills and interests before making crucial career commitments. Virtually no one is well served by the current situation. Yet inattention to the problem, inertia, or preoccupation with short-term paybacks seems to have prevented most of those in positions to undertake reform from doing so.

Upon first hearing Wagner's music, Mark Twain remarked, "it's not as bad as it sounds." Perhaps not. A situation that serves no one gives all parties incentive to change. Many may not readily recognize their self-interest. We have seen, however, that there is persuasive argument and credible evidence with which to convince them. There have also been numerous initiatives in business, business schools, and arts and science programs that can provide models for further efforts.

Incentives, arguments, evidence, and models will make little difference without the follow-through of concerned professionals in both worlds. But those who would be agents of change need to know the roles in which they can be effective and the changes that are most critical. The remainder of this chapter provides two sets of discursive recommendations. One set is for business executives. The other, for professionals in the academic community, has three parts, addressing in turn faculty in the arts and sciences, faculty in business programs, and administrators. The recommendations are, by design, broad enough to have general interest and to leave the practicing professional discretion in narrowing and applying them to particular circumstances. They are not exhaustive, but they do suggest areas of priority and some effective strategies for change.

These recommendations reflect directly the experience and ideas of many practitioners in business and higher education, for they draw not only on preceding chapters and related materials (see especially Hiley, 1982) but on the agendas for further action developed at some ten national and regional conferences held since 1982 (Mohrman, 1983a; Moyer, 1983; Association of American Colleges, 1984, 1985). Convened by the Association of American Colleges in Boston, Philadelphia, Chicago, Memphis, Los Angeles, and other cities, these working meetings pooled the insights of a total of over five hundred executives, faculty, and administrators nationwide.

Recommendations to the Business Community

The essential recommendation to the business community is that it recognize that in hiring and promoting managers it is making long-term judgments—human capital *investment* decisions. This last phrase is jargon, but it makes the point well. With people as with securities, there is investment and there is trading. Trading decisions are governed by short-term considerations. Investment judgments are not. What should count in hiring managers, with a few obvious qualifications, is a candidate's ability to produce for a substantial period of time.

The case has been made here that those most likely to possess that ability are the liberally educated. Some will be generalists. Others will be specialists who are also broadly prepared. There is a need for both in business. It is tunnel vision and a lack of flexibility that have no place there.

Insofar as generalists in particular are concerned, companies should take note that more are coming onto the market prepared by diversified course work and work experience to make an immediate contribution. Of course, some cost more than they pay back for a while. They may not be able to snap off an accelerated depreciation or define a security's *beta*. But they will often be less risky hires than more narrowly trained technicians. The breadth of their foundation makes them less likely to grow obsolete in time.

Business leaders face the task of bringing the knowledge and perspectives of liberal education into every level of their organizations. This means, first of all, working with colleges to ensure that the supply of liberally educated graduates is adequate to business's needs. Forward-looking top executives will ally themselves visibly with faculty and administrators attempting to stem the tide of vocationalism at the undergraduate level and provide moral and financial support for the maintenance of high standards of general and liberal education. They will use the influence they have on the curriculum of the business program, both undergraduate and graduate, to ensure its breadth and rigor.

Business executives should assume more responsibility for helping faculty understand the goals, procedures, and needs of business and the applicability of a liberal education in a management career. Faculty and students (nontechnical as well as technical) should be exposed firsthand to the corporation through specially arranged visits and seminars. Both can be involved in carefully planned and well-supervised internships for more extended periods. In the case of faculty, these can often be arranged as part of exchanges that send managers to a campus. There may be good opportunities for using faculty as consultants in the company. And, in what can be an enlightening experience for all involved, selected faculty can participate alongside executives in middle- and upper-level corporate management development programs.

This work of informing faculty and students will bring executives onto campus, too. They have a contribution to make there in explaining business's need for liberally educated managers and the importance of a liberal education to career success. Appropriate forums include classes, in which they can team teach with regular faculty or serve as guest lecturers; career exploration seminars; and the advising of small groups and individuals. Some executives may have the opportunity to serve on boards or on visiting and other advisory committees; they can work there very effectively both to strengthen liberal education's centrality to academic programs and to clarify its ties to managerial work. Employees planning to participate in executive loan programs or take social service leaves should routinely be encouraged to consider projects at colleges and universities that can help improve the understanding of business by students and faculty.

Business should undertake research on the career performance in business of liberally educated graduates. With their personnel systems, computer resources, and in-house research expertise, many businesses are in a good position to produce sound comparative data. Positive findings, paralleling the conclusions drawn in Chapter Four, will not only give credibility to the firm's message to students and faculty but educate many in the firm itself to the importance of recruiting and developing broadly educated managers.

Business has another role in developing the supply of optimally prepared managers; it can encourage all managers and employees to take advantage of liberal education opportunities. Many midcareer engineers and business school graduates have a sense of the personal and career value of broad education but assume that they missed their own opportunities for liberal learning years ago. It will be to both the firm's and the employee's advantage to see that they have not. Working adults are often more motivated and thoughtful learners at age thirty-five or fifty than they were at age twenty. They often make much better progress than they think possible, no matter how late they start or whatever their educational deficits. And, because liberal learning is a lifetime pursuit, it has no less value to those who have already completed degree programs. All managers at all levels can benefit. This means that liberal learning can begin benefiting the corporation today.

Business should join with colleges and universities in exploring liberal learning opportunities at the workplace as well as on campus. Chapter Five reviews a range of continuing education programs in both environments that might serve as models. If university-based programs are to be well utilized, corporations must define their tuition-reimbursement policies broadly enough not to exclude all but directly job-related course work.

On the demand side, a business will want to assure that it is competitive in identifying and securing liberally educated managerial talent. Having sometimes been faulted for inconsistencies of word and action, CEOs may want personally to order an audit of hiring practices. One large industrial firm, widely reputed to be a leader in hiring liberally educated managers, recently learned from such an audit that, in fact, fewer than 3 percent of its hires during the previous year were liberal arts graduates. Dealing with such numbers requires urging middle managers and recruiters to give every appropriate consideration to broadly prepared graduates. (At least one company president has invited recruiters in for a chat to find out more about practices in this regard and to convey directly top management's priorities, which he felt were not getting through.) Do recruiters seek candidates for entry-level jobs in the arts and sciences as well as the business school? Have they provided career development offices with good, current information on where in their operations liberally educated generalists would fit in? Are preferred candidates described in terms of skills and abilities or in terms of particular combinations of course work? If the latter, qualified and very promising candidates may be deterred even from applying. By contrast, employers who explicitly convey in their recruitment materials and job-opening announcements an interest in liberally educated graduates have found that they can attract larger and more able populations of applicants.

A firm interested in attracting high-caliber liberally educated graduates should also examine and, if necessary, redesign its provisions for management training. Such programs are often equalizers, quickly narrowing any competence gap between technical and nontechnical graduates. Firms without such programs may wish to consider instituting them as a way of attracting these candidates. Companies with established training programs may need to ensure that these are not at any point arbitrarily inaccessible to employees who, despite a broad background, may lack particular technical expertise.

Overall, the most competitive firms will be those that realize best what liberal education is, what management is, and how the two relate. They will appreciate that a college education is more than occupational training and that the successful placement of students with business employers is not one of that education's primary objectives. They will realize that, because management is a demanding and dynamic task that one grows into, the hiring and development of managers must be approached as a long-term investment. They will recognize also that the liberally educated, as a group, are well prepared for business management—in large part because they have been prepared for more.

Recommendations to the Academic Community

Faculty in the Arts and Sciences. The relationship of liberal learning and professional preparation is venerable; so is the tension between them. As Paul Zingg (1980, p. 324) points out, "Confucius lamented some 2500 years ago that it was becoming increasingly difficult to find anyone who would study for three years without thinking of money." Plato's Academy emphasized the need for broad study to build character and pursue truth for its own sake; but ancient Greece also had its Sophists, who emphasized the development of rhetorical and analytical skills as preparation for careers (Rehnke, 1982–83). Students at the earliest colleges—Bologna, Paris, and Oxford—studied a curriculum that, for all its arcane appearance, was in its time highly practical. Logic and Latin, as Arthur Levine (1983) reminds us, were then highly marketable skills. Indeed, the introduction of Greek at Cambridge, itself founded to train clerks for the king's service, was "denounced as a crude vocationalism" (Rhodes, 1985, p. 80). Like their ancient and medieval precursors, the earliest American colleges were, of course, charged with providing a practical liberal education. A major part of their mission was to produce a learned clergy fit to lead the colonial communities. Today's struggle to relate liberal learning to career preparation is not new, then. As Yogi Berra once remarked, "it's déjà vu all over again."

That is only a part of the lesson for arts and sciences faculty. For it is clear as well that history gives no reason to regard the two goals as mutually exclusive. They exist in a natural tension, and too often it is destructive. But this tension seems often to have figured constructively in distinguished programs of study that pursued both goals in an integrated fashion.

In our time, of course, there is great diversity among the missions of colleges and universities. It is a strength of our system of higher education that some institutions are traditionally more responsive to external, market considerations than others and that they differ significantly in the priority they give to preprofessional education. For every college touting a "practical liberal arts" program, there is another far more concerned that attempts to integrate liberal learning and career preparation might compromise the former's very value. As we have seen in Chapter Eight, however, there are ways that even those arts and sciences programs most committed to a "classical" curriculum can assist interested students. The range of steps by which the gap between liberal education and business can be closed includes many that are co- and extracurricular. Conversely, there is no program committed to preparing students for the world of work that cannot strengthen its ability to do so by increasing its emphasis on liberal learning. Indeed, the first priority of all arts and sciences faculty, whatever the institutional setting, should be excellence in liberal education—doing what they have always done, but with more attention to doing it well.

As some businesspeople tirelessly point out, the job begins with the basics. Neither business nor higher education nor the prospects for their mutual cooperation are served by graduates who cannot write, think, and speak clearly and who cannot handle numbers. The academy's claims for liberal arts graduates encompass far more than these abilities. Yet too often these claims only widen what Cornell president Frank H. T. Rhodes has termed the "alarming gap between the pretensions of the liberal arts and their performance" (Rhodes, 1985, p. 80).

Faculty should exercise more responsibly their influence over students' consideration of and preparation for careers. Their roles both as classroom teachers and as advisers are important in this regard. Faculty members' performance in both can be improved by efforts to learn more about business. Unfortunately, this is one subject on which some liberal arts faculty have always felt themselves free to be uninformed. They think of business and businesspeople in unwarranted stereotypes. They may be amiably indifferent or openly suspicious toward the world of commerce. But, whatever their attitudes, they communicate them willy-nilly to their students. Many faculty are at a loss to know what to say when a student expresses an interest in entering the business world, let alone when one asks for counsel on how best to prepare for such a step.

Perhaps the best way for interested faculty to develop an understanding of business and its relation to the education they provide is through personal contact with executives. Executives can be invited to the campus for occasions as formal as an evening lecture or as casual as a brown-bag lunch with students and faculty. Some faculty have found team teaching or guest-lecturer arrangements with selected business executives productive. Another vehicle for bringing business leaders to campus is the executive residency—a stay of from several days' to a year's length during which the executive may contribute to the academic and campus life as teacher, counselor, colleague, or fellow student. Career information seminars provide good occasions for visits from business representatives, and faculty can learn much by attending them. Finally, faculty interested in learning about business will in most cases find board members and former students now in business pleased to help.

Nothing can substitute for direct exposure to the world of business itself. The number of liberal arts faculty who have participated in corporate faculty-in-residence programs is small, but most agree that such arrangements are useful. Other promising means of entry include the faculty member's service as a consultant—a possibility that more nontechnical faculty should explore—and participation, alongside business colleagues, in corporate middle- and upper-level management development programs. Faculty who take opportunities such as these not only will learn more about the connection of their work and the business world but may also be able to demonstrate the relevance of the one to the other.

They will also see firsthand a reality that all faculty should appreciate: that there are, in many instances, good reasons why business cannot hire or advance individuals lacking in technical skills. Despite what some seem to think, for instance, chief executive officers do not in most cases determine the kind of candidates who are hired for entry-level positions. Nor is it appropriate as a rule to blame the problems of liberal arts graduates on recruiters and others in human resources—who are, as a group, more likely than most in business to have and to value liberal arts backgrounds. The responsibility for setting hiring priorities lies as a rule with a much larger if less visible population: middle management. The middle manager has the work to be done and specifies the qualifications of those who will do it. But the short-term operational pressures upon the middle manager are intense, and they serve to obscure the long-term view of hiring and promotion. In this environment, for the middle manager to pass over the specialist, however narrowly gauged, in order to hire any but the best-prepared products of a liberal education can seem a heroic decision. It is too easy, after all, for faculty to ask the middle manager to hire a graduate who cannot do the job now on the grounds that in time the new employee will flourish; middle managers will no more relish that prospect than faculty do the prospect of accepting unprepared students into their classes.

Thus, although much can be accomplished if more middle managers are persuaded of the value of liberally educated employees and begin in large numbers to consider and seek them out, progress will not come easily. Relatively few employers believe now that traditional liberal arts majors—without any business or computer courses, without work experience, and without access to a management training program—have the wherewithal to survive at the entry level. More and more, if they are to attract offers and last long enough to demonstrate their potential, graduates need directly job-related skills with which to make immediate contributions. Faculty have a role to play in helping interested students develop these within a coherent program of liberal education.

There is much that arts and sciences faculty can do in their classrooms to help students relate their education to the requirements of work. Proven steps include assigning readings or writing and research topics that deal at least in part with the issue and even inviting in selected course alumni or others in professional life who can thoughtfully and articulately connect the two spheres. To the extent that faculty discuss the purposes of education with their students, they may understandably stress the value of learning for its own sake, if only as a corrective to other environmental forces that promote vocationalism. In doing so, however, they risk making liberal education and career preparation seem mutually exclusive goals and leading students to think they must choose between them. A wiser course may be to help students discover the work-related abilities fostered by their studies. Emphasizing this aspect of liberal education may make good sense in advanced as well as introductory undergraduate courses, even where that entails placing somewhat less emphasis on content and scholarly apprenticeship.

Liberal arts faculty whose teaching pursues a faddish relevance to business are no more helpful than those who traffic in the old distortions. In teaching and developing curricula, however, faculty should be alert to appropriate opportunities to illuminate the powerful role of the modern corporation in American society. Courses might be considered that examine business, labor unions, and the professions as important institutions in our time—or that explore management and leadership drawing on such material as Plato's *Republic,* Machiavelli's *The Prince,* Thomas Hobbes on governance, and works by Max Weber, Henry Taylor, and Henri Fayol.

Whatever the formal division of responsibility at their institutions, faculty in the liberal arts have important roles to play as both career and academic counselors. This is not to insist that faculty develop a detailed knowledge of the occupational options available to their students. But they should have enough general knowledge of the world of work—including business—to help students think through their perennial questions: How is *this* going to help me once I graduate and what can I *do* with what I'm learning? Fortunately, faculty have, in the career development office, a particularly rich—and typically underutilized —resource for self-education. In the staff of that office, arts and sciences faculty will often find like-minded associates; unfortunately, this is not always the case, especially where the office serves an institution of which the arts and sciences program is only one part. Liberal arts faculty at such schools should introduce themselves to their career development colleagues. There are many concerns to be talked about, much support to be given on both sides. At more than one institution, for instance, faculty initiatives have now persuaded the career planning office to abandon the practice of allowing recruiters to "prescreen" candidates by major—a key step in assuring all students fair treatment in on-campus recruiting.

Business Faculty. It is at least an even bet that some business faculty think about a liberal education along the lines humorously set out by Robert Benchley (1942) in his essay "What College Did To Me." Benchley reports learning in his freshman year that "Charlemagne either died or was born or did something with the Holy Roman Empire in 800 . . . French nouns ending in "aison" are feminine, almost everything you need to know about a subject is in the encyclopedia . . . the law of diminishing returns means that after a certain margin is reached, returns begin to diminish. This may not be correctly stated, but there is a law by that name" (p. 216). But what might Benchley have written after a year in the average business school? The distance between the two parodies, the one above and the one we can imagine, defines the considerable area in which we can work toward an integration of liberal and career preparation—to the enrichment and strengthening of both.

The American Assembly of Collegiate Schools of Business (AACSB), with its 630 member institutions, does have several key policies that encourage breadth in business study. It requires that accredited undergraduate programs allow no more than 60 percent of students' course work to be in the areas of business and economics (American Assembly of Collegiate Schools of Business, 1984-85). The assembly also recommends that students concentrate their professional work in their last two years of study and use their first two for "foundation" work, which would "normally include courses in communications, mathematics, social sciences, humanities and the natural sciences" (pp. 28-29). These policies are welcome and helpful. But they leave a critical role to individual institutions in ensuring breadth of distribution. They do not address at all a more fundamental problem in business education, the dearth of liberal learning opportunities in business courses themselves.

Recommendations to business faculty must begin here, with the strong suggestion that they not leave the liberal education of business students to the liberal arts. Too often, business students see their liberal education as something to get out of the way as a preliminary to the real thing. Business faculty should bring the perspectives of the liberal arts into the business program, into business courses themselves, both basic and advanced. They should make the whole curriculum a vehicle for liberal education. Indeed, the full integration of liberal and professional business education entails not just sprinkling the business school with liberal arts courses or building liberal arts "components" into business courses. It requires the business faculty's raising those issues and employing those modes of enquiry associated with liberal learning throughout every course. It is as important—and as feasible—to do this in decision sciences as in management, and in investments as in marketing.

Most decision-science teachers, for example, are careful to expose their students to sensitivity analysis, showing how answers vary with numerical assumptions. But too few encourage students to grapple with the limitations of models in solving problems resistant to quantification—the deceptive area where clear quantities coexist with imponderables and the two cannot easily be distinguished. More attention should be given even here—especially here—to identifying the value choices inherent in alternate solutions that need to be factored into managerial deliberations. Some investments courses, to take another example, are merely statistical excursions into the world of modern portfolio theory. This body of knowledge is important, but no more so than a grasp of market psychology and history and the vagaries of an institution that, as John Kenneth Galbraith put it, has predicted seven of the last five recessions. International, ethical, and political dimensions—the market has them all, and the student of investments who has not learned about them has by definition been too narrowly trained.

A starting point for many business faculty can be the renewal of their ties with faculty in the arts and sciences (a group too often split themselves along disciplinary lines). Long separated by a variety of factors, but sharing deep intellectual roots and interests, business and liberal arts faculty have much to offer one another. Informal discussion with arts and sciences colleagues and then more formal team teaching or joint research and writing projects have enriched a number of business programs. They have led to the discovery of some effective ways of enforcing attention in business courses to oral and written communication, to ethics, to international considerations. They have helped business faculty develop alternatives to an over-emphasis on formal decision-making tools, unambiguous problems, and situations that deal simplistically with human relationships. In some instances, they have led to permanent new course offerings—with such titles as Risk, Justice and Economic Systems, Business Ethics, and Literature and Leadership—the very focus of which is the rootedness of business practice in broader contexts.

Chapters Six and Seven have also suggested other channels for collaboration—including a role for humanists and others in the liberal arts in the preparation of business cases. They have challenged business programs to employ directly some of the methods and key texts of historical, literary, and philosophical study. They have called for an entirely new commitment to the study of the management of people and still more concern with fostering not merely verbal competence but real mastery of the language.

The work done in these areas will need to be explained well to both students and employers, but there is in this need an important opportunity for education. Like their peers in the liberal arts, business students should be encouraged to think more carefully about the purposes of their education and to examine their course work for the development of broad understandings and competencies. And students and businesses both need to be aggressively sold on the practicality of reform. In recent years, the corporate community has repeatedly expressed its dissatisfaction with the business schools, in large part for failings highlighted here. If only because the changes proposed here will address many of these shortcomings, corporations are potentially the business schools' partners in these efforts. They should be briefed and enlisted and their executives and recruiters challenged to show by word and deed their support for change.

Administrators. Many of the above recommendations to faculty apply in obvious ways to those who administer arts and sciences and business programs and the institutions of which they are parts. But such administrators also have the special responsibility of creating the environment and providing the support and incentives that will make change possible and likely. Other, nonacademic administrators—particularly professionals in continuing education and career development—have distinctive roles as well.

Top administrators should take as their first priority ensuring the centrality and quality of liberal education throughout their institutions—in the arts and sciences, in the business program, and elsewhere. The arguments given here for liberal education's value to business are generalizable; its importance to the individual and society, as well as all the professions, has been argued often and powerfully before. Although this volume has argued a narrower case, provision of quality liberal education is an essential task of all a college's or university's undergraduate academic programs.

The types of support and incentives that will encourage faculty to link preparation for business and liberal education are familiar. Few faculty in business or the liberal arts will be able to do much in their classrooms to illuminate connections without research and course planning—activities that require time and money. Release time, paid and unpaid leaves, and grant funds must be made available to faculty who need them for these purposes. Unless such activity has a place alongside research and teaching as a criterion for tenure and promotion committees, few nonbusiness faculty will use their leaves and summers to learn about businesses or undertake involvements with them that might foster mutual understanding and cooperation. Similarly, few faculty are likely to see informed career advising as one of their responsibilities until it figures somehow in their evaluation. Carrots or sticks—or both—can be used by institutions wishing to relate liberal education and professional business preparation. But unless institutional priorities are in some way compellingly communicated, redirection of efforts is unlikely.

A particular kind of work in which faculty should be encouraged is research that will clarify the outcomes of liberal learning and the relationship between liberal education and management. There is a pressing need for good comparative data on companies' experiences with employees of different educational backgrounds. The collection and analysis of this data can provide opportunities for close collaboration with business. Alumni studies tracing, among other things, the career experiences of a particular institution's graduates provide another natural channel for faculty expertise.

By demonstrating the diverse contributions of liberally educated graduates in the corporate community, research can help overcome the important problem of faculty ignorance and indifference. Faculty need to be educated—those in business, typically, about the centrality of liberal learning, and those in the liberal arts about the career value of what they teach—and they need to appreciate that there is a problem. Preoccupied with their work, disinclined to get involved with institutional problems, and able to operate at several removes from the worlds of business, institutional enrollment shifts, and the entry-level job market, many faculty will never concern themselves with the situation. Yet others are not now doing what they might simply because they do not know the problem's extent or the ways it can be addressed. Shown data on the success in business of the liberally educated against a backdrop of current statistics on students' educational choices, these faculty may feel themselves motivated and equipped for the first time to confront the narrow vocationalism around them. A handful of concerned faculty can provide the critical mass of political support for programmatic and institutional change. Equipped with feasible models of reform, they are the best possible ones to bring it about.

The education of current faculty is often not enough, however, for incoming faculty may need to be oriented to the importance of these issues, too. When hiring new faculty, some institutions may even want to assess candidates' interest in helping make both career preparation and liberal education integral parts of their students' experience as learners.

Academic administrators have an obvious stake in strengthening and increasing liberal learning offerings for businesspeople. Directors of continuing education should alert businesses to the practical wisdom of encouraging lifelong liberal education and urge them to provide financial support for their employees' enrollments in nontechnical as well as technical courses. It is especially critical to extend liberal learning to middle managers, many of whom will have had little experience with it but who, as a group, have great influence over the hiring and development of others in the corporation. Continuing education courses should be made as accessible as possible to corporate audiences. The time, place, and coverage of such offerings and the credit they carry may all be appropriate variables, so long as standards of rigor and liberal learning are not compromised.

Of course, colleges and universities also need to do a better job of helping more traditional student populations bridge the worlds of liberal education and business management. This often requires some rethinking of the organizational separation of the student services and academic functions. The lack of connection and coordination between the academic and business communities is well known; but within the academic community itself, there is often little more among faculty, admissions officers, student advisers, and career planners. Because each can influence both career choice and academic planning, their functions should be closely coordinated. Admissions representatives need to be knowledgeable and aggressive in informing candidates of the value of a liberal education and in helping them to begin thinking even before their matriculation about its purposes and applications. We have presented above some of the standards to which faculty should be held as teachers and informed advisers who can encourage and help students to deal with these issues in sophisticated ways. Academic advising, whether the responsibility of faculty or of student personnel administrators, should address students' academic and career development as comprehensively as possible. And the career development function—often no more a part of the academic life of the institution than the campus health service—needs itself to serve an important and integral educational function. Senior administrators should help professionals in all these areas understand that they are engaged in a common effort, for they have much to teach one another and can do much, formally and informally, to enhance one another's effectiveness.

It is usually on the career development office, however,

that the most responsibility falls for assisting students in their search for connections between their liberal learning and possible careers. Many current professionals in career development are thoughtful and creative advocates of liberal education. But top administrators should put still more priority on obtaining or developing trained personnel for this function, sensitive to the value of liberal learning. They should also provide the budgetary support for a broader range of programs and services than many institutions now offer.

The strong career development office will repay the investment. It will reach out actively to involve students in their own career planning, helping them see that they themselves must take responsibility for it early in their college years. It will give counseling, encourage self-assessment, sponsor workshops and panel discussions, provide a career library, arrange internships and part-time or intermittent work experiences, offer non-credit skills modules, teach career development courses exploring the nature and meaning of work, assist in resumé preparation, and educate students in job search and interview techniques. It will make an extra effort to prepare female and minority students for the special difficulties they may face in the job search and beyond.

Good career development professionals will protect students not only from discrimination in recruitment but from their own premature career choices, encouraging them to keep options open and to avail themselves fully of the educational diversity around them; they will help students to plan and examine their liberal educations in terms of work-related abilities, knowledge, and skills fostered rather than as accumulations of so many courses in particular subject areas or majors; they will help the music major see in herself as much potential for management as the accounting major and, should she wish to pursue business as a career, help her consider within a balanced program electives that can give her specific and immediately applicable skills. In all these ways, strong career development offices can give students a sense of direction and of appropriate preparation—something far too many liberal arts graduates lack as they enter the job market.

Colleges and universities have had success, finally, with

public relations and "outreach" efforts. These include special events designed to highlight the connections between liberal education and business. Some have sponsored conferences, ranging in length from an afternoon to two full days, that bring together faculty and business executives to discuss those connections and consider ways of strengthening them. In some cases, these events have led to working groups that have continued to meet informally and plan collaborative efforts. But much can be done to stimulate thinking and concern even without a gathering. Thanks to the print and broadcast media, college or university administrators can get the message about liberal learning's value to business out to those who need to hear it. Television and radio spots, videotapes, brochures, and wall posters are some of the means by which institutions have done so.

If business is to appreciate its need for liberally educated managers and our institutions of higher education are to supply them, top administrators are the ones who must see that it happens. Many of the undertakings recommended here for faculty and line administrators require initiation, leadership, and even high-minded coercion from the top; and only senior administrators typically have access to corporate top management, whose support and involvement are critical. Administrators, then, must become advocates and entrepreneurs. They must broker. They must—hard news—commit funds. In these steps they have the best assurance that others will begin to do their parts and general progress will begin to be made.

At the outset, we began with a question: why should anyone—business executive, faculty member, or administrator—be concerned with the connections between liberal education and business management? We have since found our answer. Both the college and the corporation are ill served by confusion about these ties. Neither is as strong as it could be if liberal learning were more central to the preparation of business leaders. Professionals in both these institutions have important roles to play in bringing about the needed change. It is a matter of common sense and compelling self-interest for them to begin taking action now.

Thomas B. Jones

Selected Resources

The theme of this volume, liberal education for management, has attracted substantial interest throughout business and higher education recently. The result is a growing list of books, research studies, conference reports, articles, recommendations, and other resources that readers will want to consult. The bibliography and resources collected here are a brief, selected cross section of what is currently available.

Liberal Education and Career Success

George O. Klemp, Jr., "Three Factors of Success," in Dyckman W. Vermilye (ed.), _Relating Work and Education_ (San Francisco: Jossey-Bass, 1977), pp. 102–109, is a good introduction to more specific works on the link between liberal education and management. Klemp and his associates researched a wide variety of career areas, including business management, to identify which types of knowledge, skills, abilities, and characteristics distinguish the successful performer from others. Klemp found that career success primarily involved cognitive skills, interpersonal skills, and motivational characteristics. These skills and characteristics, as Arthur W. Chickering concludes in his article "Integrating Liberal Education, Work, and Human Devel-

209

opment," *American Association for Higher Education Bulletin,*
1981, *31* (7), 1, 11–13, 16, are directly related to the aims of
liberal education. Ann Bisconti and Jean Kessler, *College and
Other Stepping Stones: A Study of Learning Experiences That
Contribute to Effective Performance in Early and Long-Run
Jobs* (Bethlehem, Pa.: College Placement Council Foundation,
1980), and Ann Bisconti and Lewis Solmon, *College Education
on the Job: The Graduates' Viewpoint* (Bethlehem, Pa.: College
Placement Council Foundation, 1976), provide additional perspectives on the conclusions drawn by Klemp and Chickering.
David G. Winter, David C. McClelland, and Abigail J. Stewart,
in *A New Case for the Liberal Arts: Assessing Institutional
Goals and Student Development* (San Francisco: Jossey-Bass,
1981), have developed assessment techniques to measure liberal
education competencies, and the authors suggest significant applications of these competencies for working and living after
college.

Business Leaders on Liberal Education

Business leaders have often analyzed the contribution
that a liberal education makes to career success in management
and how a liberal education is put to use in business. Joseph
Pichler, a former business school dean and now a corporate
leader, discusses the development of the values and skills that
are necessary for executive success—with special emphasis on the
importance of the humanities disciplines—in *Executive Values,
Executive Functions, and the Humanities* (Washington, D.C.:
Association of American Colleges, 1983). Judd H. Alexander,
executive vice-president for the James River Corporation, ex-
plains how the value of liberal learning increases as managers
rise into positions of greater scope and responsibility in *Liberal
Education and Executive Leadership* (1983; a pamphlet re-
printed by the Association of American Colleges for the Associated Colleges of the Midwest). Roger B. Smith, *Why Business
Needs the Liberal Arts* (1981; a pamphlet available from the
Council for Financial Aid to Education, 680 Fifth Avenue, New
York, N.Y. 10019), points out that the public responsibilities of

business require personnel with a liberal education because of what it contributes in terms of breadth and depth as opposed to specialization. John C. Sawhill, *The Perils of Specialization or Why Corporations Should Support the Liberal Arts* (New York: Council for Financial Aid to Education, 1978), discusses the key perspectives and skills that employees with a liberal education offer to the corporations for the changing circumstances of the later twentieth century. From the vantage point of an educator and a corporate executive, Ralph Z. Sorenson, in "A Lifetime of Learning to Manage Effectively," *Wall Street Journal,* Feb. 28, 1983, p. 20, and in "The Interdependence of the Professional and Humanist Worlds," in Katherine S. Guroff (ed.), *Quality in Liberal Learning* (Washington, D.C.: Association of American Colleges, 1981), pp. 245–249, sets out desirable traits for successful managers and notes their relationship to a liberal education.

The Value of Liberal Education for Business Careers

Higher education has often made the case for liberal education and its value for business careers. A recent contribution to that case is Kathryn Mohrman's "Liberal Learning Is a Sound Human Capital Investment," *Educational Record,* 1983, *64* (4), 56–61, which argues for a broader view of human capital investment that includes the results of a liberal education. Mohrman also surveys activities in higher education that connect undergraduate study with careers in business. Paul W. Zingg, "Three Myths of Pre-Professionalism," *Liberal Education,* 1983, *69* (3), 209–224, disputes the common wisdom that training for a career and liberal learning are mutually exclusive; that premed, prelaw, and prebusiness are the only programs that really count toward success in a profession; and that to succeed in business, students should avoid the liberal arts. Christine A. Gould, *Consider Your Options: Business Opportunities for Liberal Arts Graduates* (Washington, D.C.: Association of American Colleges, 1983), is a career guide with several case examples of how a liberal education can help one attain individual success in a business career.

Liberal Education and Career Preparation

The integration of liberal learning with career preparation at the undergraduate level is an important issue in higher education. Charles S. Green III and Richard G. Salem (eds.), *Liberal Learning and Careers,* New Directions for Teaching and Learning, no. 6 (San Francisco: Jossey-Bass, 1981), contains several essays that address how the liberal arts should and can respond to the massive shift of enrollments toward vocational study. Bradley H. Sagan, "Careers, Competencies, and Liberal Education," *Liberal Education,* 1979, *65* (2), 150–166, argues for the adequacy of the liberal arts experience as preparation for modern job markets. He suggests several ways in which the liberal arts curriculum can be adapted to the career competencies necessary for undergraduates entering new job markets. Mary Ann F. Rehnke (ed.), *Liberal Learning and Career Preparation,* Current Issues in Higher Education, 1982–83, no. 2 (available from the American Association for Higher Education, One Dupont Circle, Suite 600, Washington, D.C. 20036), contains several essays on the subject, a survey of sixty-one career preparation programs, and an ERIC bibliography. William A. Cook and James C. Gonyea, *Putting Liberal Arts to Work* (1981; available through the New England Center for Career Development, P.O. Box 293, Hocksett, New Hampshire 03106), charts the results of two national surveys on the question: What career-related skills are taught in the liberal arts? Closely related to this question is Paul Breen and Urban Whitaker, *The Learner's Guide* (San Francisco: Learning Center, 1982), which contains advising and career development materials on seventy-six work-related, transferable liberal arts skills. Edwin J. Delattre, "Real Career Education Comes from the Liberal Arts," *Chronicle of Higher Education,* Jan. 5, 1983, *25,* p. 80, provides an excellent view on what a career encompasses and why students need the liberal arts as preparation.

Research Studies on Liberal Learning and Business Careers

Research evidence on the link between liberal learning and successful business careers is increasing. The most-quoted study, Robert E. Beck, *Career Patterns: The Liberal Arts Major in Bell System Management* (Washington, D.C.: Association of American Colleges, 1981), considers longitudinal data on AT&T employees over a twenty-year period, reporting on how management employees from different academic majors fare in terms of managerial potential and progress. One conclusion of the study is that students who major in the humanities and social sciences do quite well over the long run in management careers. Ann Howard's *College Experience and Managerial Performance* (New York: AT&T, 1985) follows up on Beck's study, adding new research information. Stanley T. Burns, a contributor to this volume, in *From Student to Banker: Observations from the Chase Bank* (Washington, D.C.: Association of American Colleges, 1983), demonstrates that, among other accomplishments, liberal arts graduates in one of Chase's training programs translated their learning into superior job performances. Russell G. Warren, *New Links Between General Education and Business Careers* (Washington, D.C.: Association of American Colleges, 1983), surveys almost four hundred chief executive officers and vice-presidents about broad skills, attitudes, and knowledge important to the success of college graduate employees. The study also identifies attributes that become more important as employees advance in their careers. Other studies to consult are: Alfred W. Swinyard and Floyd A. Bond, "Who Gets Promoted?," *Harvard Business Review*, 1980, *58* (5), 6–21; Liberal Arts Group, *Report on the Liberal Arts Employer Survey: Opportunities for the Liberal Arts Graduate* (Inksper, Mich.: Liberal Arts Group, Midwest College Placement Association, 1980); and Seymour Lusterman, *Education in Industry* (New York: Conference Board, 1977).

Definitions, Trends, and Issues in Liberal Education

The value of a liberal education for management is a subject that must be prefaced by some reading on the general field of liberal education—taking note of evolving definitions, trends in curriculum development and teaching, and continuing debates within higher education on the basic issues. Titles that best provide this necessary background study are: Charles H.

Wegener, *Liberal Education and the Modern University* (Chicago: University of Chicago Press, 1978); Zelda F. Gamson and Associates, *Liberating Education* (San Francisco: Jossey-Bass, 1984); James W. Hall, *In Opposition to the Core Curriculum: Models for Undergraduate Education* (Westport, Conn.: Greenwood Press, 1982); Clifton F. Conrad and Jean C. Wyer, *Liberal Education in Transition* (Washington, D.C.: American Association for Higher Education, ERIC, 1980), which does an excellent job in reviewing the literature on liberal education while advancing several answers to the issues and debates; Arthur Levine, *Handbook on Undergraduate Curriculum* (San Francisco: Jossey-Bass, 1978); and the Carnegie Foundation for the Advancement of Teaching, *Missions of the College Curriculum: A Contemporary Review with Suggestions* (San Francisco: Jossey-Bass, 1977).

The *Educational Record, Liberal Education,* and the *Chronicle for Higher Education* are publications that provide forums for current thought on liberal education and curriculum reform; they also reflect the changing opinions and evolving issues attached to liberal education over the years. For example, see David Kaiser, "Return to the Core Curriculum: A Dissenting View," *Chronicle of Higher Education,* Nov. 30, 1983, *27,* p. 64; John B. Bennett, "Liberal Education—Why?," *Liberal Education,* 1977, *63* (1), 67–79; Stephen K. Bailey, "Needed Changes in Liberal Education," *Educational Record,* Summer 1977, *58,* 250–258; and Leon Botstein, "Liberal Arts and the Core Curriculum," *Chronicle of Higher Education,* July 9, 1979, *18,* p. 17.

Historical Perspectives:
Liberal Education and Business Study

A historical perspective helps explain why liberal education and undergraduate business study have linked successfully in higher education. Perhaps the best starting point is Richard Hofstadter, *Anti-Intellectualism in American Life* (New York: Vintage Books, 1963). Hofstadter frames the developing hostility of a business society against the intellectual life and the goals of a liberal education. Interesting companion pieces are Robert Nisbet, *The Degradation of the Academic Dogma, 1945-1970* (New York: Basic Books, 1971), and Christopher Jencks and David Riesman, *The Academic Revolution* (New York: Doubleday, 1968). Paul S. Hugstad's *The Business School in the 1980s: Liberalism Versus Vocationalism* (New York: Praeger, 1983) surveys the background development of business schools with a focus on the conflict between liberal learning and specialized, vocational study. Hugstad also makes some summary suggestions on reform for business schools.

The past also reveals some notable attempts at reforming undergraduate business study as well as a continuing history of concern about higher education for business. A good introductory work is Steven A. Sass, *The Pragmatic Imagination: A History of the Wharton School, 1881-1981* (Philadelphia: University of Pennsylvania Press, 1982). Also valuable for historical backgrounds are Earl F. Cheit, *The Useful Arts and the Liberal Tradition* (New York: McGraw-Hill, 1975), Edward Chase Kirkland, *Dream and Thought in the Business Community, 1860-1890* (Ithaca, N.Y.: Cornell University Press, 1956), and Frederick Rudolph, *Curriculum: A History of the American Undergraduate Course of Study Since 1636* (San Francisco: Jossey-Bass, 1977).

Reforming the Business Schools

The late 1950s and early 1960s witnessed a flurry of studies, reports, and recommendations that criticized undergraduate business study and called for reforms, including more broad-based liberal learning. The two most important studies, Frank C. Pierson and others, *The Education of American Businessmen* (New York: McGraw-Hill, 1959), and Robert Aaron Gordon and James Edwin Howell, *Higher Education for Business* (New York: Columbia University Press, 1959), were followed shortly by the Committee on Economic Development, *Educating Tomorrow's Managers* (New York: Committee on Economic Development, 1964), and the Institute for Higher Education, *Higher Education and Business* (New York: Columbia University Press, 1963). Two surveys of business faculty and liberal arts faculty opinions on issues of liberal learning and professional education during the late-fifties reform period are Paul L. Dressel and Margaret F. Lorimer, *Attitudes of Liberal Arts Faculty Members Toward Liberal and Professional Education* (New York: Bureau of Publications, Teachers College, Columbia University, 1959), and Paul Dressel, Lewis Mayhew, and Earl McGrath, *The Liberal Arts as Viewed by Faculty Members in the Professional Schools* (New York: Bureau of Publications, Teachers College, Columbia University, 1959). A. W. Vandermeer and M. D. Lyons, "Professional Fields and the Liberal Arts, 1958–1978," *Educational Record,* 1979, *60* (2), 197–201, updated the earlier surveys of faculty attitudes, noting a decline in support for liberal learning. Gordon K. C. Chen and Edward A. Zane, "The Business School Core Curricula Eight Years After the Gordon-Howell and Pierson Reports," *Collegiate News and Views,* Oct. 1969, *22,* 5–9, measures some impacts of these major reports.

Several recent articles have criticized undergraduate and graduate study in business: Peter Baida, "MBA," *American Scholar,* Winter 1984, *54,* 23–41; Edward J. Mandt, "The Failure of Business Education—and What to Do About It," *Management Review,* 1982, *71* (8), 47–52; and Jack N. Behrman and Richard I. Levin, "Are Business Schools Doing Their Job?," *Harvard Business Review,* Jan.-Feb. 1984, *62,* 140–147. A report from the Business–Higher Education Forum, *America's Business Schools: Priorities for Change* (Washington, D.C.: Business–Higher Education Forum, 1985), recommends specific steps that business schools should take to update their programs; it further recommends how American businesses can contribute to this process.

Lewis C. Solmon, "The Humanist as Business Executive: Wishful Thinking?," *Educational Record,* Winter 1983, *64,* 32–37; Ronald Jager, "Career and Curriculum: A Philosophical Critique," in Charles S. Green III and Richard G. Salem (eds.), *Liberal Learning and Careers* (San Francisco: Jossey-Bass, 1981), pp. 87–94; and Earnest A. Lynton, "Improving Cooperation Between Colleges and Corporations," *Educational Record,* Fall 1982, *63,* 20–25, point out some important considerations and possible pitfalls to advocates of liberal learning for management and curriculum reform.

Organizational Resources

A number of national organizations have programs designed to relate higher education and business. The American Council of Life Insurance and the Woodrow Wilson Foundation, for example, have both been active in bringing managers to campus. The Business-Higher Education Forum, sponsored by the American Council on Education, looks at a wide range of issues, from high-technology innovation to curricular improvements, with occasional attention to the role of the liberal arts. That role is the sole focus of continuing programs at three other national organizations. The Career Planning Council recently established a task force on the liberal arts; as a result, the council has voted to begin a national longitudinal study of liberal arts graduates and to create a clearinghouse of research and innovative programs on the topic. The American Assembly of Collegiate Schools of Business is creating a similar task force to study the integration of liberal arts and business study and offering its new Exxon Award for innovative programs addressing this challenge in the business schools. The American Academy of Arts and Sciences, in affiliation with the newly established Corporate Council on the Liberal Arts, plans a program of research and action to give the liberal arts higher priority on the corporate agenda.

Finally, the Association of American Colleges (AAC) has in recent years sponsored numerous projects and publications on liberal education and careers. Some ten conferences since 1982 have brought together business and academic leaders in all regions of the country and produced several sets of recommendations. Janis L. Moyer, *Liberal Learning and Careers Conference Report,* and Kathryn Mohrman, *Building Bridges Between Business and Campus,* both published in 1983, summarize some of the earlier meetings. Proceedings and background papers for more recent meetings are available from the AAC and ERIC's Document Reproduction Service.

The association's Liberal Learning and Careers series includes, in addition to several monographs mentioned above, David Hiley's well-regarded *Faculty Roles in Career Advising of Liberal Arts Students* (1982). And, in addition to the journal *Liberal Education,* also mentioned above, AAC publishes the *Forum for Liberal Education,* a research newsletter reporting on innovative curricular programs. Back issues of particular relevance include 1982, *4* (6), and 1984, *6* (3). A complete list of AAC publications can be obtained by writing to the attention of Publications, Association of American Colleges, 1818 R Street, N.W., Washington, D.C. 20009.

References

Alexander, J. H. "Education for Business: A Reassessment." *Wall Street Journal,* Feb. 2, 1981, p. 16.

Alfred, R. L., and Hilpert, J. M. "The Liberal Arts and the Personnel Needs of Complex Organizations." *Liberal Education,* 1985, *71* (1), 27–38.

American Assembly of Collegiate Schools of Business. *Accreditation Council Policies, Procedures and Standards.* St. Louis: American Assembly of Collegiate Schools of Business, 1984–85.

American Society for Training and Development. "High Tech Jobs." *American Society for Training and Development National Report,* 1984a, *10* (18), 3.

American Society for Training and Development. "Training Costs 10% of Company Revenue?" *American Society for Training and Development National Report,* 1984b, *10* (21), 1.

Ansberry, C. "Feast or Famine: Managers Facing a Wide Disparity in Job Openings." *Wall Street Journal,* Aug. 7, 1985, p. 19.

Aspen Institute for Humanistic Studies. *Programs for Corporate Executives, 1984–1985.* Aspen, Co.: Aspen Institute for Humanistic Studies, 1985.

Association of American Colleges. *The Humanities and Careers in Business: Proceedings of the Conference in Princeton, New Jersey, April 1983.* Washington, D.C.: Association of American Colleges, 1984.

Association of American Colleges. *1984 Regional Conferences on the Humanities and Careers in Business.* Washington, D.C.: Association of American Colleges, 1985.

Astin, A. W. "Student Values: Knowing More About Where We Are Today." *American Association of Higher Education Bulletin,* 1984, *36* (9), 10–13.

Astin, A. W., Green, K. C., Williams, S., and Maier, M. J. *The American Freshman: National Norms for Fall 1984.* Los Angeles: Higher Education Research Institute, Graduate School of Education, University of California, 1984.

Baida, P. "MBA." *American Scholar,* 1984, *54,* 23–41.

Baker, J. S. "An Analysis of Degree Programs Offered by Selected Industrial Corporations." Unpublished doctoral dissertation, University of Arizona, 1983.

Beck, R. E. *Career Patterns: The Liberal Arts Major in Bell System Management.* Washington, D.C.: Association of American Colleges, 1981.

Behrman, J. N., and Levin, R. I. "Are Business Schools Doing Their Job?" *Harvard Business Review,* 1984, *62,* 140–147.

Bell, D. "Notes on the Post Industrial Society." *Public Interest,* 1967, *6–7,* 24–35.

Benchley, R. "What College Did to Me." In R. Benchley, *Inside Benchley.* New York: Harper & Row, 1942.

Berle, A., Jr., and Means, G. C. *The Modern Corporation and Private Property.* New York: Harcourt, Brace, Jovanovich, 1967. (Originally published 1932.)

Birch, D. L. "Who Creates Jobs?" *Public Interest,* 1981, *65,* 3–14.

Bisconti, A. S. *Who Will Succeed? College Graduates as Business Executives.* Bethlehem, Pa.: College Placement Council Foundation, 1978.

Bisconti, A. S., and Gomberg, I. L. *The Hard-to-Place Majority: A National Study of the Career Outcomes of Liberal Arts Graduates.* Bethlehem, Pa.: College Placement Council Foundation, 1975.

Bisconti, A. S., and Kessler, J. G. *College and Other Stepping Stones: A Study of Learning Experiences That Contribute to Effective Performance in Early and Long-Run Jobs.* Bethlehem, Pa.: College Placement Council Foundation, 1980.

Bisconti, A. S., and Solmon, L. C. *College Education on the Job: The Graduates' Viewpoint.* Bethlehem, Pa.: College Placement Council Foundation, 1976.

Boettinger, H. "Is Management Really an Art?" *Harvard Business Review,* Jan.-Feb. 1975, pp. 54-64.

Bond, F. A., Leabo, D. A., and Swinyard, A. W. *Preparation for Business Leadership.* Ann Arbor: University of Michigan Press, 1964.

Bonfield, P. *U.S. Business Leaders: A Study of Opinions and Characteristics.* New York: Conference Board, 1980.

Bowen, H. R. *Investment in Learning: The Individual and Social Value of American Higher Education.* San Francisco: Jossey-Bass, 1977.

Branscomb, L. M., and Gilmore, P. C. "Education in Private Industry." *Daedalus,* Winter 1975, pp. 222-233.

Brazziel, W. F. "College-Corporate Partnerships in Higher Education." *Educational Record,* Spring 1981, pp. 50-52.

Brown, C. L. Keynote address to the Conference on the Humanities and Careers in Business, Princeton, N.J., Apr. 27, 1983.

Brown, P. A. "University of Florida Humanities Perspectives on the Professions." *The Forum for Liberal Education,* 1982, *4* (6), 9-10.

Brown, P. A. "Extending Liberal Education to New Audiences." *Forum for Liberal Education,* 1985, 7 (3), 2-19.

Burck, C. G. "A Group Profile of the *Fortune* 500 Chief Executive." *Fortune,* May 1976, pp. 173ff.

Burns, S. T. *From Student to Banker: Observations from the Chase Bank.* Washington, D.C.: Association of American Colleges, 1983.

Business and the Humanities: A National Conference. Lawrence: School of Business, University of Kansas, 1981.

Business–Higher Education Forum. *America's Business Schools: Priorities for Change.* Washington, D.C.: Business–Higher Education Forum, 1985.

Career Placement Council. "Supply and Demand." *Spotlight on Career Planning, Placement and Recruitment,* 1985, *8* (1), 1.

Cheit, E. F. *The Useful Arts and the Liberal Tradition.* New York: McGraw-Hill, 1975.

Chen, G. K. C., and Zane, E. A. "The Business School Core Curricula Eight Years After the Gordon-Howell and Pierson Reports." *Collegiate News and Views,* 1969, *22,* 5–9.

College Entrance Examination Board. *National Report of College-Bound Seniors.* New York: College Entrance Examination Board, 1985.

Collins, R. "Functional and Conflict Theories of Educational Stratification." *American Sociological Review,* 1971, *36,* 1002–1019.

Committee on Economic Development. *Educating Tomorrow's Managers.* New York: Committee on Economic Development, 1964.

Committee on Public History. *Educating Historians for Business.* Bloomington, Ind.: Organization of American Historians, 1983.

Cox, A. *The Cox Report on the American Corporation.* New York: Delacorte Press, 1982.

Craig, R. L., and Evers, C. J. "Employers as Educators: 'The Shadow Education System.' " In G. G. Gold (ed.), *Business and Higher Education: Toward New Alliances.* San Francisco: Jossey-Bass, 1981.

Dartmouth Institute. *The Dartmouth Institute.* Hanover, N.H.: Dartmouth College, 1985.

DiMaggio, P. "Cultural Capital and School Success: The Impact of Status Culture Participation on the Grades of U.S. High School Students." *American Sociological Review,* 1982, *47,* 189–201.

Dobrzynski, J. H., Tarpey, J. P., and Aikmann, R. "Small Is Beautiful." *Business Week,* May 27, 1985, pp. 88–90.

Dressel, P. L., and Lorimer, M. F. *Attitudes of Liberal Arts Faculty Members Toward Liberal and Professional Education.* New York: Bureau of Publications, Teachers College, Columbia University, 1959.

Dressel, P. L., Mayhew, L. B., and McGrath, E. J. *The Liberal Arts as Viewed by Faculty Members in the Professional Schools.* New York: Bureau of Publications, Teachers College, Columbia University, 1959.

Dun and Bradstreet, Inc. *Reference Book of Corporate Management.* Parsippany, N.J.: Dun and Bradstreet, 1982.

Edgerton, R. "The New Economy and the Old Liberal Arts." In *The Liberal Arts College: The Next Quarter Century.* Chicago: Great Lakes Colleges Association, 1984.

Ehrenhalt, S. H. "No Golden Age for College Graduates." *Challenge,* 1983, *26,* 42–50.

Eurich, N. P. *Corporate Classrooms: The Learning Business.* Princeton, N.J.: Carnegie Foundation for the Advancement of Teaching, 1985.

Feldman, K. A., and Newcomb, T. M. *The Impact of College on Students.* San Francisco: Jossey-Bass, 1969.

Feldstein, M., Poterba, J., and Dicks-Mireaux, L. *The Effective Tax Rate and the Pretax Rate of Return.* Cambridge, Mass.: National Bureau of Economic Research, 1982.

Friedrich, O. "The Money Chase." *Time,* May 4, 1981, pp. 58–69.

Frye, N. "Speculation and Concern." In T. B. Stroup (ed.), *The Humanities and the Understanding of Reality.* Lexington: University of Kentucky Press, 1966.

Gamson, Z. F., and Associates. *Liberating Education.* San Francisco: Jossey-Bass, 1984.

Garis, J. W., Hess, H. R., and Marron, D. J. "Curriculum Counts —for Liberal Arts Students Seeking Business Careers." *Journal of College Placement,* 1985, *45,* 32–37.

Georgeson, C. "MBA, Ideally: M(ore) B(asic) A(nalysis)." *New York Times,* Aug. 31, 1982, p. 21.

Gordon, R. A., and Howell, J. E. *Higher Education for Business.* New York: Columbia University Press, 1959.

Gorlin, H. *Personnel Practices I: Recruitment, Placement, Training, Communication.* New York: Conference Board, 1981.

Gorlin, H., and Shein, L. *Innovations in Managing Human Resources.* New York: Conference Board, 1984.

Grantham, S. "Zen and the Art of Corporate Maintenance." *Dartmouth Alumni Magazine,* Jan.-Feb. 1985, pp. 47–50.

Gutis, P. S. "Teaching Arts Instead of Accounting." *New York Times,* Mar. 24, 1985, p. F17.

Hambrick, D. C., and Mason, P. A. "Upper Echelons: The Organization as a Reflection of Its Top Managers." Academy of *Management Review,* 1984, *9,* 193–206.

"Harper's Index." *Harper's,* Dec. 1984, p. 10.

Harvard Business School. *The MBA Program, 1984–85.* Boston: Harvard University, 1984.

Hastie, K. L. "A Perspective on Management Education." *Financial Management,* Winter 1982, pp. 55–62.

Hayes, R. H., and Abernathy, W. J. "Managing Our Way to Economic Decline." *Harvard Business Review,* 1980, *58,* 67–77.

Heidrick and Struggles, Inc. *Mobile Manager 1981.* Chicago: Heidrick and Struggles, Inc., 1981.

Herman, E. S. *Corporate Control, Corporate Power.* New York: Cambridge University Press, 1981.

Hildebrandt, H. H. *Learning from Top Women Executives— Their Perceptions on Business Communication, Careers, and Education.* Ann Arbor: Graduate School of Business, University of Michigan, 1985.

Hiley, D. R. *Faculty Roles in Career Advising of Liberal Arts Students.* Washington, D.C.: Association of American Colleges, 1982.

Hofstadter, R. *Anti-Intellectualism in American Life.* New York: Vintage Books, 1963.

Holusha, J. "A New Leader Who Stresses Design: Donald Eugene Petersen." *New York Times,* Oct. 30, 1984, pp. D1, D5.

Howard, A. *College Experience and Managerial Performance: Report to Management.* New York: American Telephone and Telegraph Company, 1984.

Howard, A. *College Experience and Managerial Performance.* New York: American Telephone and Telegraph Company, 1985.

Hoyt, D. P. *The Relationship Between College Grades and Adult Achievement: A Review of the Literature.* Iowa City, Ia.: ACT Research Reports, 1965.

Hugstad, P. S. *The Business School in the 1980s: Liberalism Versus Vocationalism.* New York: Praeger, 1983.

Interindustry Forecasting Project of the University of Maryland. *INFORUM Forecast.* College Park: Interindustry Forecasting Project, University of Maryland, 1983.

Jacob, N. "The Internationalization of Management Education." *Selections,* Winter 1985, pp. 3–8.

Jenkins, R. L., and Reizenstein, R. C. "Insights into the MBA: Its Contents, Output, and Relevance." *Selections*, Spring 1984, pp. 19–24.

Jenkins, R. L., Reizenstein, R. C., and Rodgers, F. G. "Report Cards on the M.B.A." *Harvard Business Review*, 1984, *62*, 20–30.

Johnson, E. C., and Tornatzky, L. G. "Academic and Industrial Innovation." In G. G. Gold (ed.), *Business and Higher Education: Toward New Alliances*. San Francisco: Jossey-Bass, 1981.

Jones, L. *Great Expectations*. New York: Coward, McCann, and Geoghegan, 1980.

Jones, T. B. "Introduction." In T. B. Jones (ed.), *Liberal Learning and Business Careers*. St. Paul, Minn.: Metropolitan State University, 1982.

Kanter, R. M. *The Change Masters: Innovation for Productivity in the American Corporation*. New York: Simon & Schuster, 1983.

Kanter, R. M. *The Roots of Corporate Progressivism: How and Why Corporations Respond to Changing Societal Needs and Expectations*. New York: Russell Sage Foundation, 1984.

Kemeny, J. G. Address to Dartmouth alumni, New York, Apr. 8, 1980.

Kerr, C. "The Schools of Business Administration." In *New Dimensions of Learning in a Free Society*. Pittsburgh: University of Pittsburgh Press, 1958.

Kiernan, C. J. "The Rise of the American School of Business." In B. Opulente (ed.), *Thought Patterns: Toward a Philosophy of Business Education*. New York: St. John's University Press, 1960.

Kimberly, J. R., and Evanisko, M. J. "Organizational Innovation: The Influence of Individual, Organizational and Contextual Factors on Hospital Adoption of Technological and Administrative Innovations." *Academy of Management Journal*, 1981, *24*, 689–713.

Kirkland, E. C. *Dream and Thought in the Business Community, 1860–1900*. Ithaca, N.Y.: Cornell University Press, 1956.

Koontz, H., O'Donnell, C., and Weihrich, H. *Management.* New York: McGraw-Hill, 1976.

Levine, A. "Myths in the Anti-Liberal Arts Kingdom." *New York Times,* Aug. 21, 1983, p. 61.

Lipset, S. M., and Schneider, W. P. *The Confidence Gap: How Americans View Their Institutions.* New York: Macmillan, 1981.

Livingston, J. S. "Myth of the Well-Educated Manager." *Harvard Business Review,* Jan.-Feb. 1971, pp. 79-89.

Louis, M. "The First Years Out Study: A Report Card on MBA Programs." Unpublished manuscript, Boston University, 1985.

Lusterman, S. *Education in Industry.* New York: Conference Board, 1977.

Lusterman, S. *Managerial Competence: The Public Affairs Aspect.* New York: Conference Board, 1981.

Lynton, E. A. "Colleges, Universities, and Corporate Training." In G. G. Gold (ed.), *Business and Higher Education: Toward New Alliances.* San Francisco: Jossey-Bass, 1981a.

Lynton, E. A. "A Role for Colleges in Corporate Training and Development." In American Association for Higher Education, *Partnerships with Business and the Professions.* Washington, D.C.: American Association for Higher Education, 1981b.

Lynton, E. A. *The Missing Connection Between Business and the Universities.* New York: Macmillan, 1984.

McGarraghy, J. J., and Reilly, K. P. "College Credit for Corporate Training." In G. G. Gold (ed.), *Business and Higher Education: Toward New Alliances.* San Francisco: Jossey-Bass, 1981.

McGrath, E. J. *Liberal Education in the Professions.* New York: Bureau of Publications, Teachers College, Columbia University, 1959.

McGrath, P. S. *Developing Employee Political Awareness.* New York: Conference Board, 1980.

McQuigg, B. "The Role of Education in Industry." *Phi Delta Kappan,* Jan. 1983, pp. 324-325.

Mandt, E. J. "The Failure of Business Education—and What to Do About It." *Management Review,* 1982, *71* (8), 47-52.

Merenda, M. J. "The Process of Corporate Social Involvement: Five Case Studies." In L. E. Preston (ed.), *Research in Corporate Social Performance and Policy.* Vol. 3. Greenwich, Conn.: JAI Press, 1981.

Mitroff, I., and Kilmann, R. H. "Corporate Tragedies: Teaching Companies to Cope with Evil." *New Management,* 1984, *1* (4), 48–53.

Mohrman, K. *Building Bridges Between Business and Campus.* Washington, D.C.: Association of American Colleges, 1983a.

Mohrman, K. "Liberal Learning Is a Sound Human Capital Investment." *Educational Record,* 1983b, *64* (4), 56–61.

Moore, D. G. *Politics and the Corporate Chief Executive.* New York: Conference Board, 1980.

Morgan, B. S., and Schiemann, W. A. (eds.). *Supervision in the '80s: Trends in Corporate America.* Princeton, N.J.: Opinion Research Corporation, 1984.

Moyer, J. L. *Liberal Learning and Careers Conference Report.* Washington, D.C.: Association of American Colleges, 1983.

Naisbett, J. *Megatrends: Ten New Directions Transforming Our Lives.* (Rev. ed.) New York: Warner Books, 1984.

National Center for Education Statistics. *The Condition of Education, 1985, Statistical Report.* Washington, D.C.: National Center for Education Statistics, 1985.

O'Toole, J. "Getting Ready for the Next Industrial Revolution." *Washington Post Fall Hi Tech 1984 Supplement,* Oct. 7, 1984, pp. 23, 43.

Parrish, J. B., and Duff, F. L. "Job Experience of College Graduates: A Case Study." *Quarterly Journal of Economics and Business,* 1975, *15,* 25–36.

Pattison, R. "The Literacy of Power." *Communicator's Journal,* 1983, *1* (3), 46–50.

Perelman, L. J. *The Learning Enterprise: Adult Learning, Human Capital and Economic Development.* Washington, D.C.: Council of State Planning Agencies, 1984.

Peter, L. *Peter's Quotations: Ideas for Our Time.* New York: Bantam Books, 1977.

Peters, T. J., and Waterman, R. H., Jr. *In Search of Excellence: Lessons from America's Best Run Companies.* New York: Harper & Row, 1982.

Pierson, F. C., and others. *The Education of American Business-men.* New York: McGraw-Hill, 1959.

Pierson, G. W. *The Education of American Leaders: Comparative Contributions of U.S. Colleges and Universities.* New York: Praeger, 1969.

Randall, W. C. "The Experience of Liberal Arts Graduates in Business Positions." In The University of Kansas School of Business and the Center for Humanistic Studies (eds.), *Business and the Humanities: A National Conference.* Lawrence: School of Business, University of Kansas, 1981.

Randle, C. W. "How to Identify Promotable Executives." *Harvard Business Review,* 1956, *34,* 122-134.

Rawlins, V. L., and Ulman, L. "The Utilization of College-Trained Manpower in the United States." In M. S. Gordon (ed.), *Higher Education and the Labor Market.* New York: McGraw-Hill, 1974.

Rehnke, M. A. F. "Introduction." In M. A. F. Rehnke (ed.), *Liberal Learning and Career Preparation.* Current Issues in Higher Education, no. 2. Washington, D.C.: American Association for Higher Education, 1982-83.

Rhodes, F. H. T. "Reforming Higher Education Will Take More Than Just Tinkering with Curricula." *Chronicle of Higher Education,* 1985, *30* (12), 80.

Riche, R. W., Hecker, D. E., and Burgan, J. U. "High Technology Today and Tomorrow: A Small Slice of the Employment Pie." *Monthly Labor Review,* 1983, *106* (11), 50-58.

Rothberg, J. O. "What They Say About Liberal Arts." *Career Opportunities News,* Mar.-Apr. 1985, p. 7.

Rumberger, R. W. "The Job Market for College Graduates, 1960-90." *Journal of Higher Education,* 1984, *55,* 433-454.

Sargent, J. "The Job Outlook for College Graduates Through the Mid-1990s." *College Guidance Research,* Spring 1985, pp. 1-7.

Sass, S. A. *The Pragmatic Imagination: A History of the Wharton School, 1881-1981.* Philadelphia: University of Pennsylvania Press, 1982.

Shaeffer, R. G. *Top-Management Staffing Challenges: CEOs Describe Their Needs.* New York: Conference Board, 1982.

Shaeffer, R. G., and Janger, A. R. *Who Is Top Management?* New York: Conference Board, 1982.

Shaiken, H. "A Robot Is After Your Job." *New York Times,* Sept. 3, 1981, p. 10.

Shapiro, I. "Business and the Public Policy Process." Paper delivered at the Symposium on Business and Government, Harvard University, May 9, 1979.

Sheils, M., and others. "And Man Created the Chip." *Newsweek,* 1980, *95* (26), 50–56.

Shingleton, J. D., and Scheetz, L. P. *Recruiting Trends 1984–85.* East Lansing: Placement Services, Michigan State University, 1984.

Silk, L. S. *The Education of Businessmen.* A supplementary paper of the Business-Education Committee, Committee on Economic Development. New York: Committee on Economic Development, 1960.

Simon, H. A. "The Business School: A Problem in Organizational Design." *Journal of Management Studies,* 1967, *4,* 1–16.

Solmon, L. C. "New Findings on the Links Between College Education and Work." *Higher Education,* 1981, *10,* 615–648.

Stanford University. *Stanford 1984–85 MBA Brochure.* Stanford, Calif.: Stanford University, 1984.

Steckmest, F. W. "Career Development for the Public Policy Dimension of Executive Performance." *Public Affairs Review,* 1981, *2,* 71–87.

Steckmest, F. W. *Corporate Performance: The Key to Public Trust.* New York: McGraw-Hill, 1982.

Stine, G. H. "Future Technology and the Manager." *New Management,* 1984, *2* (1), 44–47.

Swinyard, A. W., and Bond, F. A. "Who Gets Promoted?" *Harvard Business Review,* 1980, *58* (5), 6–21.

Thomas, M. M. "Business Education: A Study in Paradox." *Business and Society,* Spring 1983, pp. 18–21.

Unger, D. "Educating Tomorrow's Managers: Liberal Arts or Business School?" *Professional Training,* Winter 1985, pp. 1, 12.

Useem, M. *The Inner Circle: Large Corporations and the Rise of Business Political Activity in the U.S. and U.K.* New York: Oxford University Press, 1984.

Useem, M. "The Rise of the Political Manager." *Sloan Management Review,* 1985, *27* (Fall), 15–26.

Useem, M., and Karabel, J. "Pathways to Top Corporate Management." Boston: Center for Applied Social Science, Boston University, 1985.

Useem, M., and Kutner, S. I. "Corporate Contributions to the Arts and Culture: The Organizations of Giving and the Influence of the Chief Executive Officer and Other Firms on Company Contributions in Massachusetts." In P. DiMaggio (ed.), *Nonprofit Organizations in the Production and Distribution of Culture.* New York: Oxford University Press, 1985.

Vandermeer, A. W., and Lyons, M. D. "Professional Fields and the Liberal Arts, 1958–1978." *Educational Record,* 1979, *60* (2), 197–201.

Wabash College. *The Wabash Executive Program.* Crawfordsville, Ind.: Wabash College, 1985.

Wade, O. J. "Remarks." Conference on the Humanities and Careers in Business, Northwestern University, May 22, 1984 (and personal communication with Illinois Bell).

Ward, L. B. "Education for Careers in Management." In F. C. Pierson (ed.), *The Education of American Businessmen.* New York: McGraw-Hill, 1959.

Warren, R. G. *New Links Between General Education and Business Careers.* Washington, D.C.: Association of American Colleges, 1983.

Washington and Lee University. *Institute for Executives. A Program in the Humanities: Business Ethics and Decisions.* Lexington, Va.: Washington and Lee University, 1985.

Weiner, B. "Train Up an MBA in a Way He Can Think." *Christian Science Monitor,* 1984, *76,* 12.

Whitelaw, W. (ed.). "The Economy and the College Student." In M. A. F. Rehnke (ed.), *Liberal Learning and Career Preparation.* Current Issues in Higher Education, no. 2. Washington, D.C.: American Association of Higher Education, 1982–83.

"Who's Excellent Now? Some of the Best Seller's Picks Haven't Been Doing So Well Lately." *Business Week,* Oct. 5, 1984, pp. 76–78.

Whyte, W. H., Jr. *The Organization Man.* New York: Simon & Schuster, 1956.

Williams, D. A., and King, P. "Getting a B.A. at the Office." *Newsweek,* Dec. 21, 1981, p. 74.

Williams College Executive Program. *Williams College Executive Program.* Williamstown, Mass.: Williams College, 1985.

Winter, D. G., McClelland, D. C., and Stewart, A. J. *A New Case for the Liberal Arts: Assessing Institutional Goals and Student Development.* San Francisco: Jossey-Bass, 1981.

Wolfbein, S. "New Alliances for Economic Growth: Can Business and Education Collaborate?" Address at Temple University, Philadelphia, Apr. 1985.

Woodington, D. "Some Impressions of the Evaluation of Training in Industry." *Phi Delta Kappan,* 1980, *61,* 326–328.

Wriston, W. Address at meeting of the Security Industry Association, New York, Jan. 21, 1981.

Zingg, P. W. "The Liberal Arts Student—A Sphinx on the Land of Academe?" *Liberal Education,* 1980, *66* (3), 321–326.

Index